W

New Case

JOHN DONN

New Casebooks

New Casebooks

JOHN DONNE

Edited by
ANDREW MOUSLEY

First published in Great Britain 1999 by
MACMILLAN PRESS LTD
Houndmills, Basingstoke, Hampshire RG21 6XS and London
Companies and representatives throughout the world

A catalogue record for this book is available from the British Library.

ISBN 0–333–67188–0 hardcover
ISBN 0–333–67189–9 paperback

First published in the United States of America 1999 by
ST. MARTIN'S PRESS, INC.,
Scholarly and Reference Division,
175 Fifth Avenue, New York, N.Y. 10010

ISBN 0–312–21640–8

Library of Congress Cataloging-in-Publication Data
John Donne / edited by Andrew Mousley.
p.   cm. — (New casebooks)
Includes bibliographical references and index.
ISBN 0–312–21640–8
1. Donne, John, 1572–1631—Criticism and interpretation.
I. Mousley, Andrew.   II. Series.
PR2248.J58   1998
821'.3—dc21   98–6886
                                                                    CIP

Selection, editorial matter and Introduction © Andrew Mousley 1999

This book is printed on paper suitable for recycling and made from fully managed and sustained forest sources.

10   9   8   7   6   5   4   3   2   1
08   07   06   05   04   03   02   01   00   99

Printed in Hong Kong

For Debbie and Dan and my parents

Contents

Acknowledgements

I would like to thank John Peck for his comments, Martin Coyle for all the time, advice and support he's given me, Janet Lewison for her insight and friendship, and Debbie for all these things and much more besides.

I have, with the authors' permission, shortened all of the essays in the present collection.

The editor and publishers wish to thank the following for permission to use copyright material:

David Aers and Gunther Kress, for, '"Darke texts need notes": Versions of Self in Donne's Verse Epistles', in *Literature, Language and Society in England 1580–1680*, ed. D. Aers, B. Hodge and G. Kress (1981), Gill and Macmillan, pp. 23–48, by permission of David Aers and Gunther Kress; Catherine Belsey, for material from *Desire: Love Stories in Western Culture* (1994), pp. 130–49, by permission of Blackwell Publishers; Barbara Estrin, for material from *Laura: Uncovering Gender and Genre in Wyatt, Donne and Marvell* (1994), pp. 149–79. Copyright © 1994 Duke University Press, by permission of Duke University Press; Stanley Fish, for 'Masculine Persuasive Force: Donne and Verbal Power' from *Soliciting Interpretation: Literary Theory and Seventeenth-Century English Poetry*, ed. Elizabeth D. Harvey and Katharine Eisaman Maus (1990), pp. 223–52, by permission of the University of Chicago Press; Achsah Guibbory, for '"Oh, let mee not serve so": The Politics of Love in Donne's *Elegies*', *English Literary History*, 57 (1990), 811–33. Copyright © 1990 the Johns Hopkins University Press, by permission of the Johns Hopkins University Press; Richard Halpern, for 'The Lyric in the Field of Information: Autopoiesis and History in Donne's *Songs and Sonnets*', *The Yale School of Criticism*, 6

(1993), 185–215, by permission of the Johns Hopkins University Press; Elizabeth Harvey, for material from *Ventriloquized Voices: Feminist Theory and English Renaissance Texts* (1992), pp. 76–115, by permission of Routledge; William Kerrigan, 'The Fearful Accommodations of John Donne', *English Literary Renaissance*, 4 (1974), 337–63, by permission of the editors of *English Literary Renaissance*; Tilottama Rajan, for '"Nothing sooner broke": Donne's *Songs and Sonets* as Self-Consuming Artifact', *English Literary History*, 49 (1982), 805–28. Copyright © 1982 the Johns Hopkins University Press, by permission of the Johns Hopkins University Press; Nancy Wright, for 'The *Figura* of the Martyr in John Donne's Sermons', *English Literary History*, 56 (1989) 293–309. Copyright © the Johns Hopkins University Press, by permission of the Johns Hopkins University Press.

Every effort has been made to trace the copyright holders but if any have been inadvertently overlooked the publishers will be pleased to make the necessary arrangement at the first opportunity.

General Editors' Preface

The purpose of this series of New Casebooks is to reveal some of the ways in which contemporary criticism has changed our understanding of commonly studied texts and writers and, indeed, of the nature of criticism itself. Central to the series is a concern with modern critical theory and its effect on current approaches to the study of literature. Each New Casebook editor has been asked to select a sequence of essays which will introduce the reader to the new critical approaches to the text or texts being discussed in the volume and also illuminate the rich interchange between critical theory and critical practice that characterises so much current writing about literature.

In this focus on modern critical thinking and practice New Casebooks aim not only to inform but also to stimulate, with volumes seeking to reflect both the controversy and the excitement of current criticism. Because much of this criticism is difficult and often employs an unfamiliar critical language, editors have been asked to give the reader as much help as they feel is appropriate, but without simplifying the essays or the issues they raise. Again, editors have been asked to supply a list of further reading which will enable readers to follow up issues raised by the essays in the volume.

The project of New Casebooks, then, is to bring together in an illuminating way those critics who best illustrate the ways in which contemporary criticism has established new methods of analysing texts and who have reinvigorated the important debate about how we 'read' literature. The hope is, of course, that New Casebooks will not only open up this debate to a wider audience, but will also encourage students to extend their own ideas, and think afresh about their responses to the texts they are studying.

John Peck and Martin Coyle
University of Wales, Cardiff

Introduction

ANDREW MOUSLEY

I

> Twice or thrice had I loved thee,
> Before I knew thy face or name.

If adventures entice by removing us, for a while, from our normal places, then the adventure of reading John Donne is manifested in these opening lines of 'Air and Angels'.[1] One of the excitements of reading Donne, the poet and the preacher, is the thrill of not knowing where one is being taken. We may falteringly pursue a Donne text in all its intricacy, eventually catching up with the speaker and his argument only to find that he and it have moved on elsewhere. If this suggests that Donne's speakers are always in control, always one step ahead of us, seeming to know how the various parts of an argument will finally knit together, then this speaks to the attempt to create of an individual poem an auto-nomous verbal artifact, driven and ultimately resolved by its own special logic. A Donne text may often only hold together, however, by virtue of a virtuoso performance which flirts continually with the risk of 'things ... scatt'ring'.[2] Donne's giddy verbal excursions max-imise possibilities of meaning and metaphor, and may leave us – and him – looking in vain for a place of rest and recollection.

Even in a work as structured as *Devotions Upon Emergent Occasions*, written at a time of illness, Donne travels beyond the confines of his sick-bed to explore the multiple metaphorical and religious implications of his dis-ease, the sick-bed itself becoming the occasion for a vertiginous movement of thought and language:

Whither shall I come to thee? To this bed? I have this weake, and childish frowardnes too, I cannot sit up, and yet am loth to go to bed; shall I find thee in bed? Oh, have I alwaies done so? The bed is not ordinarily thy *Scene*, thy *Climate*: Lord, dost thou not accuse me, dost thou not reproach to mee, my former sinns, when thou layest mee upon this bed? Is not this to hang a man at his owne dore, to lay him sicke in his owne bed of wantonnesse? When thou chidest us by thy *Prophet* for lying in *beds of Ivory*, is not thine anger vented? not till thou changest our *bedds of Ivory*, into *beds of Ebony*; *David* sweares unto thee, *that hee will not goe up into his bed, till he had built thee a* House. To go up into the bed, denotes strength, and promises ease; But when thou saiest, *That thou wilt cast Jesubel into a bed*, thou mak'st thine own comment upon that, Thou callest the bed *Tribulation*, great *Tribulation*: How shal they come to thee, whom thou hast nayled to their bed?[3]

The effort to discover, amidst competing possibilities, what God meant by laying 'mee upon this bed' (to show his anger? his favour? even his desire?) points to the hoped for existence of a definitive meaning, a transcendent receptacle, which would arrest the infinite movement of metaphor.

Another bed, for which Donne attempts to find a central, stable meaning, but this time in an explicitly amorous context, appears in 'The Sun Rising'. 'Shine here to us', the speaker commands of the sun in the final stanza, 'and thou art everywhere; / This bed thy centre is, these walls, thy sphere.'[4] In a sermon of 1626, Donne speaks of the way 'new Philosophy' (meaning Copernican philosophy) 'denies a settlednesse, an acquiescence in the very body of the Earth, but makes the Earth to move in that place, where we thought the Sunne had moved'.[5] The relativism implied by the thought that one generation's truth may become another's fiction, and that phenomena do not have a settled place in the scheme of things but are subject to re-evaluation, finds its expression, on a microcosmic level, in poems like 'The Sun Rising'.[6] Here, the sun as a physical centre of gravity and a potent symbolic centre is supplanted by the lovers' bed. Love is what makes the world go round, and the bed is at its fixed centre. The divine cosmology, sought after in works like *Devotions*, a cosmology which attempts to map the world as God's text, is supplanted within the secularised religion of love by the special geographies created by Donne's amorous speakers. But these special geographies, in which lovers' beds are placed at the centre of the universe instead of God, earth or sun, are as equally susceptible to falsification or change as the larger cosmologies which they displace. Donne's love poems may present, as in 'The Ecstasy', some beautifully still, arresting images, which capture a moment of absolute intimacy. They may assert, as in 'The Sun Rising', the authority, autonomy and centrality of the lover's subjectivity: 'She'is all states, and all princes, I, / Nothing else is.'[7] They may elevate love, as in 'The Canonization' and 'The Relic', to the status of an alternative religion, by canonising the lovers and appropriating to them the mainly Catholic languages of ritual, miracle and transubstantiation. Such were the possibilities for creating new geographies, new centres of authority in a world whose co-ordinates were no longer fixed. But these domains of love are themselves subject to the same forces and impulses which produce them. Thus what Donne creates through his manipulation of language in one poem or text, he can always un-create in another.

Donne's astonishing versatility of perception may therefore prompt the suspicion that there is nothing which cannot be transformed or reconceived through language. In a verbal universe in which God can be troped in any number of ways, in which love can be likened to a pair of compasses ('A Valediction: Forbidding Mourning'), and in which a bed can become the centre of the cosmos, the independent existence of things is continually called into question. Instead of revealing the true nature of an experience (like love), or the essential identity of a phenomenon (like God), Donne's verbal gymnastics vary perceptions to such an extent that the essence of these experiences and objects disappears. Of course, one might suggest here that there is nothing essential to these experiences and phenomena in the first place, and that what Donne is showing us is the vacuity, the emptiness of things that can be variously filled by language. However, I would suggest that Donne himself was sufficiently worried by the idea of things lacking their own distinctive identity to try to counteract it by searching for significant distillations of experience, knowledge and identity. Donne's repeated embrace of words like 'essence', 'quintessence', 'elixir' and 'soul' suggests the possible but problematic existence of an animating spirit behind concepts, emotions, relationships and moments in time otherwise in danger of scattering and fragmenting through the endless play of language.

In the love poem 'A Nocturnal upon S. Lucy's Day, being the shortest day', for example, the nothing that the speaker feels himself to have become as a result of the death of a beloved, is described as an absolute, quintessential nothingness: 'I, by love's limbeck, am the grave / Of all, that's nothing'; 'I am by her death (which word wrongs her) / Of the first nothing, the elixir grown.' To become nothing in this poem is paradoxically to become a something, the feeling of non-being producing a sharper sense of being, a more acute sense of what the 'I' essentially is. Disembodied and vaporised, the extraordinary nothingness of the I now hearkening after its absent beloved leaves no signs whatsoever of its being in the world: 'If I an ordinary nothing were, / As shadow, a light, and body must be here.'[8] Unlocatable, the speaker in this poem takes leave of all confining places. He is no-where, the ultimate nomad, celebrating his freedom from all definitions and identities, but euphorically affirming this state of no-thingness to be a moment of authentic self-discovery: 'Study me then ... '; 'I am every dead thing ... '; 'I, by love's limbeck ... '[9]

'A Nocturnal' thus searches for essences, in this case, for a sense of true being, even as it destabilises essentialist thinking by under-mining the stable reality which a concept like nothing might embrace. Donne frequently disturbs the usual definitions of words, and in doing so creates a space for linguistic, intellectual and psychic play and experimentation. The pressing problem which arises as a result of this experimentation is the question of what survives of people, things and concepts once their identity has been subjected to the alchemy of Donne's language. Is gold still recognisable as gold once it has been beaten to 'aery thinness' ('A Valediction: Forbidding Mourning')?[10] What survives of a relationship, or experience, or way of knowing and feeling, once vertigo has been established as a central, decentring category?

Donne's mobility of mind is also manifested in his ability to trans-late himself into diverse genres and idioms, and by the permeability of the boundaries which separate these genres. Thus political and socioeconomic concerns can be read into his poetry of seemingly pure metaphysical speculation, and, likewise, metaphysical questions are discoverable in those verse letters addressed to actual or poten-tial patrons/patronesses, whose primary motivation might otherwise be seen as being wholly pragmatic. It is these kinds of overlap which invite interdisciplinary approaches to his work. Religious, intellec-tual, social and literary historians are all welcomed by the inter-textual allusiveness and extensive cultural and intellectual reference of Donne's writing. There is no end, it seems, to the contexts in which individual genres, or Donne's work as a whole, can be placed: Calvinism, Catholicism, the patronage system, Petrarchism, new phil-osophy, coterie poetry, Renaissance didactic theory, and so forth.[11] However, if the displacement of one context by another speaks to the hospitality of Donne's writing, its availability for different contexts, concerns and approaches, then it also suggests the inadequacy of any one single perspective. For every apparently definitive context which is produced by critics as a map for locating Donne, a further, often alternative context is always likely to dislodge previous frameworks. Thus Donne remains other to the attempt to reduce his work to one or another philosophy, attitude, or social and political context. Perhaps it is this resistance of Donne to translation that defines his problematic, intangible identity.

II

I want now to turn more explicitly to those other intangible or disputedly tangible objects of our own time: literature and literary criticism. If religious belief and religious language were in crisis in Donne's time, then a similar crisis has befallen that body of texts once known as Literature, a body of texts that has itself often been constituted, by many critics and readers, as an alternative religion.[12] This crisis is, or has been seen as, part of a larger crisis of belief in all forms of essentialism.[13] Again this larger crisis has its equivalent reverberations in Donne's own search for essences. If, of a sudden, Donne seems curiously or conveniently modern, if it seems as though Donne is being manipulated to fit current concerns, then these are aspects of the very problem, of the relationship between the essential and the contingent, that I now wish to address. For do we inevitably reconstruct writers like Donne, and literature in general, in our own image? Or does Donne – does literature – possess an inviolable identity, an essential reality, which are independent of contingent historical constructions of them?

One of the differences that the intensively theoretical moment or series of moments of the 1970s and 1980s made was to doubt the kind of essentialism that granted concepts like literature a relatively stable and independent reality.[14] In 1972, the year of publication of the original Casebook on Donne, it was still possible to avoid or not to have been affected by new theory, and to affirm an identity for literature. Thus A. E. Dyson writes, in that Casebook:

> The critical forum is a place of vigorous conflict and disagreement, but there is nothing in this to cause dismay. What is attested is the complexity of human experience and the richness of literature, not any chaos or relativity of taste. A critic is better seen, no doubt, as an explorer than as an 'authority', but explorers ought to be, and usually are, well equipped.

> The effect of good criticism is to convince us of what C. S. Lewis called 'the enormous extension of our being which we owe to authors'. A Casebook will be justified only if it helps to promote the same end.[15]

The 'vigorous conflict and disagreement' referred to here are reflected in the essays included in the original Casebook, and indicate that the canon invoked by traditional criticism is not as fixed as some of the later critiques of the notion of canonicity claimed it to be.[16] What is not so much at stake in traditional criticism is the category of literature itself. Donne's place in the literary canon may be disputed, but the idea that critical commentary should attempt to mark off a special body of writing called literature is not. Significantly, it is almost exclusively Donne's love poetry, rather than his sermons or other prose works, that constitutes Donne's claim upon literary status. By contrast, the essays in this volume cover a diversity of genres, in addition to Donne's love lyrics.

The privileging of poetry within traditional criticism is largely the result of the highly influential New Criticism which flourished in the 1940s and 1950s and which emphasised and isolated the text-in-itself as the proper object of literary study. Poetry being especially amenable to close scrutiny and isolation, it was frequently poetry which sustained claims about the autonomy of literature. A classic and influential example of the old New Criticism in action is Cleanth Brooks' *The Well Wrought Urn*, the title of which is taken from a phrase in Donne's 'The Canonization'. For Brooks, the autonomy of the poem as literary artifact mirrors the affirmation of the lovers' own autonomy and independence:

> The poem is an instance of the doctrine which it asserts; it is both the assertion and the realisation of the assertion. The poet has actually before our eyes built within the song the 'pretty room' with which he says the lovers can be content. The poem itself is the well-wrought urn which can hold the lovers' ashes and which will not suffer in comparison with the prince's 'halfe-acre tomb'.

As the lovers remove themselves from the world of ordinary time and history, so, too, does the poem. For Brooks, the poem creates its own distinctive space or 'pretty room' by employing the language of paradox:

> almost any insight important enough to warrant a great poem apparently has to be stated in such terms. Deprived of the character of

paradox with its twin concomitants of irony and wonder, the matter of Donne's poems unravels into 'facts', biological, sociological, and economic.

According to Brooks, words in poetry 'are continually modifying each other, and thus violating their dictionary meanings'.[17] It is paradox's specific violation of ordinary sense upon which poetry depends for its transgression and transcendence of ordinary language.

New Criticism is a species of formalism. As the term suggests, formalism emphasises a text's formal features (such as the use of paradox in 'The Canonization'). In doing so, it provides us with a vocabulary with which to articulate those characteristics thought to be peculiar, or at least especially pertinent to, literary texts. Paradox, metaphor, omniscient narrator, narrative voice, imagery, persona, sestet, octet and so on are examples of a formalist vocabulary, which treats literature as a special form of expression, demanding a specialised or semi-specialised terminology. This emphasis upon the supposed extra-ordinariness of literary language links New Criticism, and other manifestations of formalism, to a Romantic and Modernist aesthetic, which grants to art, and especially to poetry, a capacity to transcend or transgress the limitations of their host culture. T. S. Eliot is the figure that links Romanticism, Modernism, New Criticism and Donne. Eliot's Prufrock may be a failed Romantic, and Eliot's ideas about the function of poetry significantly different from those of the Romantics, but Eliot nevertheless inherited from the Romantics a belief in the countercultural effectiveness of poetry. In championing Donne's ability to amalgamate disparate experience, Eliot paved the way for the New Critical appreciation of the metaphysicals' use of paradox to press ordinary language into new complex meaning.[18]

The original Donne Casebook of 1972 is largely based upon the premises of New Criticism, with literature taken to be a special category of writing, demanding close attention to its dense and complex language. Intellectual and social contexts are brought to bear upon Donne's poetry, but only as these illuminate the primary objects of analysis, the poems themselves. Although different accounts, deploying different criteria, are given of Donne's literary value, the assumption is that literature is the place where one can find, and keep on finding, special things. These special things might be the 'diversity of experience and feeling' that Joan Bennett claims to be 'among Donne's singular merits'; or 'the explosive dissonances ...

the sustained intensity and the dazzling nimbleness' which Arnold Stein finds in 'The Good Morrow'; or the notion, proffered by Helen Gardner, that

> Certain books, and certain ideas which we meet with in our reading, move us deeply and become part of our way of thinking because they make us conscious of the meaning of our own experience and reveal us to ourselves.[19]

Canonical texts may come and go as a result of the different criteria employed for evaluating them. Nevertheless, the idea that there is a valuable, but contestable, body of texts deserving of, in Frank Kermode's phrase, '"special forms of attention"',[20] grants to literature an albeit precarious reality, analogous to the problematic essences searched for in Donne's writing.

A contrasting, anti-essentialist perspective, which post-dates the theoretical explosion of the 1970s and 1980s, is Arthur Marotti's article of 1989, entitled 'John Donne, author':

> Thanks partly to poststructuralist criticism, we are able to see literary authorship as a cultural product rather than as a Platonic idea: we know that historically the 'author-function', like literature itself, has changed, shaped by the social and material conditions of writing.[21]

Eroded here is the precarious reality of the concept of literature, for literature is an empty term which different social formations construct differently. It is seen, in other words, as a wholly contingent rather than tentatively essentialist category. Marotti is not so much preoccupied with the question of what literature essentially is than with how such a notion gets constructed and whose social purposes and interests it serves.

One of the principles which the various recent forms of criticism share in common is a constructivist notion of language. Modern theoretical criticism has as one of its centrally informing ideas the notion that language constructs rather than simply reflects reality. Words like 'literature', 'author', 'self' do not mirror permanent, or to use Marotti's term, Platonic realities. They bring those realities into existence and, as words change their meanings over time, so, too, do the realities which they signify. What this means in practical terms, at least for Marotti, is that devices like paradox and ambiguity are treated less as essentially literary phenomena than as part of a complex social text or context, in which Donne and his coterie audience of fellow gentlemen-poets were involved. This context was one in which youthful aspirants to prestigious positions within the Elizabethan and Jacobean courts would characteristically compete with one another for employment and patronage, whilst maintaining an air of independence and detachment from the court and its power structures. For the paradoxes which form the basis of Brooks' autonomously literary version of Donne, Marotti, in his book, *John Donne, Coterie Poet*, substitutes a broader notion of paradox which resituates Donne within his social and historical context:

> As verse paradoxes, they [i.e. Donne's *Elegies*] draw on different literary antecedents and relate to the prose paradoxes Donne composed at the same time. And yet, both they and most of the other *Elegies* grew out of the same Inns-of-Court environment, which provided the social co-ordinates as well as the primary audience for the poems.[22]

From Marotti's perspective, a poem like 'The Canonization' only appears to be privileging the private world of the lovers over the public world which it invokes. The apparent independence of the lover disguises his political ambition, and the apparent autonomy of the poem as a literary and linguistic world unto itself disguises its porousness, its actual connectedness to the larger world of which it claims to be independent.

The questions Donne asks of the survival of God, or the beds of lovers, or 'gold to aery thinness beat', could be similarly asked of literature once its identifying characteristics have been called into question. One, but not the only, outcome of an emphasis, such as Marotti's, upon the cultural construction of concepts like literature, is the erosion of the identity of literature and literary criticism as autonomous practices. During the 1970s and 1980s, literary criticism rapidly imported a range of concepts from disciplines which might once have been thought foreign to the study of literature. As Annabel Paterson puts it:

> Literary studies was caught up in a series of paradigm shifts, in a whirlwind of larger ideas and projects: the philosophy of language (from Chomsky to Saussure); structuralist anthropology (from Lévi-Strauss to Northrop Frye); deconstructive critique of rationalism by Derrida and de Man; a revival of philosophical pragmatism by Richard Rorty; Marxist political philosophy as resuscitated by Althusser; a wave of academic feminism; the civil rights movement and its logical consequence, Afro-American studies; and the related

though not identical movements for multiculturalism and interdisciplinary studies. It may later occur to analysts of the past half century as decidedly odd that literary study, rather than sinking into insignificance as a result, expanded to meet the challenge, became indeed so voracious of concepts and knowledge systems seemingly extraneous to its central concerns that it is now, as I write in the 1990s, and in certain quarters where these developments are deemed reprehensible, held responsible for the whole affair.[23]

Literary critics now perform a diverse range of intellectual tasks, beyond and above the study of the words on the page of a literary text, presumed to be relatively self-sufficient. The purist's anxiety, intimated by Patterson, that literature is now dead, is based upon this diversification, or, to put it more perjoratively, this fragmentation of literary studies.

Arguments for and against theory vary, but a fair number of them turn upon the issue of the (supposed) hijacking by theory of the (supposed) specificity and autonomy of literature. However, this opposition seems to me to be too stark. One outcome of modern theory's suspicion of essentialism may be an unceremonious disregard for things-in-themselves, but there are strands of theory whose preoccupation with the albeit erasable traces and identifying marks of things maintains a respect for their specificity and particularity.[24] It seems to me that the best kinds of modern theoretical criticism straddle the dividing line between essentialist and anti-essentialist thinking by preserving a notion of literature's otherness and difference, whilst calling into question the idea of its absolute autonomy.

III

The rest of this introduction will do several things: introduce the essays; outline some of the theories (deconstruction, psychoanalysis, feminism, New Historicism) on which they draw; and continue to address and develop the question, when is a door not a door? This question, asking about the identifying marks which separate one thing off from another thing, will form the basis of the narrative I want to weave around the essays. Can a phenomenon, like a poem, or a person, or love, ever be entirely itself, or are these things more or less empty categories which different cultural formations contingently fill, and which are subject to the endless substitutions and disfigurements effected by language? I should perhaps confess here to a belief in the inviolable uniqueness and particularity of things: in the uniqueness of a Donne poem, for example, and the particularity of a style that bears his own unique signature. But this has to be said carefully, because Donne, as I have already suggested, was also preoccupied and exhilarated by experimentation and dispersal, by movements away from a centred self. The notion of particularity, which I think Donne himself is partly responsible for encouraging, should not be taken to imply a one-dimensionality, for an object may have many different characteristics whilst maintaining its identity as that thing and no other. These questions of particularity and identifying marks will be located by focusing upon the attestedly internal dynamics of phenomena, like desire and lyric poetry. At the same time, attention will be given to the effects which Donne's use of analogy and metaphor has upon the ostensible identity of things, people and concepts. The essays' own integrity and internal dynamics will hopefully be preserved, in the threading of this connecting narrative between them.

IV

The first four essays represent four influential strands of modern theoretical criticism: New Historicism; poststructuralism; psychoanalysis; and feminism. Variations and combinations of these approaches will appear in subsequent essays, and each of these first four essays itself combines a variety of perspectives. Nevertheless, the main theoretical trajectory of each essay is identifiable.

It seems appropriate to begin the collection with an example of New Historicist criticism, as New Historicism has bulked large in Renaissance studies in recent years. If the newness of New Historicism is taken to imply that historical approaches to texts are new, then the term is misleading, particularly in the context of Renaissance Studies, where historical scholarship has for a long time thrived. What is new is the *kind* of history undertaken by New Historicists. Where older forms of historical writing maintain a sense of literature's difference by distinguishing between the background of historical influences, and the foreground of the text itself, New Historicists tend to be more subversive of the concept of boundaried space.[25]

So Achsah Guibbory's essay (1), '"Oh, let mee not serve so": The Politics of Love in Donne's *Elegies*', calls into question modern

separations between private and public, love and politics, by disclosing the political nature of love and love poetry in the Elizabethan
period. Guibbory argues that the *Elegies* compensate for the destabilisation of patriarchal gender hierarchies generated by the powerful female monarchy of Elizabeth I, by debasing women and
attempting to restore male control within the erotic relationships
which the poems present. This attempt is only partially successful,
however, as both patriarchal boundaries in particular, and cognitive
boundaries in general (between love, politics and religion), remain
fluid. It is the perceived traffic in Donne and other Renaissance
writers between *apparently* disparate kinds of language (the language of love and language of patronage), and different kinds of
genre (political poetry and love poetry), which has fuelled the
mobile, interdisciplinary, anti-essentialist work of New Historicists
such as Guibbory and Marotti.

The second essay, Tilottama Rajan's '"Nothing sooner broke":
Donne's *Songs and Sonets* as Self-Consuming Artifact', is another
powerful and resolutely anti-essentialist piece of modern theoretical
criticism. Rajan discusses the inability of Donne's poetry to express
essential truths of any kind, whether these are about the personality
of the author; God; Donne's historical context; love; or the human
condition. For the poems to be about something, and to illuminate
the essence of that something, they would have to be able to refer to
objects and experiences as if they existed outside of language.
Donne's poetry instead subverts its own referential or expressive aspirations: aspirations which would ground truths or realities outside
of the poems' provisional and precarious creation of them. This is
because there is no outside to language. Language is all we have,
and language is irredeemably anti- or non-foundational, meaning
that it creates unstable realities, instead of accurately mirroring a
stable one.

Rajan's poststructuralist method is a development of Ferdinand
de Saussure's hugely influential theory of language, which held that
words lack positive, autonomous meaning because meaning is only
ever created relationally, through difference.[26] The word or signifier
'red' has a number of possible meanings or signifieds: for example,
danger, passion, socialist and stop. The meaning of a signifier can
only be determined by the linguistic context in which it is placed (as
in red/amber/green), in other words, by the other signifiers which
surround it. We know red means stop in the context of the traffic
light sequence, by virtue of red's difference from amber and green.

Elsewhere, in another system of contrasting terms (for example, red/blue), red signifies differently. There are two casualties that this theory of language creates. One is any notion of an external reality: reality is created through language and its internal organisation of signifiers. The other casualty is stability, for signifiers do not have a stable one-to-one correspondence with their signifieds. 'Red' is never entirely itself because it has a number of different meanings.[27] There is, then, an emptiness about language, born of the signifier's lack of a stable content, and it is this emptiness, this tendency of verbal constructs to cancel themselves out which Rajan finds in Donne's 'self-consuming' artifacts.

The third essay, Catherine Belsey's 'John Donne's Worlds of Desire', is again broadly anti-essentialist in that it refuses to recognise the separate identity of the literary text in general, and of the love lyric in particular. The essay begins, like Guibbory's, by pointing to the interchangeable realms of love, gender politics and history, the most glaring example of which is the analogy frequently drawn by male love poets between exploration and conquest of the female body, and exploration and conquest of the new world. However, Belsey is also keen to attend to the internal dynamics of love and desire, for desire, she suggests, 'has its own political history',[28] which is separate from other kinds of history: for example, the history of imperialism or of representations of women by men. The psychoanalytic perspectives which Belsey makes use of might be seen as the analytical equivalent of 'getting involved', of passing beyond the threshold of a lover's bedroom. The cultural historian, on the other hand, may be more inclined to remain on the threshold. Refusing to acknowledge love's own special décor/geography, s/he sees love as the merely secondary symptom of a primary reality located elsewhere, in socioeconomic conditions.[29] But who is to say what comes first? For many psychoanalysts, love is primary, the mother being the first and primal love object. What comes after love is society and the Symbolic (meaning language, and the symbolic/cultural creation of desire). From this perspective, Donne's love poems can be seen as attempting to discover or recover something more essential, more primary, than his merely social self.

However, the naming of this more primary 'something else' is deeply problematic for Belsey, as language never allows us to attain full recognition of what it is we lack. Utilising the poststructuralist psychoanalytic theories of Julia Kristeva and Jacques Lacan, Belsey explores the elusiveness of desire, an elusiveness that is initiated by language itself. For Belsey, language is the breeding ground of desire. To grasp this, think of language, think of this sentence as an ...

You want to know the end? There is no end to language. Sentences end, only to begin again.

And again.

Through language's tantalising deferral of gratification, we learn desire; and we learn the lack upon which desire is predicated. Principal amongst language's deferred objects of desire is the subject's own subjectivity, for language tantalises us by almost but not quite making possible a full sense of ourselves as differentiated and autonomous. If the difference inscribed in language between I and you compensates for separation (from the maternal body), by giving us a means of identifying ourselves, then this is misleading, as the linguistic differentiation of the I actually entails endless differentiation and dispersal. Just as 'red' is never entirely itself, neither is 'i', for that sIgn, like red, can be used in a multiplicity of linguistic and social contexts.[30] Belsey sees Donne as attempting to overcome this situation of lack and dispersal by placing himself as the 'origin of difference, and not merely its effect'. Through his seeming verbal mastery Donne recovers a fullness of being beyond that of the subject endlessly unsettled by the cultural symbolic. The historical dimension which Belsey gives to this account of psycho-linguistic processes is to locate Donne in the context of a culture 'in the process of producing as the heart of society a private world of intimacy and personal experience, to be distinguished from the world of work, and to be valued above the public and the political'.[31] The lyric, as the utopian expression of an untrammelled subjectivity, is itself implicated in the emerging demarcations described by Belsey, for the lyric will eventually come to epitomise literature's own transcendence of history and politics.

The fourth essay, Barbara Estrin's 'Small Change: Defections from Petrarchan and Spenserian Poetics', is a feminist reconsideration of the hierarchies which have been seen to exist, by previous feminist critics, between Donne's male speakers and their female addressees. Such claims as Janel Mueller's, that 'Donne acutely delineates a whole range of male attitudinising about love', is a salutary antidote to the kind of unthinking canonisation which would confer upon male attitudes to love the specious legitimacy of a universal norm.[32] For Estrin, however, feminist critics have not been sufficiently attentive to lyric poetry as a form of '"dream-work"' which 'refigures desire in ways that are not always definable by the biographical self or apparent to the historian'.[33]

Estrin is interested, then, in the utopian potential of poetry to transcend the constraints of history and biography, whilst resisting the temptation to close in upon itself and its own powers of creation. Donne's love poetry achieves this balance, according to Estrin, by defecting from those Petrarchan poetic traditions where the lover/poet rests contented with his own narcissistic creation of the beloved. Within these traditions, poetry functions as a compensatory substitute for the erotic encounter itself. For Estrin's Donne, however, 'no alternative feeling can substitute for love'.[34] The poems create their own verbal universes, but they do not shut themselves off from the imagined influence and potency of the love object, for the love object offers the speaker the possibility of discovering those positive differences within himself which prevent him, and his love poetry, from stagnating. This, for Estrin, is what constitutes the dream-work of poetry. Like Belsey and Rajan but from a different perspective, Estrin thus emphasises the utopianism which may be thought of as one of the lyric's distinguishing traits, and which prevents its complete assimilation to existing realities. At the same time, Donne's poetry is not so narcissistically self-enclosed and self-regarding as to remain impervious to the influence of the other. For Estrin, subject and object, self and other exist in a state of mutually dependent, utopian possibility.

V

Essays 5 and 6 can be grouped together (alongside Guibbory's essay), under the heading 'Forms of Historicism'. Taken together, these essays stage a debate about historical approaches to literature, and raise questions about the extent to which literature, once historicised, survives as a meaningful category. In the fifth essay, entitled 'The Lyric in the Field of Information: Autopoiesis and History in Donne's *Songs and Sonnets'*, Richard Halpern provocatively rehabilitates (old) New Critical and Modernist notions of literature's autonomy, by proposing that the concepts of autonomy and boundaried space are themselves Renaissance inventions. In contrast to the insistence of other historical approaches, such as Guibbory's, upon interchangeability, Halpern argues that the lyric, like other aspects of life within an increasingly specialised society, forms its own closed system. 'Autopoiesis' is the term Halpern borrows from the natural and social sciences to describe the diversification of modern culture which leaves systems or practices like literature, the law, love, and sexuality, in worlds of their own.

Focusing in particular on the discourse of love, Halpern shows how Donne's idiosyncratic employment of metaphor allows love to disappear into an impenetrable space of its own. Metaphor, suggests Halpern, 'does not work ... as a window which allows us to peer voyeuristically into love's pretty rooms; it is, rather, a mirrored surface which simply reflects the public world back onto itself'.[35] This is because the incongruity of such metaphors for love as the compasses image in 'A Valediction: Forbidding Mourning' hides rather than illuminates the reality which the metaphor purportedly describes. Love is elsewhere, other to a metaphor which so obviously belongs to another field of experience.

Taking together the approaches thus far discussed, it is tempting to suggest that Donne exists on the cusp of two contrasting principles: one based on analogy, connectedness and interchangeability; the other on difference and particularity. In 'Air and Angels', the idea that the body functions as a physical house/container for an otherwise unhoused and ethereal soul indicates an analogical mode of thinking which conceives of the world in terms of intersections and meeting places. Yet also registered within the same poem is the notion of things, like the body, having a life separate from the place assigned to them within any given or invented system of correspondences.[36] Extending this perspective to Donne's writing itself, we might say that a typical Donne text is at once that densely populated place where diverse ideas, feelings and cultural references meet, clash, and interchange; and at the same time a distinctive verbal construct, driven by its own idiosyncratic logic.

The sixth essay, by David Aers and Gunther Kress, entitled '"Darke texts need notes": Versions of Self in Donne's Verse Epistles', bears out some of the above points, and can be situated somewhere between the contrasting historical approaches of Halpern's essay, on the one hand, and Achsah Guibbory's, on the other. For if Guibbory's historical method is broadly connective in its insistence upon the relationship between realms (such as the literary and the non-literary, or the private and the public), and if Halpern's contrasting historical emphasis is upon the developing autonomy of cultural practices (such as literature), then the essay by Aers and Kress is poised between these two models. Their Donne is a Donne who himself inhabits two contrasting realms, which correspond to two competing models of self: one realm is a Platonic realm where the self is viewed, in essentialist terms, as unchanging and transcendent of society; the other is the alchemicising realm of Donne's 'present historical world ... a world where value is a function of contingent market relations, supply and demand, mere "circumstance"'.[37] Thus where the Platonic self maintains its own distinct shape, the worldly, mutable self is available for endless translation.

The diverse vocabularies (metaphysical, economic, ethical, profane and so on) which Aers and Kress find at work in a single, closely analysed verse letter, in themselves indicate Donne's ability, referred to earlier, to translate himself into different idioms and genres. At the same time, Donne resists translation, either through appeals to an inviolable self, or through the obscurity of poems and texts which defy easy appropriation to one or another context. The essay by Aers and Kress is especially useful in this respect, for in dealing with a genre so explicitly rooted in social, not to say, pragmatic circumstances as the patronage poem, they simultaneously reveal the ways in which Donne's poems de-contextualise themselves.

VI

The next two essays present further examples of feminist approaches at the same time as they develop the concerns of previous essays, with history, language and (in the case of essay 7) psychoanalysis. The seventh essay, Elizabeth Harvey's 'Matrix as Metaphor: Midwifery and the Conception of Voice', focuses principally upon the *Anniversaries*, and explores the encroachment of men and male poets into areas, such as midwifery, birth and the female body, previously marked off as exclusively female spaces. Harvey's essay forms interesting connections with Halpern's theory of autopoiesis, and with the emphasis of other essays upon emerging divisions between public and private, in that it, too, acknowledges the inward turn taken by male poets like Donne. Noticing the connection drawn in the period between birthing and creativity, the uterus and the imagination, Harvey explores the way in which the female body became the site of renewed interest for men looking to reveal the secrets, plenitude and creativity thought to inhere in the maternal body. The crucial difference between Halpern's and Harvey's essays is that where Halpern tends to credit Donne and other male lyric poets with the invention of private spheres and autonomous

spaces, Harvey draws attention to the prior existence of autonomous female spaces which men, looking beyond the public realm
of the Symbolic, appropriate.

Central, once again, to this process of appropriation is the principle of substitution embodied in the use of metaphor and analogy.
Elizabeth Drury, the ostensible source of the *Anniversaries'* inspiration, loses her individual, bodily identity in the transfers which are
effected by the poems' method of likening her to other things: 'her
physical body is conflated with the world's, and synecdochised, it
continues to inform Donne's description of it.' Donne's desire to
restore coherence and connectedness to a fragmented macrocosm
drains microcosms of their specificity: 'What is specific to woman
(the womb) is generalised to all humanity.'[38] Harvey's exploration
of metaphor thus returns us once again to the issue of particularity
and its dispersal via the use of analogy.

In the eighth essay, 'Masculine Persuasive Force: Donne and
Verbal Power', Stanley Fish explores Donne's pervasive use of
analogy, and its implications for those on its receiving end.
Discussing a wide range of poems, which include elegies, satires and
religious sonnets, Fish shows how Donne's verbal power effectively
annihilates the resistance of others to his conceit, his textualisation
of them. In the highly mediated world (similar to the world of
market relations described by Aers and Kress) of a Donne poem,
nothing is ever so completely itself that it cannot become, be compared to, or rewritten as, something else.

Donne's speakers, as creators rather than creatures of creation,
may presume to stand outside of this principle of unfettered substitution and exchange, but they, too, are implicated in it. The I of
'Elegy 7', for example, 'wants to bear his own sense, wants to be inscribed by convictions to which his will has assented; he doesn't
want to be someone else's text'.[39] Nevertheless, he shares the same
fate as those upon whom he writes, which is to become passively
palimpsestic texts, 'worked on, ploughed, appropriated, violated'.[40]

VII

The final essays extend the range of genres discussed in the collection still further by exploring Donne's sermons and *Holy Sonnets*.
The volume ends with two essays exclusively devoted to Donne's
religious writing because, as Debora Shuger has suggested, religion

in this period 'is the cultural matrix for explorations of virtually every topic: kingship, selfhood, rationality, language, marriage, ethics, and so forth'.[41] Religion is, in other words, as nomadic, multi-faceted and connective a discourse as a typical Donne text. Indeed, it was largely from religious discourse that Donne fashioned his own analogical ways of thinking. Thus the same question that I have been asking of Donne, poetry, love, literature, self and so on, may be asked of God. What survives of God after the translation of him/her/it into different tongues?

Emphasis upon the real or presumed particularity of things (poems, bodies, literature, selves, love, desire, God) should not be taken to suggest, though, that their Platonic natures are so static and so essential as never to be questionable, relocatable or differently in-scribed. The liquidity of things and concepts fascinated Donne, and was the motor for social, religious and personal transformation. The ninth essay, Nancy Wright's 'The *Figura* of the Martyr in Donne's Sermons', explores the state of linguistic, religious and ideological de-regulation that existed in the Renaissance. Wright focuses in par-ticular upon the failed attempt by secular authorities to monopolise religious truth. The principle of analogy is again important to Wright's argument, 'analogical predication' being the principle whereby an equivalence was created between divine and secular spheres.[42] Wright suggests that while this principle was used to strengthen hierarchy (by creating a correspondence between monar-chial and divine authority), it could be redeployed to sanctify and consecrate other aspects of secular life, such as, for example, love.

Building on Wright's thesis, it is possible to suggest that this unfixing of analogical correspondences actually depends upon a per-ception of incommensurability: a king may be like God, but the re-lationship is approximate rather than exact. Donne himself was not such a committed literalist (or believer in transubstantiation) that he took metaphors completely seriously all of the time. To affirm liter-alistically that wine is the blood of Christ erases the difference of wine from blood (to the extent of putting one off the drink, perhaps). It was the perceived inexactness or speciousness of ho-mologies that allowed Donne to invent the alternative analogical systems described by Wright (and, in previous essays, by Fish, Belsey and Halpern). In Wright's discussion, Donne is seen as conferring upon individual testimony to the word of God, the sanctity and rev-erence which the state would have preferred to have monopolised for itself. In this revised form of correspondence between the secular and the sacred, it is subjective testimony, rather than the state, that functions as the conduit for God.

The final essay, William Kerrigan's 'The Fearful Accommodations of John Donne', is a fitting conclusion to the collection in its eloquent and wide-ranging rearticulation of the contrasting principles, variously explored and/or practised by other contributors, of interchangeability, on the one hand, and incommensurability, on the other. Accommodation is the term Kerrigan uses to describe the anthropomorphic mediation of God through the use of analogies between the secular and the sacred. The essay explores the extent to which theologians and religious writers from Augustine to Milton either embraced or resisted the construction of God in one or another human image, and ends by discussing the crude anthropomorphism of two of the *Holy Sonnets*, including the 'Batter my Heart' poem in which God is likened to a rapist.

For Kerrigan, however, a sense of the incommensurability between the human and divine is redeemed by the superhuman paradox of *chaste* ravishing, and by the perversity of a metaphor which says more about the (male) perceiver than the perceived. The point Kerrigan goes on to make, that when 'the metaphor turns perverse, God vacates the metaphor', is similar to Richard Halpern's discussion of Donne's use of metaphor to veil, rather than to illuminate, the object of a comparison. Thus against a God who would be rendered knowable through 'the unfolding of anthropomorphic metaphors', Donne posits a God who remains mysteriously other to his appropriations of him.[43]

Might the same, to risk one final analogy, be said of Donne's writing, and more generally, of those categories, of the literary and the aesthetic, which we still maintain as special and distinctive whilst continuing to use them for a variety of other purposes?[44] Modern theoretical approaches have excitingly extended the boundaries of literary criticism, but there is a danger of collapsing discrete or semiautonomous discourses into one another in the name of a flattened out notion of cultural representation. It seems to me that while all of the essays in this volume provokingly question the absolute autonomy of the literary, many of them maintain a sense of its Platonic or historically rooted particularity. If literary criticism has at least one of its origins in a modernist aesthetic which saw literature as an antidote to uniformity, then there are still good reasons for wanting to preserve its identity as a site of creativity, resistance and special insight.

NOTES

1. *John Donne: The Complete English Poems*, ed. A. J. Smith (1971; rpt. Harmondsworth, 1984), p. 41, ll. 1–2.

2. Ibid., p. 41, ll. 21–2.

3. *Devotions Upon Emergent Occasions*, ed. Anthony Raspa (Montreal, 1975), p. 16.

4. *Complete English Poems*, p. 81, ll. 29–30.

5. *The Sermons of John Donne*, ed. George R. Potter and Evelyn Simpson, 10 vols (Berkeley, CA, 1953–62), 7.10.271. The reference is to volume, sermon, and page.

6. A similar point about the relativism implied by Copernican philosophy is made by Thomas Docherty in *John Donne, Undone* (London, 1986), pp. 23–4.

7. *Complete English Poems*, p. 80, ll. 21–2.

8. Ibid., pp. 72–3, ll. 21–2; 28–9; 35–6.

9. Ibid., p. 72, l. 10; 12; 21.

10. Ibid., p. 72, l. 24.

11. Examples of these various contextual approaches include, respectively: John Stachniewski, 'John Donne: The Despair of the "Holy Sonnets", *English Literary History*, 48 (1981), 677–705; John Carey, *John Donne: Life, Mind and Art* (London, 1981); Joan Faust, 'John Donne's Verse Letters to the Countess of Bedford: Mediators in a Poet–Patroness Relationship', *John Donne Journal*, 12 (1993), 79–99; Donald Guss, *John Donne, Petrarchist* (Detroit, 1966); William Empson, 'Donne the Space Man', in John Haffenden (ed.), *William Empson: Essays on Renaissance Literature* (1993; rpt. Cambridge, 1995), pp. 78–128; Arthur F. Marotti, *John Donne, Coterie Poet* (Madison, WI, 1986); and Rosemond Tuve, *Elizabethan and Metaphysical Imagery* (Chicago, 1947).

12. Elizabeth Harvey and Katharine Maus draw a similar analogy between the crisis precipitated by new philosophy in Donne's time and by modern theory in our own, in their introduction to *Soliciting Interpretation: Literary Theory and Seventeenth-Century English Poetry*, ed. Elizabeth D. Harvey and Katharine Eisaman Maus (Chicago, 1990), p. ix.

13. Modern theories have repeatedly questioned the idea that there is, for example, an unchanging human nature and that every human being possesses an essential, 'core' self. Subjectivity has been an especially debated topic in modern theory. One of the reasons for this may be that the self is theory's 'litmus paper': if the self, which is often seen as

the cornerstone of essentialist thought, can be proved to be invented rather than 'real', then all the other givens of essentialism are similarly questionable. See, as an example of the (Renaissance) self perceived as construct rather than essence, Stephen Greenblatt's influential *Renaissance Self-Fashioning: From More to Shakespeare* (Chicago, 1980).

14. Theorists importing structuralism, poststructuralism, semiotics, feminism and Marxism into literary study in the 1970s and 1980s variously contributed to the interrogation of essentialist concepts of reality. See, for example, Terence Hawkes, *Structuralism and Semiotics* (London, 1977); Terry Eagleton, *Literary Theory: An Introduction* (Oxford, 1983); and Catherine Belsey, *Critical Practice* (London, 1980).

15. A. E. Dyson, 'General Editor's Preface', in Julian Lovelock (ed.), *Donne: Songs and Sonets* (1973; rpt. Basingstoke, 1987), p. 9.

16. See Frank Kermode's similar argument in *An Appetite for Poetry* (London, 1989), p. 15.

17. Cleanth Brooks, *The Well Wrought Urn*, revised edn (London, 1968), pp. 12, 13, 6. John Guibbory also discusses Brooks' interpretation of 'The Canonization', contrasting it with Arthur Marotti's historicist analysis. The conclusions he draws, however, are different from mine. See John Guibbory, 'Canon', in *Critical Terms for Literary Study*, ed. Frank Lentricchia and Thomas McLaughlin (Chicago, 1990), pp. 244–8.

18. T. S. Eliot, 'The Metaphysical Poets', in *Selected Essays*, 3rd edn (London, 1966), pp. 281–91.

19. Joan Bennet, 'The Love Poetry of John Donne – A Reply to Mr. C. S. Lewis'; Arnold Stein, 'The Good-Morrow'; Helen Gardner, 'The Argument about "The Ecstasy"', in Julian Lovelock (ed.), *Donne: Songs and Sonets*, pp. 154, 157, 242.

20. Kermode, *Appetite*, p. 16.

21. Arthur F. Marotti, 'John Donne, author', *Journal of Medieval and Renaissance Studies*, 19 (1989), 69–82, 69.

22. Marotti, *Coterie*, pp. 45–6.

23. Annabel Patterson, *Reading Between the Lines* (London, 1993), p. 4.

24. For example, Jacques Derrida's concept of the trace presupposes the capacity of signs to leave their own distinctive marks upon one another. See Jacques Derrida, *Positions*, trans. Alan Bass (London, 1981), pp. 24–9.

25. For further discussions of new and old versions of historicism, see Marjorie Levinson, Marilyn Butler, Jerome McGann and Paul Hamilton (eds), *Rethinking Historicism* (Oxford, 1989); Paul Hamilton, *Historicism* (London, 1996); Ramon Selden, Peter Widdowson and

Peter Brooker, *A Reader's Guide to Contemporary Literary Theory*, 4th edn (London, 1997), pp. 187–95; Richard Strier, Leah Marcus, Richard Helgerson and James G. Turner, 'Historicism, New and Old: Excerpts from a Panel Discussion', in Claude J. Summers and Ted-Larry Pebworth (eds), *'The Muses Common-Weale': Poetry and Politics in the Seventeenth Century* (Columbia, MO, 1988), pp. 207–17; and Harold Veeser (ed.), *The New Historicism* (New York, 1994).

26. For a clear and concise account of Saussure's theory of language, see David Robey, 'Modern Linguistics and the Language of Literature', in *Modern Literary Theory: A Comparative Introduction*, 2nd edn (London, 1986), pp. 46–51.

27. For further discussions of poststructuralist theories, see Christopher Norris, *Deconstruction: Theory and Practice* (London, 1982); and Selden, Widdowson and Brooker, *A Reader's Guide*, pp. 150–99.

28. See p. 64 below.

29. See Achsah Guibbory's similar point about Arthur Marotti's approach in particular, at the beginning of her essay (p. 25 below).

30. For further discussions of psychoanalytic criticism, see Maud Ellman (ed.), *Psychoanalytic Literary Criticism* (London, 1994); Shoshana Felman (ed.), *Literature and Psychoanalysis: The Question of Reading – Otherwise* (Baltimore, MD, 1982); Selden, Widdowson and Brooker, *A Reader's Guide*, pp. 161–70; and Elizabeth Wright, *Psychoanalytic Criticism: Theory in Practice* (London, 1984).

31. See pp. 69, 71 below.

32. Janel Mueller, 'Women Among the Metaphysicals: A Case, Mostly, of Being Donne For', *Modern Philology*, 87 (1989), 142–58, 145. For further discussion of feminist theory, see Mary Eagleton (ed.), *Feminist Literary Theory: A Reader* (Oxford, 1986); Maggie Humm, *The Dictionary of Feminist Theory* (Hemel Hempstead, 1989); Toril Moi, *Sexual/Textual Politics* (London, 1985); and Selden, Widdowson and Brooker, *A Reader's Guide*, pp. 121–49;

33. See p. 83 below.

34. See p. 91 below.

35. See p. 114 below.

36. Debora Kuller Shuger, *Habits of Thought in the English Renaissance* (Berkeley, CA, 1990) makes the interesting point that the 'impulse to define and distinguish ... results from a prior sense of confusion and lack of demarcation' (p. 10). See also John Carey's discussion of Donne's fascination with joins and divisions (*Life, Mind and Art*, pp. 261–79); and Michel Foucault's discussion of similitude in the Renaissance, in *The Order of Things*, trans. Alan Sheridan (London, 1970), pp. 34–44.

37. See p. 124 below.

38. See pp. 149, 152 below.

39. Stanley Fish, 'Masculine Persuasive Force: Donne and Verbal Power', in *Soliciting interpretation: Literary Theory and Seventeenth-Century English Poetry*, ed. Elizabeth Harvey and Katharine Eisaman Maus (Chicago, 1990), p. 230. [This is a quotation from Fish's original essay, which, for reasons of space, has had to be cut. Ed.]

40. See p. 162 below.

41. Debora Shuger, *Habits of Thought*, p. 6.

42. See p. 185 below.

43. See pp. 211, 207 below.

44. The notion that the aesthetic is in excess of any attempt to conceptualise it has (one of) its influential origins in the work of Immanuel Kant. See *The Critique of Judgement*, trans. J. C. Meredith (Oxford, 1928). As a 'postmodern' variation on the Kantian insistence upon the ineffable as the basis of aesthetic experience, see Jean-François Lyotard, 'Answering the Question: What is Postmodernism', trans. Régis Durand, in *The Postmodern Condition: A Report on Knowledge*, trans. Geoff Bennington and Brian Massumi (1984; rpt. Manchester, 1994), pp. 71–82.

1

'Oh, let mee not serve so': The Politics of Love in Donne's *Elegies*

ACHSAH GUIBBORY

For modern readers, accustomed to distinct separations between private and public, love and politics may seem strange bedfellows. But recent studies have made us aware of important connections between amatory poetry and patronage, between the discourse of (courtly) love and the seeking of advancement by aspiring men at Queen Elizabeth's court.[1] Arthur Marotti, especially, has analysed the political circumstances and dimensions of Donne's amatory poetry, arguing that we should see it as 'coterie' poetry written in an 'encoded' language, embodying Donne's frustrated ambitions for socioeconomic, political power even when, *especially* when, he is writing about love.[2]

Marotti's discussion of the interrelations between politics and the languages of love is deservedly influential. But his argument (both in the book on Donne and in his important earlier article on Elizabethan sonnet sequences) fosters a certain distortion, for repeatedly Marotti's language implies that the *real* subject of this poetry is socioeconomic power and ambition. While he brilliantly shows the political dimensions of the languages of courtly love as used in Elizabethan poetry, the effect of his argument is to suggest not so much the *inter*relations between love and politics but the centrality of socioeconomic concerns. Love becomes merely the vehicle of the metaphor; the tenor is invariably political. In the interest of deciphering this political 'meaning', amatory relations between men and women tend to all but disappear.

I want to build on Marotti's sense of the political dimension of Donne's witty love poetry, by arguing not that love is a metaphor for politics but that love itself is political – involves power transactions between men and women. By privileging neither Donne's ambitions for socioeconomic power nor his personal need for a fulfilling emotional relationship with a woman, I re-evaluate the interrelationship between love and politics. I will focus on Donne's depictions of amatory relationships – his representation of the female body, sexual relations, and sexual difference – to show how he represents power relationships in love and how love repeatedly intersects public politics. In Donne's treatment of love in the *Elegies*, the public world of politics and the intimacies of the private world are often inseparable.[3]

The 'direct, natural, and necessary relation of person to person is the *relation of man to woman*'.[4] Though the words are Karl Marx's, the notion was well understood in the Renaissance. As Milton's portrayal of the 'society' of Adam and Eve makes clear, the relationship between man and woman is thought to constitute the basic unit of society. Apparently natural but also culturally determined, that relationship offers a potential image of the organisation and distribution of power in the larger society. Milton's treatment of Adam and Eve in *Paradise Lost* reveals his awareness of a political dimension to interpersonal, sexual relations. Donne, too, understood the political dimension of amatory relations, exploiting it in his *Elegies*. Donne repeatedly in these poems envisions relations between the sexes as a site of conflict, thereby mirroring a larger society in which there is considerable anxiety about the lines and boundaries of power.

Exploring male/female relations, Donne's *Elegies* focus insistently on the body, especially the female body. The human body commonly functions as what the anthropologist Mary Douglas has called a 'natural symbol' of society – a 'model' symbolically expressing the values and orders, powers and dangers, of the social body.[5] Thus it is not surprising that Donne's representations of the body, as well as of male/female sexual relations, have a sociopolitical significance.

In discussing the male/female relations in the *Elegies*, I will deal with the misogyny evident in many of these poems, but often repressed in critical readings of Donne.[6] There is in many of the *Elegies* a persistent misogyny, indeed a revulsion at the female body, which has provoked various responses. Some readers give these poems scant attention, preferring to focus on the more easily admired poems of the *Songs and Sonnets* like 'The Good-morrow', 'The Canonization', or 'The Ecstasy', which celebrate a mutual love that attributes to the mistress special importance and value. Others see the misogyny as simply a matter of 'literary convention' (which skirts the issue of why authors are attracted to some literary conventions and not to others), or as an example of Donne's desire to shock or his outrageous wit, or as one posture among many that Donne tries out in his poetry. But these critical responses effectively tame Donne's *Elegies*. Yes, Donne is being outrageously, shockingly witty, but why are women the subject of degradation in so much of the wit? Granted there is humour in these poems, but jokes often have a serious dimension and reveal much about the person. And though Donne adopts various personae and tries out a variety of postures, at some level he possesses an ability to identify (even if briefly) with these roles. It is unfair to Donne's poetry, and inconsistent, to treat the mysogynous, cynical poems as rhetorical posturing or as exercises in witty manipulation of literary convention (hence, not 'really' meant) while reading the celebrations of mutual love as indicative of Donne's 'true' feelings. Though we may not like to admit the presence of misogyny in one of the greatest love poets in the English language, we need to come to terms with it, especially in the *Elegies* where it appears so strongly. What I will be arguing about the *Elegies* is not meant to be taken as the whole picture of Donne – obviously, the canon is extensive and various, and his attitudes are quite different in many of the *Songs and Sonnets* – but it is one part of Donne's works that needs to be understood and historicised rather than repressed if we are to have a fuller understanding of the poet and the canon.

Many if not most of Donne's *Elegies* were written in the 1590s, when England was ruled by a female monarch who demanded faithful service and devotion from aspiring men.[7] The mere presence of a female monarch is insufficient to account for the *Elegies*, but it does suggest an initial historical context for these poems. Elizabeth, the 'woman on top' (to use Natalie Zemon Davis's phrase) was an anomaly in a strongly patriarchal, hierarchical culture in which women were considered subordinate to men.[8] It is difficult to ascertain the effect that rule by a female monarch had on the position of women. Though she may have provided an encouraging example for women, it is likely that, as the exception, she actually confirmed the rule of patriarchy in English society. But for men there were tensions inherent in submission to the authority of a queen in what was otherwise a culture in which power and authority were invested in men. As Constance Jordan remarks, the prospect of a female ruler 'could hardly have been regarded with anything but concern'; and the actual presence of a woman on the throne in England gave focus to a debate about the legitimacy of woman's rule.[9]

Tensions over submission to female rule are strikingly evident in Donne's representation of private love relationships in the *Elegies*. Many poems attack or reject female dominance in love and attempt to reassert male control. Though Marotti has well described fantasies of control in these poems, it has not been sufficiently appreciated how much the degradation and conquest of women is presented as essential to that control, nor how these efforts to control woman have a special sociopolitical meaning. 'Private' relations between man and woman are closely connected to the pattern of relations in the larger social body – a point recognised by Milton in his divorce tracts, for example, when he set about to reform the institution of marriage. Though the private and public spheres became increasingly separated in England during the seventeenth century, in the world of Donne's *Elegies* they are still closely interrelated.[10] Repeatedly, the attack on female rule in amatory relations spills over into an attack on female rule in the public world. Private love and public politics become subtly intertwined as Donne's amatory elegies are inscribed in politically resonant language. Many of the poems are both explicitly amatory *and* covertly political. Hence they possess a politically subversive potential at the same time as they probe the dynamics of amatory relations.

The conventions of courtly love poetry, with its chaste, unattainable, superior woman, desired and sought by an admiring, subservient, faithful male suitor, were especially appropriate for articulating complex relationships between Queen Elizabeth and the ambitious courtiers seeking her favours.[11] That Donne rejects and mocks these conventions in his poetry has not gone unnoticed. As Marotti well puts it, Donne in his *Elegies* is rejecting 'the dominant social and literary modes of the Court, substituting plainspeaking directness for polite compliment, sexual realism for amorous idealisation, critical argumentativeness for sentimental mystification, and aggressive masculine self-assertion for politely self-effacing subservience' (*Coterie*, p. 45). But it has not been sufficiently appreciated that the rejection of courtly love and the assertion of self are achieved in large part through a ritualised verbal debasement of women. It is common to speak of Donne's Ovidian 'realism', but in some elegies, 'realism' seems too mild a term for the debasement Donne substitutes for idealisation.

Repeatedly, Donne's *Elegies* represent women, not as idealised creatures, closed and inviolable in their chastity, but as low, impure, sometimes even disgusting creatures. Donne rejects 'classical' representations of the female body (finished, elevated, pure), which characterised courtly and Petrarchan love poetry, in favour of the 'grotesque' female body – not so much out of an attraction toward the vitality of the grotesque body as out of an impulse to demolish the idealised image of woman, thereby making her undesirable and hence, no longer an object of worship.[12]

Elegy 2: The Anagram wittily, systematically subverts the conventions of female beauty as the speaker tells how Flavia has 'all things, whereby others beautious bee' (l. 2), but in the wrong order, proportion, places, or forms. Her small and dim eyes, large mouth, jet teeth, and red hair make her grotesque and 'foule' (l. 32). Like Shakespeare's sonnet 130 ('My mistress' eyes are nothing like the sun'), this elegy playfully mocks conventional Petrarchan descriptions of female beauty (golden hair, small mouth, pearly white teeth), but Donne's details may also glance at the physical appearance of the ageing Queen Elizabeth, who in her later years had visibly rotten teeth and wore a red wig. The poem itself re-enacts the descent from high to low not only in its announced subject (the ugly mistress) but also in its movement from describing her face to describing her genitals, which are guarded by a 'durty foulenesse' (l. 42) that will keep out all rivals and ensure her chastity for the man who dares marry her. 'Though seaven yeares, she in the Stews had laid, / A Nunnery durst receive [her], and thinke a maid' (ll. 48–9). Even 'Dildoes' would be 'loath to touch' her (ll. 53–4). The language of the poem unpleasantly links her face and her genitals – both are 'foule' (ll. 32, 42). Just as the foulness of the one reflects the foulness of the other (and Donne uncovers both), so the larger implication of the poem is that this low grotesque female body mirrors, even in its distortion, the traditionally beautiful female body. She has all of 'beauties elements' (l. 9) and is thus an 'anagram' of beauty. As in his *Paradoxes and Problems*, Donne delights in being outrageous, in exercising his wit in defending the indefensible. The paradox here serves to undermine the idea of female beauty (and hence desirability) and to suggest that 'beauty' (and the power of beautiful forms) is humanly constructed – Donne suggests that the man can rearrange Flavia's 'parts' to make her beautiful just as we arrange 'letters' different ways in order to produce a variety of pleasing 'words' (ll. 15–18). ...

Donne's emphasis on sex, on the body, and notably on female genitals in these poems has typically been seen as characteristic of the Ovidian influence, and of his 'realism'. But it is a peculiar realism that focuses so exclusively on one part of the body. The speaker in the witty, satirical *Elegy 18: Loves Progress* assumes a superior posture as he denies woman the qualities of 'virtue', 'wholesomeness', 'ingenuity' (ll. 21, 13) and defines her essence as her genitals, the 'Centrique part' that men love (l. 36). Men should pay no attention to the face and those higher parts of the female body, which are dangerous distractions that threaten to waylay or even 'shipwracke' (l. 70) men on their journey to the harbour of love: her 'hair' is 'a forrest of ambushes, / Of springes, snares, fetters, and manacles' (ll. 41–2), her lips give off 'Syrens songs' (l. 55), her tongue is a 'Remora' (l. 58); her 'navell' (l. 66) may be mistaken as the port; even her pubic hair is 'another forrest set, / Where some doe shipwracke, and no farther gett' (ll. 69–70). Seduction becomes a journey of exploration and discovery, but also potential entrapment for the unwary male. The female body he traverses actively seeks to thwart him.

Satirising Petrarchan idealisations of women, Donne implies that such refinements are new and monstrous perversions of nature: 'Love's a beare-whelpe borne; if wee'overlicke / Our love, and force it new strange shapes to take / We erre, and of a lumpe a monster make' (ll. 4–6).

If worshipping woman from a distance and praising her virtue and beauty are modern, monstrous innovations, Donne implies he is restoring older, natural and correct amorous relations. Mocking the platonic ladder of love (set forth first by Diotima in Plato's *Symposium* and later by Bembo in Castiglione's *The Courtier*) whereby the lover ascends from the beauty of a particular person to an admiration of beauty generally to a vision of ideal, transcendent beauty, Donne sets up a different pattern of love whereby men may 'ascend' if they 'set out below' and start from 'the foote' (ll. 73–4).[13] The 'progress' of love is thus a journey of progressive mastery, in which the goal or 'right true end of love' (l. 2) (the female genitals) is kept firmly in sight at all times. The refusal to idealise, indeed the impulse to debase that 'end' of love shapes the poem's final lines, which first describe sexual intercourse as paying 'tribute' to woman's 'lower' 'purse' and then compare the man who uses the wrong means to attain this end to a person who foolishly tries to feed the stomach by purging it with a 'Clyster' (ll. 91–6).

What we have here, as in so many of the *Elegies*, are strategies for reasserting male control in love. To some extent these are reminiscent of Ovid. Alan Armstrong's description of Ovid's contribution to the development of the elegy suggests both his special appeal for Donne and also a parallel in these two poets' redistribution of power in love relationships. Much as Donne would subvert Petrarchan conventions, Ovid himself undercut Latin elegiac conventions such as the enslaved lover, asserting instead that love is an art with the lover in control rather than ruled by his passions and mistress. Ovid gave the 'elegiac lover a degree of rationality and self-control reflected in his urbane wit and complete self-consciousness'.[14] Such a description of Ovid, with its emphasis on mastery, is more valuable in explaining the appeal and usefulness of Ovid to Donne than the commonplace label of 'Ovidian realism'. Ovid's concern with control may have had a political dimension (though obviously not identical to Donne's), expressing a desire for independence in a society of limited freedoms, in which one could be exiled at the pleasure of the emperor. (One thinks of the premium Cicero and Horace in their own ways placed on rationality, self-control, and self-sufficiency as means of insulation from dangerous political vicissitudes.) Ovid's love elegies continue the stance of political nonconformity evident even earlier in Catullus and Propertius. But there are differences between Ovid's and Donne's elegies, for gender assumes a special importance in Donne's efforts at mastery. The misogyny that surfaces in Donne's poems, and becomes a strategy for defining the male speaker's superiority, recalls not Ovid's elegies so much as Juvenal's *Satires*.[15]

Since the conventions of courtly love were an integral part of the ideology of Queen Elizabeth's court, appropriated and encouraged by the queen as articulating and confirming her power, Donne's sharp rejection and subversions of these love conventions might be expected to have political implications. His choice of genre itself reflects not simply his literary taste but a political stance, for he is distancing himself from the preferred discourse of the Elizabethan court. He elects in the 1590s to write not sonnets of courtly love but satires and elegies – genres marked by misogyny and insistence on the male speaker's power and control. The anti-establishment implications of his choice of genres and of the misogyny in Donne's elegies accord well with our knowledge that in the mid 1590s Donne was associated with the Essex circle, having embarked on two expeditions against Spain under Essex in 1596 and 1597.[16]

Throughout the 1590s Essex was engaged in a prolonged struggle for power with the queen that set him against the court establishment and that ended only in 1601 with his trial and execution for treason. His conflicts were not only with Cecil and Ralegh, his rivals for political favour, but also with the queen herself – a point evident in J. E. Neale's conclusion that 'had she let a man of Essex's nature pack the royal service and the Council with his nominees, she would probably in the end have found herself a puppet-Queen, in tutelage to him'. Disdaining the subservience that characterised his stepfather Leicester's relation with the queen, Essex found it difficult to subject himself to Elizabeth's will, repeatedly betraying in his actions and letters a particular and growing dislike of serving a woman.[17] ...

Such sentiments find an echo in Donne's privately circulated *Elegies*. The *Elegies* embody attitudes toward female rule that were also being expressed by Essex and his circle. The whole pattern of Donne's anti-Petrarchanism and revisions of gender relations betrays a discomfort with (indeed, a rejection of) the political structure headed by a female monarch. Intimate private relations between man and woman and the power structure of the body politic mirror and reinforce each other. If the private and the public are so closely related, perhaps a change in relations in the private realm will generate a corresponding change in the world of politics.

The political dimension of Donne's love elegies is particularly evident in the sense of seduction as mastery that pervades *Elegy 19: To his Mistres Going to Bed*, in which Donne moves easily between the bedroom and the political realm of empires and monarchs. In this witty, exuberant poem we are far from the degradation and disgust of *The Anagram* or *Comparison*. For the speaker joy, enthusiasm, and delight reign. But even here, as the speaker commands his mistress to undress, Donne transfers power from the woman, desired and praised, to the man who hopes to possess her. She is wittingly idealised and commodified through a variety of stunning conceits that aim to conquer her (his 'foe' [l. 3]) through hyperbolic praise: she is a 'farre fairer world', a 'beauteous state', 'flowery meades', an 'Angel', 'my America', the repository of 'whole joys' (in Donne's wicked pun) (ll. 6, 13, 14, 20, 27, 35). But the other side of compliment, admiration, and reverence is the desire to possess and thus master the colonised woman. The speaker affirms his power not only through the accumulated verbal commands of the poem but also through a crucial shift in metaphor in lines 25–32:

> License my roving hands, and let them goe
> Before, behind, above, between, below.
> O my America, my new found lande,
> My kingdome, safeliest when with one man man'd,
> My myne of precious stones, my Empiree,
> How blest am I in this discovering thee.
> To enter in these bonds, is to be free,
> Then where my hand is set my seal shall be.

At the beginning of this passage the woman is the monarch, providing a licence; but the moment she gives this licence she loses her sovereignty. What was implicit from the first now is clear. The man becomes not only explorer but conquerer, and she becomes *his* land and kingdom. The repeated possessives reinforce the sense of his mastery, and by the end of this passage he has now become the monarch, setting his 'seal'. Self-aggrandisement, of course, characterises much of Donne's poetry, even his divine poems, but the metaphors and images in these lines have a distinctive political resonance as they dethrone the woman and restore sovereignty to man.

As soon as this politically subversive note has been sounded, Donne momentarily retreats from its implications, first praising 'full nakedness' (l. 33) then flattering the woman as both a 'mystique book' and a divinity who imputes 'grace' to the special few allowed to see her mysteries 'reveal'd' (ll. 41–3). But once her confidence in female superiority has been re-established, Donne gives a final twist to the argument that conclusively and wittily reasserts male supremacy by placing the man 'on top': 'To teach thee, I am naked first: Why than / What need'st thou have more covering than a man' (ll. 47–8). The act of sex confirms what is seen as the legitimate, rightful mastery of man – a mastery that conflicts both with the conventions of courtly love and with the political situation in England in the 1590s. Seduction fantasies, even as they represent woman as supremely desirable, complement Donne's strategy of debasement, for both aim at restoring male sovereignty.[18]

But, as readers have noticed, the mastery and control Donne's speakers strive for in the *Elegies* is often frustrated or incomplete.[19] The very metaphors describing women contain a disturbing potential for suggesting women's resistance to any individual man's control. The *Elegies* show a recurring tension between the male mastery asserted and an implicit female resistance to mastery which undermines the restoration of male sovereignty. The land, despite man's attempts to enclose and possess it, is always vulnerable to being 'possessed' by other men, as the speaker of *Elegy 7* ('Natures lay Ideot ... ') only too well has learned. His mistress's husband may have 'sever'd' her 'from the worlds Common' (l. 21), enclosed her as private property, and her lover may have further 'Refin'd' her into a 'bliss-full paradise' (l. 24), but these acts prove inadequate attempts to civilise her. For all the speaker's position of superiority (he claims to be her teacher, even her God-like creator who has 'planted knowledge' and 'graces' in her [ll. 24–5]), she has thrown off his authority and is leaving him for other lovers. The poem ends with angry, impotent outbursts, in which verbal degradation reveals both the desire to control the woman through what *Elegy 16: On his Mistris* calls 'masculine persuasive force' (l. 4) and the striking inability to do so:

> Must I alas
> Frame and enamell Plate, and drinke in Glasse?
> Chafe wax for others seales? breake a colts force
> And leave him then, beeing made a ready horse?
> (ll. 27–30)

The female body's 'openness' subverts all attempts at permanent masculine control, and ensures that dominance will always be unstable and precarious. As the speaker in *Elegy 3: Change* puts it, 'Women are like the Arts, forc'd unto none, / Open to'all searchers' (ll. 5–6). The conventional representations of woman as land/earth and as water convey a sense of her openness, her essential resistance to boundaries or limits, which Donne wittily exploits:

> Who hath a plow-land, casts all his seed corne there,
> And yet allowes his ground more corne should beare;
> Though Danuby into the sea must flow,
> The sea receives the Rhene, Volga, and Po.
> (ll. 17–20)

Embodying the Aristotelian identification of woman with the supposedly lower elements of earth and water, such representations both suggest the difficulty of mastering woman and reinforce the notion of her necessary inferiority to man, making male sovereignty seem natural and imperative. Though the receptiveness of their bodies shows women were not made to be faithful to one man, the speaker argues that women are made for men in much the same sense as nature, in the Judaeo-Christian scheme of creation, was made for man – hence, the comparisons of women to birds, foxes, and goats in this poem. Given such hierarchy and 'natural' inequality, for a man to submissively serve a woman would be as wrong as for animals to rule man.

Donne's discomfort with serving a woman is perhaps most obvious in *Elegy* 6, the opening of which draws a rich, complex analogy between love and politics:[20]

> Oh, let mee not serve so, as those men serve
> Whom honours smoakes at once fatten and sterve;
> Poorely enrich't with great mens words or lookes;
> Nor so write my name in thy loving bookes
> As those Idolatrous flatterers, which still
> Their Princes stiles, with many Realmes fulfill
> Whence they no tribute have, and where no sway.
> Such services I offer as shall pay
> Themselves, I hate dead names: Oh then let mee
> Favorite in Ordinary, or no favorite bee.
>
> (ll. 1–10)

Distinguishing himself from others, he rejects in both political and amatory spheres a service in which the lover/suitor is submissive, flattering, and unrewarded, and the woman falsely idealised, made into an idol by her admirer. Instead, Donne offers a different kind of 'service', clearly sexual, which 'pay[s]' the woman (compare the 'tribute' paid into the woman's 'purse' in *Elegy 18*) and is in turn rewarded. This kind of service restores male dignity, for it is not servitude but mastery. But mastery is desire rather than accomplishment, for the poem's fictive occasion is the discovery that his mistress is unfaithful.

Recounting their relationship, he represents her as a destructive 'whirlpoole' (l. 16) or 'streame' (l. 21), himself as the delicate 'carelesse' (innocent) 'flower' which is 'drowne[d]' in the water's 'embrace' (ll. 15–17). This image of the destructive stream also appears near the end of *Satyre III*, where the stream is explicitly identified with royal power:

> That thou may'st rightly' obey power, her bounds know;
> Those past, her nature and name's chang'd; to be
> Then humble to her is idolatrie;
> As streames are, Power is; those blest flowers that dwell,
> At the rough streames calme head, thrive and prove well,
> But having left their roots, and themselves given
> To the streames tyrannous rage, alas, are driven
> Through mills, and rockes, and woods, and at last, almost
> Consum'd in going, in the sea are lost:
>   So perish Soules, which more chuse mens unjust
>   Power from God claym'd, then God himselfe to trust.
>   (100–10)[21]

The dating of this satire is uncertain, but the anxiety about royal power (figured as female and identified with the watery female element) would seem to place the poem in the company of those clearly written during the reign of Elizabeth.[22] These complex lines of *Satyre III* articulate both fear of and resistance to royal power, as the speaker, identifying himself with the 'blessed flowers' and unjust monarchs with tyrannous streams, rejects idolatrous submission to earthly rulers and hopes to find ultimate (though not necessarily earthly) safety by dwelling at the calm head (God, the source of all power).

In *Elegy 6*, the deceptive mistress, likened to the whirlpool or stream, takes on conventionally 'masculine' attributes. She is active, aggressive; he becomes the vulnerable, passive victim. Not the man but the mistress is associated with fire when like the 'tapers beamie eye / Amorously twinkling, [she] beckens the giddie flie' to his destruction (ll. 17–18). He is the 'wedded channels bosome' (l. 24) which she, the 'streame' (l. 21), has deserted:

> She rusheth violently, and doth divorce
> Her from her native, and her long-kept course,
> And rores, and braves it, and in gallant scorne,
> In flattering eddies promising retorne,
> She flouts the channell, who thenceforth is drie;
> Then say I; that is shee, and this am I.
>   (ll. 29–34)

The cumulative effect of this language, transferring conventionally 'masculine' terms (for example, 'brave', 'gallant') to the woman, is not to question traditional distinctions between male and female but to show her unnaturalness, thereby reinforcing conventional distinctions between the sexes.

These distinctions were being re-examined in medical circles, as Ian Maclean has shown.[23] During the late sixteenth century a limitedly revisionist medical discourse emerged as anatomists and physicians, attacking the Aristotelian idea of woman as imperfect man, argued that women and men were equally perfect in their respective sexes. But in contrast to medical discourses, ethical, legal, theological, and political discourses remained conservative in their view of woman. For all the remarkable innovation of Donne's *Elegies*, they are conservative, even reactionary, in their representations of the sexes. Like Aristotle, Donne presumes clear sex distinctions. Aristotle had justified what he saw as clear sex differentiation among the 'higher' animals according to the principle that 'the superior one should be separate from the inferior one': 'wherever possible and so far as possible the male is separate from the female, since it is something *better* and more divine'.[24] In the *Elegies*, Donne like Aristotle is concerned to enforce firm sex distinctions. But whereas Aristotle assumes fixed, stable categories, Donne's poems embody strong anxiety about transgressions of hierarchical distinctions between the sexes – an anxiety understandable in a culture in which those categories, both physiological and social, could no longer be assumed to be fixed or stable. Indeed, Queen Elizabeth herself was effectively destabilising these clear sex distinctions by publicly cultivating an androgynous image of herself as both a desirable maiden to be courted and a strong, martial ruler who was master of all her subjects and noted for her 'masculine' qualities of judgement and prudence.[25]

In Donne's *Elegy* 6 the rebellious woman, imaged as both fire and water, has transgressed the supposedly natural, proper boundaries distinguishing the sexes (as did the promiscuous mistress in 'Natures lay Ideot', which is, I believe, why the gender changes in the last lines, where the woman is compared to a male 'colt', broken in only to be enjoyed by another). The woman's assimilation of 'masculine' attributes has effectively 'feminised' the man (he is like a flower, or the earth that is the stream's channel). Donne's strategy is first to expose the blurring of gender distinctions as unnatural and then to restore those boundaries and reassert masculine dominance. Once he has exposed her betrayal, the speaker can reassert the 'proper' male authority and supremacy as he warns her:

Yet let not thy deepe bitternesse beget
Carelesse despaire in mee, for that will whet
My minde to scorne; and Oh, love dull'd with paine
Was ne'r so wise, nor well arm'd as disdaine.
Then with new eyes I shall survay thee, and spie
Death in thy cheekes, and darknesse in thine eye.
Though hope bred faith and love; thus taught, I shall
As nations do from Rome, from thy love fall.
My hate shall outgrow thine, and utterly
I will renounce thy dalliance: and when I
Am the Recusant, in that absolute state,
What hurts it me to be'excommunicate?

(ll. 35–46)

His warning effectively gives him control as he suggests that her beauty, and thus her power and authority over him, depends on *him*. Questioning the conventions that idealise the mistress, Donne suggests that the lover empowers the mistress and thus ultimately holds the reigns of control. Perhaps this is all just wishful thinking on the speaker's part, and Donne is just wittily playing with literary conventions; but in this poem which brings together love, religion, and politics, these lines have a dangerous subversive potential. When one returns to the opening analogies between amorous and political service, this ending implies that just as the power of the mistress depends upon the good will of her lover (and the power of the Roman Church depends upon the willing consent of nations), so the power of the queen depends upon her subjects.

Elegy 6 is not the only poem to imply that monarchs can be deposed. In *Elegy 17: Variety*, the speaker rejects constancy for variety in love and invokes political language that suggests that no allegiance is permanent:

I love her well, and would, if need were, dye
To do her service. But followes it that I
Must serve her onely, when I may have choice?

(ll. 21–3)

Constancy in love entails a loss of man's original 'liberty' (l. 62) – it ties him to a single person and makes him subservient to a woman. Rather than being faithful to one woman (and submitting to 'opinion' and 'honor' [ll. 50, 45], which Donne associates with woman in the ideology of courtly love), he chooses to follow a male monarch, making a 'throne' (l. 64) for the deposed Cupid. The political implications of this poem, in which worship/administration of a single woman is replaced by loyalty to a king, would not have been lost on Donne's Elizabethan readers. But the poem might well have been unsettling even after Elizabeth's reign, for by the poem's end the attack on woman's rule has expanded to question the sovereignty of all rulers. Though the speaker proclaims he will now loyally serve the king of love by pursuing a variety of women, eventually even this pursuit will become tiresome and this new loyalty bondage.

> But time will in his course a point discry
> When I this loved service must deny,
> For our allegiance temporary is.
>   (ll. 73–5)

Paradoxically, continual variety itself will prove boring, so for a change he will become faithful to a single mistress, if he can find one beautiful and worthy. Then the cycle of constancy and change will begin again. Envisioning a succession of allegiances, all of which are provisional and temporary, the poem both explores the psychology of desire and undermines an absolutist interpretation of monarchy.

In their revisions of power the Elegies thus have a politically subversive aspect which helps explain why Donne not only did not want his poems published but also in later years apparently regretted having written them (or at least, regretted not having destroyed them). Five elegies (including *Loves Progress* and *To his Mistress Going to Bed*) were refused a licence to be published with his other poems in 1633. Probably it was not simply their eroticism that offended. Donne's elegies might have seemed dangerous not just during Elizabeth's reign but even later in James's and Charles I's, when Donne had finally achieved a position of prominence in the church, for repeatedly they imply that allegiances can be withdrawn, that monarchs can be deposed – which was precisely the fate that awaited Charles.

But for all their extended political resonance, I see these poems as distinctly (though not narrowly) the product of, and a reaction to, the historical situation of England's rule by a woman. Donne's anti-Petrarchanism, his debasement of women, his various subversions of women's rule, and his repeated attempts to reassert masculine sovereignty embody both the problematics of male submission to a female ruler and Donne's not unrelated personal sense that male desire requires an element of conflict, a feeling of superiority (however precarious) and the promise of mastery. Participating in the debate about women's rule as they contribute to the development of the love elegy, Donne's elegies embody a central tension: while basically conservative, even reactionary, in their insistence on male superiority and rule, they repeatedly demonstrate woman's unruliness, her subversion of permanent male rule. Thus power (whether in private, interpersonal relations, or in public, social ones) is seen as radically unstable.

The *Elegies* suggest that Donne was deeply disturbed by the sense that the old hierarchical order was threatened by a blurring of gender and sex distinctions (he attacks effeminacy as well as voracious, rebellious, aggressive women), by conventions such as neo-Petrarchan courtly love that seemed to invert the 'proper' order in male/female relations, and by rule of a female monarch which seemingly enabled these other disruptions. Clearly, many things in late sixteenth-century English culture besides the presence of the queen on the throne contributed to the unsettling of traditional orders. But even if Queen Elizabeth's reign actually reinforced the existing hierarchies, Donne's *Elegies* are striking evidence that he may have perceived in it a threat to patriarchy, with its assumption of stable, permanent hierarchies. These poems reveal a deep sense of the connectedness of private and political human relations – and a strong sense that hierarchical power relations characterise the most personal and private area of human experience.

From *ELH*, 57 (1990), 811–33.

NOTES

[Achsah Guibbory's article is an example of the rehistoricising work which has been influential in recent studies of Renaissance texts. The so-called New Historicism differentiates itself both from formalism (the conviction that literary texts are relatively self-sufficient), and from those older historical approaches which imply or assume a distinction between the 'backstage' of (usually intellectual or literary) history, and the stage 'proper', which is the literary text. In contrast, New Historicist criticism tends to be more aggressively subversive of such boundaries. Moreover, the contexts supplied by New Historicists, of power, patronage, gender, and socioeconomic motivations, are less amenable to incorporation within an idealist account of literature as the repository of transcendent humane values. So Guibbory begins her article by calling into question modern divisions between private

and public, love poetry and politics, and proceeds to examine the misogynistic politics of love in Donne's *Elegies*, arguing that Donne's debasement
of women was a response to the threat posed to patriarchal gender hierarchies by the existence of the powerful female monarchy of Elizabeth I.

Guibbory's skilfully combined feminist and historicist perspectives might be
usefully compared with the similar historical approach of David Aers and
Gunther Kress, and contrasted with the alternative perception of love
poetry's relationship to history presented in Richard Halpern's essay. For
further discussion and contextualisation of Guibbory's essay, see Introduction,
pp. 11–12. Ed.]

1. See, e.g., Arthur F. Marotti, '"Love is not love": Elizabethan Sonnet
   Sequences and the Social Order', *ELH*, 49 (1982), 396–428; Louis
   Montrose's two essays, 'Celebration and Insinuation: Sir Philip Sidney
   and the Motives of Elizabethan Courtship', *Renaissance Drama*, n.s., 8
   (1977), 3–35, and '"Shaping Fantasies": Figurations of Gender and
   Power in Elizabethan Culture', *Representations*, 1 (1983), 61–94; and
   David Javitch, 'The Impure Motives of Elizabethan Poetry', in *The
   Power of Forms in the English Renaissance*, ed. Stephen Greenblatt
   (Norman, OK, 1982), pp. 225–38. Lauro Martines has suggested similarly complex relationships between courtly love poetry and politics in
   a paper 'The Politics of Love Poetry in Renaissance Italy', given at a
   conference on 'Historical Criticism in an age of Deconstruction'
   (University of Illinois at Urbana-Champaign, 13–15 October 1989).

2. Arthur F. Marotti, *John Donne, Coterie Poet* (Madison, WI, 1986).
   Further references to this work will be cited parenthetically in the text.
   See also John Carey, *John Donne: Life, Mind and Art* (New York,
   1981), chs 3–4, who similarly argues that 'power is the shaping principle in Donne's verse' (p. 117).

3. A. LaBranche, '"Blanda Elegeia": The Background to Donne's
   "Elegies"', *Modern Language Review*, 61 (1966), 357–68, argues that
   'the study of essential human relationships' is a 'principal theme of the
   love elegy' as developed by Catullus and Ovid and later by Donne
   (357). LaBranche's argument should make us wary of concluding too
   narrowly that Donne's concern is only socioeconomic politics.

4. Karl Marx, 'Private Property and Communism', in *Economics and
   Philosophic Manuscripts of 1844*, ed. Dirk J. Struik, trans. Martin
   Milligan (New York, 1973), p. 134.

5. See Mary Douglas, *Natural Symbols: Explorations in Cosmology*
   (London, 1970), p. 12; and *Purity and Danger: An Analysis of
   Concepts of Pollution and Taboo* (New York, 1966), ch. 7.

6. Marotti's otherwise excellent reading of *The Anagram*, for example,
   glosses over the anti-feminism when he comments 'The point of the
   exercise is not to indulge in a virtuoso anti-feminism, but to question

an entire range of amorous customs and rituals' (*Coterie*, p. 48). Other critics simply ignore those poems where the misogyny is difficult to avoid. In *The Metaphysics of Love: Studies in Renaissance Love Poetry from Dante to Milton* (Cambridge, 1985), A. J. Smith, gracefully describing Donne's celebration of mutual love and the interdependency of body and soul, lavishes attention on 'The Ecstasy' but nowhere mentions the *Elegies* (ch. 3, 'Body and Soul'). Recently, George Parfitt has correctly directed attention to the 'reductive', 'immature' view of women in the *Elegies* (*John Donne: A Literary Life* [London, 1989], pp. 39–9), but the misogyny of these poems still remains to be historicised and the political implications explored.

7. I have used Helen Gardner's edition of *The Elegies and Songs and Sonnets* (Oxford, 1965) for the texts of the poems, though I refer to the elegies by the numbers assigned to them by Grierson in his 1912 Oxford edition. Specific references are cited parenthetically in the text by line number. I accept Gardner's dating of the *Elegies* as generally belonging to the 1590s (pp. xxxii–xxxiii), though it is possible a few are later. *The Autumnall* has long been assigned a later date. Annabel Patterson, reminding us to be wary of assuming that all the elegies are early, argues that several belong to the period of James I (see 'John Donne, Kingsman?', in *The Mental World of the Jacobean Court*, ed. Linda Levy Peck [Cambridge, forthcoming]). [This book was published in 1991. Ed.]

8. Natalie Zemon Davis, 'Women on Top: Symbolic Sexual Inversion and Political Disorder in Early Modern Europe', in *The Reversible World: Symbolic Inversion in Art and Society*, ed. Barbara Babcock (Ithaca, NY, 1978), pp. 147–90.

9. Constance Jordan, 'Woman's Rule in Sixteenth-Century British Thought', *Renaissance Quarterly*, 40 (1987), 421–51 (421). Jordan examines the writings for and against gynaecocracy prompted by the accessions of Mary I and Elizabeth I. Most notorious is John Knox's *The First Blast of the Trumpet against the Monstrous Regiment of Women* (Geneva, 1558), published the year Elizabeth ascended the throne, though it was written specifically against the Catholic Mary I. Knox insisted that woman's rule is 'monstrouse', 'repugnant to nature', and a 'subversion of good order' (see, for example, 5v, 9r, 12v, 17r, 27v, though his charges are repeated throughout). Knox's diatribe was impelled by his anti-Catholic Protestantism, but the treatise is also an exhausting argument for woman's natural inferiority to man. Knox's treatise was answered by John Aylmer's *An Harborowe for faithfull and trewe Subjectes, against the Late blowne Blaste* ... (London, 1559), which in counselling obedience to the queen suggested Knox's position was seditious (B1r, B1v, R2v). On the tensions for men posed by obedience to a female monarch, see also Montrose, 'Shaping Fantasies', 61, 64–5, 75.

10. Francis Barker, *The Tremulous Private Body: Essays on Subjection* (London, 1984), argues that during the seventeenth century the 'division between the public and the private [was] constructed in its modern form' (p. 14).

11. See Javitch, 'The Impure Motives', and especially Marotti, 'Love is not love' and *Coterie*, ch. 1.

12. See Mikhail Bakhtin's useful distinction between the 'classical' aesthetic and 'grotesque realism' as two manners of representing the human body (*Rabelais and His World*, trans. Helene Iswolsky [Bloomington, IN, 1984], pp. 18–30). But as Peter Stallybrass and Allon White well point out (*The Politics and Poetics of Transgression* [London, 1986], pp. 5–6), Bakhtin idealises the grotesque when he identifies it with festivity and vitality. Donne's representation of the female body in the *Elegies* betrays a sense of revulsion that contradicts Bakhtin's sense that the bodily element is always 'deeply positive' in 'grotesque realism' (p. 19).

13. *Symposium*, in *The Dialogues of Plato*, trans. B. Jowett, vol. 1 (Oxford, 1892), pp. 580–2; Baldassare Castiglione, *The Book of the Courtier ... done into English by Sir Thomas Hoby* [1591] (London, 1900), The Fourth Book, pp. 357–63.

14. Alan Armstrong, 'The Apprenticeship of John Donne: Ovid and the *Elegies*', *ELH*, 44 (1977), 419–42, esp. 433. Armstrong comments that Donne's elegies show 'a more aggressive version of the techniques used by Ovid' (434) though the implications and the significance of this aggressiveness are not the concern of his important article.

15. L. P. Wilkinson, *Ovid Recalled* (Cambridge, 1955), p. 44, describes Ovid's continuation of the nonconformist stance in Catullus and Propertius. For the misogynist strain in Juvenal taken up by Donne, see especially Juvenal's sixth satire. Though Ovid depicts love as an art, a game, and a hunt, Wilkinson finds him 'a sympathiser with women' with 'an unusual inclination to see things from their point of view' (pp. 25, 86).

16. On Donne's connection with Essex, see Carey, *Life*, pp. 64–9, and especially M. Thomas Hester, 'Donne's (Re)Annunciation of the Virgin(ia Colony) in *Elegy XIX*', *South Central Review*, 4 (1987), 49–64. Hester argues that the opposition to the dominant court establishment that is inherent in Donne's association with Essex's circle underlies the anti-establishment implications of *Elegy 19*.

17. J. E. Neale, *Queen Elizabeth I: A Biography* (1934; rpt. New York, 1957), p. 350.

18. Cf. Montrose's analysis of the seditious political implications of the seductive mastery of a queen ('Shaping Fantasies', 62, 65). Marotti argues that Donne's seduction poems are vehicles for expressing fantasies of

achievement and triumph in the social world (*Coterie*, pp. 89–90). Both Montrose and Jordan ('Woman's Rule, 450) recognise that for Elizabeth virginity was a source of power, that to yield to a man in marriage entailed a diminution of her power.

19. Marotti, *Coterie*, pp. 52–3; also Stanley Fish's paper at the 1987 MLA, 'Masculine Persuasive Force: Donne and Verbal Power', which argued that in the *Elegies* Donne and his surrogate speakers can never achieve the control they desire. [Reprinted in this volume. Ed.]

20. See Marotti, *Coterie*, pp. 56–7.

21. For the text of this satire, I have used W. Milgate's edition of *The Satires, Epigrams and Verse Letters* (Oxford, 1967).

22. Paul R. Sellin, 'The Proper Dating of John Donne's "Satyre III"', *Huntington Library Quarterly*, 43 (1980), 275–312, questions the traditional dating of this satire as belonging to the 1590s, arguing that the poem grows out of Donne's experiences in the Netherlands in 1619.

23. On the revision of Aristotelian thought, see Ian Maclean, *The Renaissance Notion of Woman* (Cambridge, 1980), pp. 43–6.

24. Aristotle, *De generatione animalium [Generation of Animals]*, trans. A. L. Peck, Loeb Library (Cambridge, MA, 1953), 2.1.732a.

25. On the queen's androgynous image, see Montrose, 'Shaping Fantasies', 77–8.

2

'Nothing sooner broke': Donne's *Songs and Sonets* as Self-Consuming Artifact

TILOTTAMA RAJAN

In sketching what can be no more than a preliminary and theoretical approach to Donne, I will argue that while the *Songs and Sonets* are poems about love in its variety, they are also poems about language itself. A reading which treats the poems non-mimetically as poems about the status of their own discourse as well as poems about concepts of love is clearly poststructuralist in tendency. But such a reading is not as heterodox or anachronistic as it may seem. It receives a certain degree of generic sanction from the fact that Renaissance sonnet sequences from Sidney through Shakespeare are often reflexively concerned with the act of writing poems about love, such that the poems as a group become not only the story of an emotional relationship but also the narrative of their own construction (or, in this case, deconstruction).

It is appropriate to begin with the poems of mutual love since they are often seen as the apex of Donne's achievement, in a post-Romantic reading (institutionalised by Gardner's arrangement of the *Songs and Sonets*) which views him as the monarch of love in all its moods. 'A Valediction: Forbidding Mourning' may serve as an initial example of a poem whose rhetoric seems to be self-authenticating but turns out, on closer inspection, to call attention to the insufficiency of its own procedures. Crucial to a more complex reading of the poem is a recognition that the speaker is a persona, and hence a partial but not a total projection of the author. But particularly because of Walton's comment that the poem was composed on the occasion of Donne's departure for the Continent, our first instinct is to read it straightforwardly as a personal lyric in which speaker and author can be identified. We therefore accept sympathetically the poem's central image, which draws on inherited associations of the circle with perfection, with alchemical gold, and even with the creation of the universe. Such associations contribute to an interpretation of the poem itself as a second nature, in which the use of imagery with a sacred potency to describe a profane experience actually converts that experience into something transcendent. Because this transubstantiation is effected by an imaginative conceit, it is not simply the natural supernaturalism of human love which is being claimed here, but also the power of poetic rhetoric to validate that claim in a world that contradicts it, or in Harold Toliver's words, the sense of the poem 'as its own kind of transforming locality capable of reshaping nature in art'.[1] Moreover, the poem, as Rosalie Colie points out, possesses a circular structure which authenticates the claims made for love by its central image.[2] The text can therefore claim to embody the doctrine that it asserts: it can claim to be as well as to mean, and thus to close the gap between truth and the deceptive simulation of truth in words.

It is clear that the speaker wants us to feel he has created a love 'mixt equally'[3] by actualising in the form of the poem his hyperbolical analogy between the circle and the experience of love. But the curious intellectualism of the compass image, used of an experience that is intensely emotional, is Donne's first indication to the reader that this love is short of absolute perfection. The celebration of a love which can endure 'ab-sense' and abstraction (ll. 13–16) because it is intellectual rather than sensuous is also an admission that this love is absent rather than present, because it cannot assume limbs of flesh and thereby become concrete. The very image of a mathematical instrument whose arms are linked at one point yet separate at another remains ambivalent. The speaker claims to have absorbed the separation of the lovers into a higher spiritual union. But he also concedes, through the use of such an image, that this ideal union must be asserted in the face of a real separation which makes it necessary for him to forbid mourning rather than simply to affirm immortality. Revealingly, his love is said to endure 'not yet' a breach but an expansion (ll. 22–3), an indication that he feels his arguments may deceive time but not her daughter truth.

More significantly, the stiffness of the analogy between lovers and compasses – an analogy which yokes together things which are heterogeneous and incompatible except on an imaginary plane – exposes the fact that the supreme claim made by the speaker is based on a poetic fiction, on invention rather than logic. The artificiality of the compass image builds into Donne's poem an element of self-irony which inhibits the reader's acceptance of those arguments for the perfection of love in which the speaker's intensity almost persuades him to believe. By creating a split between the tenor of its argument and the vehicle, the awareness of artifice suspends the imitation of perfection by secular love at the level of imitation. This awareness of the poem as metaphor rather than truth is crucial to the effect that Donne intends the text to have upon the reader. Maynard Mack points out that the Renaissance work of art, 'though composed to be experienced as a Second Nature, is likewise to be experienced as art; the mirror remains a mirror [: there is] a system of built-in balances between the forces drawing the spectator to identify with the faces in the mirror and those which remind him that they [are] reflections'.[4] Behind the poem's evident claim for human discourse as vatic is an awareness that the assertions of art remain within the prison-house of language: an awareness radically at odds with the 'Romantic' view of Donne's discourse taken by a New Criticism which seeks to identify the artifacts of consciousness with the organisms of nature. For the Metaphysicals the words in a poem are not things, except when the wit of a poem is (as it is for Herbert) the wit of God. Given the deconstruction by theorists like de Man of the logocentric view of Romanticism with which the organicist aesthetics of the New Criticism is affiliated, it seems particularly appropriate at this point in time to raise similar questions about the relevance of a holistic poetics to an analysis of Metaphysical discourse.

The dissociation of feeling and intellect, the emotion that does and the irony that contemplates, prevents the total effect of a poem by Donne from coinciding with the effect that the persona claims for it. There is, as Stein observes, 'a second argument or form emerging from the first ... an implied point of opposition' which stems from the location of the poems on the boundary between the sacred and the profane, and of language itself on the threshold between being and nothingness.[5] The reader must therefore be cautious about taking at face value the 'rhetoric of hyperbole' that critics such as Brian Vickers see as sustaining the truth of the affirmations reached in the poems of mutual love, which appear to establish love as an inviolable centre, within and yet immune to the world of temporality.[6] Such rhetoric is rhetoric only, not logic. The form of Donne's poems, which simulate the dramatic immediacy of oral communication, may seem to call for a logocentric hermeneutics abolishing the duality between text and reader: a reading which enters into the spirit of the poem and grants the authority of the speaking voice. But more to the point for a consideration of Donne's secular poetry is A. E. Malloch's description of the reading process as it operates in Donne's prose paradoxes:

> The true nature of the paradox is revealed when the reader overturns it, just as the true nature of the swaggerer appears only when he is resisted. And further, the paradoxes do not really have natures at all; they are nothings. They exist only within the antithetical action of the reader. ... Thus the paradox may be said to present one part in a verbal drama (truly a word play): the other part is not written out, but is supplied by the reader as he tries 'to find better reasons'.[7]

Two factors undermine the claim of love's rhetoric to be self-authenticating. Donne's use of personae to speak his poems results in a poetry that is conscious of an audience and therefore dependent on the reader's assent to validate its claims. At least in part, it is the reader's role in the verbal drama to withhold this assent. Equally significant, perhaps, there are poems in the *Songs and Sonets* which themselves serve to overturn the assertions made in the poems of mutual love and thus to support the reader's hesitation.

Removed from, or placed at the climax of, the cycle as a whole, the poems of mutual love appear to form an ascending series that creates and successively strengthens the egotistically sublime sense of love as an expression of a human victory over temporality. 'The Sunne Rising', the most fantastical of these poems, concludes by making the lovers the centre of the universe. The poem is a witty poem and justifies its assertions by its wit, which sets aside as irrelevant the limiting truths of the external world and the cycle of nature. Again, the impulse behind it is a belief that the alchemy of language can actually transform the world of fact represented by the motions of the sun, and create through rhetoric what cannot be affirmed through logic. That the extravagant hyperbole of the poem asks to be resisted is fairly obvious. It is by means of an optical illusion that the lover eliminates the sun (l. 13), and the poem is aware of itself as a sleight of hand, no different from the 'mimique' and 'alchimie' of the world it rejects. If, by the time that Donne wrote this poem, the Copernican view of the cosmos as heliocentric rather than geocentric was gaining currency, then the hyperbolical claim that the sun revolves around a pair of earthly lovers knows itself to be based on an exploded cosmological fiction. The originality of the poem's wit, which is the speaker's rhetorical declaration of independence from the paternity of the temporal cycle, becomes antiquarian rather than revolutionary. Although it is nowhere acknowledged in the poem itself, this alliance of anti-Petrarchan literary radicalism and scientific reaction functions as an undermining subtext which the reader reconstructs as he withholds assent from the speaker's claims.

'The Sunne Rising' is one of those paradoxes which Donne dismissed as 'swaggerers'.[8] But its attempt to affirm an integral centre in love is a serious one which recurs in 'The Canonization' and 'The Good-Morrow', poems which are not normally read as self-compromising. Inasmuch as a poem, through its choice of language, registers a commentary on the status of its own discourse, 'The Canonization' claims to put the assertions of 'The Sunne Rising' on a securer basis by moving beyond the self-deflating metaphors of a merely extravagant wit. It is the ornamental Petrarchan conceits of the second stanza which correspond in mood to 'The Sunne Rising'. By replacing these with metaphysical conceits the speaker implicitly claims to create a discourse which is logical rather than rhetorical. The Petrarchan lover alluded to in the second stanza succeeds in dissenting from the actual world, but in a style whose decorative quality concedes, through the incongruity of tenor and vehicle, a certain irrelevance of words to matter. A more potent transvaluation of poetic discourse is claimed by the speaker when he replaces the conventional paradoxes of love poetry with sacred paradox in the third stanza of the poem. As a reversal of the laws of nature through the power of human inventiveness, Petrarchan paradox can only represent the reaching of an impasse: the world accepts the lover's wresting of invention and his use of giddy metaphors not because it knows his love to be a higher truth, but because it knows him to be, in Drayton's word, 'Lunaticke'. The paradox is one of duality and allows the lover to construct a separate but illusory world existing only at the level of words. Sacred paradox, on the other hand, transforms reality because it fuses contradictories in a single unity, and asserts a higher and not simply a divergent reality. Through it the lover is able to assert a love which is 'mixt equally' through a language which is beyond discrepancies between tenor and vehicle, substance and shadow. The 'ridle' (l. 23) becomes the 'patterne' of the final stanza (l. 45), and the particularity of 'wee' (l. 28) is left behind in a universally valid 'you' (l. 37) – or so the speaker claims. In the final stanza the poem moves from the present tense to the past tense, from the assertion which is constantly in the process of being made and is therefore liable to lapse, to the affirmation which is recognised as a legend and as a victory won once and for all.

Of equal importance to the claim of a discourse that is permanent and not evanescent is the formal symmetry of the poem, not evident in 'The Sunne Rising'. As in 'A Valediction: Forbidding Mourning', the speaker, by embodying the poem's doctrine in its form, seeks to eliminate the hiatus between meaning and being characteristic of verbal artifacts. The poem claims for human love a certain comprehensiveness attained precisely through its self-enclosedness. The first and last lines of each stanza end with the word 'love', and the poem is a structure of such stanzas, each self-enclosed and each 'one little roome' which is 'an every where' ('The Good-Morrow', l. 11). The fact that the poem itself as a pattern of such stanzas concentrates all experience in a small space makes its form a concrete embodiment of the microcosmic image at the end, which affirms with reference to the lovers' eyes the encapsulation of the great world in the small:

> Who did the whole worlds soule extract, and drove
> Into the glasses of your eyes
> So made such mirrors, and such spies,
> That they did all to you epitomize,
>
> (ll. 40–3)

The culminating lines of the poem have important consequences for the status of verbal imitation in terms of image and truth. The image of the lovers' eyes as mirrors reverses the traditional relationship between copy and model, by giving the copy or reflection in the eyes a higher authority than the original which it reduplicates. As such, it comments on the status of the miniaturised repetition or copy of experience in the poem, which is now to be read not as an imitation but as truth.

The poem in effect claims for itself the power of reshaping nature in art. If the reader accepts the claim to authority implicit in the poem's metaphorical mode and formal symmetry, he accepts a complete cleavage between the Donne of *Songs and Sonets* and the intensely self-doubting author of the sermons and *Anniversaries*. As

already suggested, a reading of the *Songs and Sonets* in their continuity, a consideration of the affirmations made within the enclosure
of the individual poem from such external vantage-points as 'Love's
Alchymie', immediately fractures the illusion that the little world of
the poem can convert its self-centredness into a self-enclosedness
that excludes the real world. But the counterarguments supplied by
the more realistic poems simply make explicit for the reader under-
mining elements or subtexts already present within the poems of
mutual love themselves. It is a significant if deliberately muted fact
that the speaker of 'The Canonization', having claimed for his love
the phoenix-like power to 'dye and rise the same' (l. 26), goes on to
concede in the next stanza: 'We can dye by it, if not live by love'
(l. 28). The careful reader recognises that in the space intervening
between the climactic affirmations of the third stanza and the consolidation of these affirmations in the final stanza, the phoenix has
been replaced by the urn and fire by ashes. The 'pretty roomes' or
stanzas of the poem, a source of fame, have also been acknowledged
as a place of entombment (ll. 32–4). Moreover, it is surely a deliberate irony on Donne's part that the phoenix, the image by means of
which the speaker claims to translate his love to a new and uncon-
ventional plane, is in fact a commonplace of Petrarchan poetry. The
transvaluation of values claimed by the speaker through his linguistic inventiveness thus turns out to be, on closer inspection, nothing
but a piece of Petrarchan wit.

Of further importance are the reading instructions provided by the
poem itself through its choice of rhetorical mode. According to
speech-act theory there is no such thing as a constative utterance:
one that unambiguously means what it says, and does not occur in a
context which limits and complicates it. All verbal utterance is pos-
itional: it is, in other words, a role played in response to a certain
situation, and not a set of precepts with absolute validity. Whether or
not one accepts as a critical principle the psychoanalysis of linguistic
motivation which must result from such a theory, the point is that
Donne here invites us to accept it by describing for us a situation of
utterance. The speaker of 'The Canonization' is not simply an invisible vehicle for the poem's discourse; he is a dramatised narrator,
characterised as being under attack from his friend and therefore
insecure. His gestural use of hyperbole involves a deliberate exploit-
ation of the credibility gap, and invites questioning because of the
situation in which we see him. To put the matter differently, the use
of dramatic monologue rather than lyrical effusion jeopardises the

speaker's argument by making us aware of an auditor to whom the poem is defensively addressed. The reference to this auditor undermines the speaker's claim for the self-enclosedness of mutual love by conceding within the poem itself an implied reader who has the power to resist or overturn the speaker's argument. Were the poem a subjective effusion in the manner of many love lyrics, the sceptical reader might well resist absorption into its mood, but there would be no direction to him *in the poem* to do so. The dramatic monologue, while it avoids the open scepticism of the dialogue poem, also acknowledges the impossibility of a self-enclosed lyrical subjectivity. ...

The poems we have considered thus far deliberately call into question the hermeneutics of immediacy associated with the love lyric, which makes of poetry the true voice of feeling, and substitute for it a hermeneutics of suspicion designed to make the reader aware that the truths arrived at through human emotion are unstable. Irony, paradox, and hyperbole are all self-questioning verbal devices. Donne himself, more conservative than his New Critical followers who claim for the language of paradox the power to constitute new and complex realities, points to the self-defeating nature of his paradoxes:

> But indeed they were made rather to deceave tyme than her daughter truth; although they have beene written in an age when anything is strong enough to overthrow her ... they are but swaggerers. ... If perchance they be pretly guilt, that is their best for they are not hatcht: they are rather alarums to truth to arme her than enemies: and they have only this advantage to escape from being called ill things that they are nothings.[9]

The paradoxical reconstitution of realistic logic through human invention, and the corresponding belief in language as myth-making, are here dismissed as hollow.

Although this comment on *Certain Problems and Paradoxes* does seem to isolate a 'true' as opposed to a false language, it is important to remember that for Donne paradox is ubiquitous. There is no language free of paradox and metaphor: to be committed to self-expression is, hence, to be caught in a language that calls itself into question. The problem of a rhetoric that is not identical with truth reflects on the ultimate value of all temporal and human solutions, and not simply on the element of deception and fallacy in a particular witty argument. In contrast to Donne's view of truth as entrapped in a rhetoric that causes its assertions to exist in bad faith is

Bacon's notion of a language in which rhetoric and logic, or words and matter, coincide.[10] The concept of a plain style, a zero degree of figurality at which words become the 'very images of matter', assumes that language can, by stripping itself of pretence, refer directly to truth. A style that is characterised by metaphor and equivocation rather than statement, on the other hand, concedes the limitations of human language as a vehicle of truth. It renounces what to it is the fiction of a plain style able to grasp and consolidate truth within this world, and points towards the consuming of a vehicle that yields only fictions about truth.

The rhetoricity of Donne's poetry, disparaged by post-Ramists like Jonson who condemn him for not writing in a plain style,[11] is then integral to the process by which the poetry finally negates itself as a representation of truth. In looking at the structure of wit and invention in Donne's poetry, we have considered the text's self-conscious display of its own wit as the means by which it discovers its own status as fiction. Inasmuch as language is one of the primary human activities, Donne's exploration of its possibilities and limits is related to his dramatisation of the dialogue between human aspiration and the acknowledgement of post-lapsarian limits. His use of wit is initially Romantic, but is finally sceptical. It expresses, at first, a desire to redefine the canons of reality through imagination. But in poem after poem, the use of wit rather than logic to reach a conclusion ends by casting doubt on the conclusion reached. The paradoxical ability to make 'absent things present',[12] to create something *ex nihilo*, ends by disclosing a sense of nothingness that verbal self-display can hide but cannot dispel.

'A Valediction: of Weeping' might almost serve as a paradigm for the action of wit, inasmuch as it reveals literature as simultaneously a counterfeit creation, and an 'evaporation' of that which is created.[13] Donne himself describes the paradoxical nature of the verbal medium:

> How empty a thing is Rhetorique? (and yet Rhetorique will make absent and remote things present to your understanding). How weak a thing is Poetry? (and yet Poetry is a counterfait Creation, and makes things that are not, as though they were).[14]

One is struck by the closeness of his recognitions to those of more recent theorists, who comment on the ambivalent nature of verbal representation as acknowledging the absence of what is being made present again or re-presented.[15] Thus the speaker of 'A Valediction' insists on the power of the imagination's alchemy as a fictional over-coming of an experience of nothingness and separation, but in the process admits those very flaws in the artifice of love that his use of witty language is supposed to repair: 'thou and I are nothing then, when on a divers shore' (l. 9). The poem, as an attempt to restore the presence of the beloved, is aware of itself as growing from an experience of loss and absence, and therefore as an enterprise whose compensatory nature only serves to heighten the realities that it fights off. An awareness of the paradoxical structure of witty lan-guage is present at the heart of the poem's central image. The striv-ing to convert tears into globes continues the rhetoric of maximisation present in the poems of mutual love, but bases this rhetoric on an image of dissolution, a falling tear. The attempt to create solid worlds out of the nothingness of tears dissolves in itself, inasmuch as it serves only to call forth further tears. ...

Donne's poems are thus pervaded by a feeling that language is a protective fiction, aware of itself as a figurative rather than a literal structure, and therefore unable to embody within itself any final reality. The sense of verbal structures as either self-consuming or con-sumed by the communicative process is not the only one that emerges from a reading of *Songs and Sonets*, but it is at least the final sense. 'The Funerall' and 'The Relique', both poems which are built around the image of a bracelet of bright hair left in a grave, attempt to prove the equivocal status of the tokens and symbols that man leaves behind him. We may consider these texts as poems in which the latent or secondary theme is the status and reception of the poetic discourse itself. They are, in other words, poems which are self-referentially in-volved in reflecting on whether the human voice can make credible the fiction that something exclusively human, a love which has no au-thority higher than that given it by another human being, can survive death. As tokens themselves (tokens to a future reader who survives the poet), the poems are at once attempts to reunite the physical and spiritual orders sundered by the body's dissolution, and explorations of the power of human language to re-beget the soul from absence and darkness. Neither poem affords to itself the idolatry of claiming 'all that a Soule can doe' ('The Funerall', l. 22). Yet it can be argued that from the extraordinary mixture of a bravado that demands to be resisted and a humility that almost invites our assent to the poem's miracles, there does emerge a sense that something may endure even in the dissolution of human tokens. Even so, it is too tentative a sense to dominate our final view of *Songs and Sonets* as a cycle.

The 'subtile wreath of hair' in 'The Funerall' poses the difficult question of whether the linguistic token is to be viewed in spiritual or naturalistic terms: whether the hair is an emblem of the soul (l. 5) and the token an incarnation of reality, or whether the hair is a pair of manacles (l. 16) and the token therefore an emblem of its own dissolution. In the description of it as 'The mystery, the signe you must not touch' (l. 4), there is an equivocal sense that the images made by human consciousness may perhaps possess an esoteric power, or may perhaps be empty and on the verge of crumbling. Further complicating the status of the token is the ambiguous, almost mistrustful quality of the love it seeks to recapture, evident in the silence by which the lady addressed calls into question the fiction of a mutuality corroborated only by the single voice of the speaker. A similar ambivalence informs 'The Relique', where the modesty of the tone almost persuades the reader to support the claim of miraculous qualities for the bracelet of bright hair, but where the status of fiction as sacramental or merely metaphoric cannot really be resolved.

Donne's poems as dramatised lyrics addressed to a second person are deliberately hermeneutic: concerned with their own interpretation and aware of their potential dissolution in the reading process. Occasionally, as in 'The Good-Morrow' or 'A Valediction: Forbidding Mourning', the person addressed is a loyal lover, and the reader is called on to attempt a firmness which will draw into a circle the flawed ellipse of the speaker's circuit of analogies. But more often the addressee is a critic or a lover emotionally at variance with the speaker – a fact which guides the reader away from a fusion of horizons with the speaker. Particularly crucial for an understanding of how the *Songs and Sonets* problematise their own reception are poems like 'The Funerall' and 'The Relique', where the speaker addresses himself in part to someone who comes to bury him or dig up his grave, and questions the fiction of the reader as lover through the image of the reader as someone who probes and excavates. These poems no longer address themselves in the dramatic present to an initiated reader or to one who is familiar even if hostile,[16] but to someone completely unknown to the poet. Hence they renounce all pretence at a logocentric hermeneutics, in which to speak is to be understood sympathetically; they open up the enclosed spaces of a coterie poetry to the anonymous gaze of posterity.

The question which 'The Relique' poses is whether human tokens are symbols or mere signs. A distinction between the two terms is made by Paul Ricoeur, who observes that in the sign the link between the word and the reality it designates is wholly arbitrary, whereas in the symbol the word actually does embody and incarnate – as a sacred presence – the reality it evokes.[17] Ontologically, the word as sign is an emptiness, a merely intentional structure. In attempting to communicate the perfection of mutual love through the image of stiff twin compasses, Donne throws into relief the arbitrariness of the image as sign; in describing this same love through the image of a relic, he brings out the reservoir of richness within the word as symbol. But the tentative sense of the creative authority of language, which sometimes survives the deconstructive tendencies of the individual text, survives only for the duration of that text. Read in succession, the *Songs and Sonets* are not incarnational but self-emptying, and point away from themselves to a literature in which the Word is genuinely symbol and light and is no longer consumed by the shadows which separate words from matter.

So far we have considered the dissolution of the text's argument in the dialectic of the reading process with reference only to the individual poem. The same process operating intertextually between the poems has significant consequences for the poems considered as a cycle – consequences which undermine even further the ability of language to capture truth. The implication of this argument is that despite the wide variety of forms and attitudes in *Songs and Sonets*, the poems are far from being what one critic describes as 'discrete' in nature, a heterogeneous compilation of lyrics representing 'different amorous situations'.[18] While they do not formally make up a sequence in the manner of *Amoretti* or *Ideas Mirrour*, they are nevertheless part of a continuous enterprise, an anti-sequence which precipitates the progress of the soul towards the *Anniversaries* and the sermons. One may look to Donne himself, and to his often repeated concept of the two circles, for an image of how the *Songs and Sonets* are related as a structure and of what the seemingly discrete nature of individual lyrics says about the structure of experience itself:

> This life is a Circle, made with a Compasse, that passes from point to point; That life is a Circle stamped with a print, an endlesse, and perfect Circle, as soone as it begins. Of this Circle, the Mathematician is our great and good God; The other Circle we make up our selves; we bring the Cradle, and Grave together by a course of nature.[19]

The speaker of Donne's poems passes through a variety of incomplete points of view, annulling in each poem the seemingly final recognitions reached in the previous poem. Thus a poem like 'The Canonization' is often followed at some point by a poem like 'Loves Alchymie', and the latter in turn is often followed by a poem such as the former. While it might seem as though it is the poems of mutual love that are overturned by profane and libertine poems such as 'The Flea', the point is rather that the *Songs and Sonets* are continuously self-reversing: the reader can no more find a resting place in the worldly cynicism of the profane poems than in the neo-platonic romanticism of the poems of mutual love. The poems as they stand mutually qualify each other within a larger structure which cannot be grasped in its entirety from the standpoint represented by any one poem. Moreover, individual poems are themselves binary in form, and if they do not stand like Janus in the field of knowledge, they are at least incipiently self-questioning, and point to the need for other poems to overturn their conclusions, and beyond that to the need for a higher standpoint to overturn the cycle as a whole. The 'meaning' of the poems does not reside in the explicit propositions that emerge from them, but rather in the disintegration of those propositions that occurs in the individual poem through the interaction between text and subtext, and in the cycle as a whole between text and countertext. It exists not as a content of the poem, but as a recognition reached by the reader in the interstices within and between poems.

Behind a literary structure in which each poem is a point or segment of a circle which is never possessed in its entirety, and in which the sequence of the poems is a homeless movement from one point to another, there is also a view of language very different from the one which seemed to inform 'The Canonization' in isolation. Paul de Man has said that it is in the nature of poetic language that it 'can do nothing but originate over and over again: it is always constitutive, able to posit regardless of presence but, by the same token, unable to give a foundation to what it posits except as an intent of consciousness'.[20] But because poetry cannot confirm what it creates, its fictions are always collapsing again:

> yet he [man] hath raised up nothing, nothing appears in his circle. If these things could fill us, yet they could not satisfie us, because they cannot stay with us, or not we with them.[21]

Crucial to this notion of the *Songs and Sonets* as a deliberate anti-sequence is the assumption that the poems were intended to form a collection, and that within this collection they were arranged according to certain principles. While no authoritative text of the poems was published in Donne's lifetime, it does seem clear that the posthumous editions were not compiled by an editor from copies of single, 'occasional' poems given to Donne's friends and that Donne did circulate the poems as a substantial (though not fixed) corpus of work.[22] The fact that he intended the poems to be read as a group in turn suggests the legitimacy of looking for some principle of order in the collection. The 1633 edition, while posthumous, does derive from manuscripts which presumably reflect (or at least do not contravene) Donne's general intentions.[23] Though the order of poems in the 1633 and 1635 editions differs, the principle of arrangement in both is apparently random. It is therefore clear that Donne was not concerned that his poems follow a set order. My own view is a more radical one: namely that Donne deliberately randomised the arrangement of his poems in order to challenge the conventional assumption of the reading process as a linear movement in which a 'truth' is progressively explored and consolidated as the reader moves forward. The only obvious principle of arrangement in both editions is the juxtaposition of disparate poems or groups of poems.[24] The constant disorienting self-negation of the text which results from this arrangement extends, to the collection as a whole, the principle of paradoxy which destabilises our reading of individual poems. ...

Richard Hughes has spoken of the importance for the Italian Renaissance of the 'summa complex' and of what he calls a 'holoscopic epistemology': 'This amazing vision of unity that decries flux, of form that resolves all accidents, of a symbolic centre for all phenomenological fragments, is ubiquitous in the Italian Renaissance.' But as against the holoscopic sense of experience there is also the 'meroscopic ... awareness of multiplicity, of an infinitude or unresolved singularities'.[25] The point of insisting that *Songs and Sonets*, although not a sequence, can be read as a structure, is that its very lack of unity involves a decentring of holoscopic epistemology. Dante's love for Beatrice is a series of successive transcendences, beginning in the *Vita Nuova* and culminating in the *Paradise* with the perception of Beatrice as theology. It embodies a feeling that human knowledge, aided by grace, is capable of the ascent towards perfection. Astrophil's love for Stella derives from a somewhat different tradition, the more Augustinian tradition of Petrarch, which sees a cleavage rather than a continuity between nature and grace, and which therefore ends by admitting a final frustration in the attempt to ascend towards perfection and to find in a love a way of transcending the finite towards the infinite. Yet the intention behind *Astrophil and Stella* remains holoscopic, and although no poem in fact succeeds in bringing the lover's quest to any conclusion, or marking an advance beyond the stage reached in the previous poem, the arrangement of the poems as a sequence in a definite order seems to involve a continued faith that somehow all the accidents and contradictions will add up to a final statement. The lover in the last sonnet continues to feel that his love for Stella can provide a centre for all phenomenological fragments, even though the nature of his experience should have convinced him of the contrary.

By contrast, the order of *Songs and Sonets* could easily be changed without changing the total effect of the poems, as long as the fundamental organising principle of juxtaposing disparate poems was preserved. Donne's love poetry is therefore in another category altogether, although his editors have not always recognised this fact. Helen Gardner's arrangement puts the poems of mutual love after the libertine poems and introduces into the *Songs and Sonets* a movement from the profane to the sacred based on her assumption that Donne's stylistic evolution went hand in hand with a conversion to neo-platonism. Such an arrangement, while it does not exactly convert the poems into a sonnet sequence, gives to the poems of mutual love a climactic position within Donne's development as a secular poet, and thus virtually grants their holoscopic and logocentric claims. But the early arrangements seem truer to the spirit of the poems, and what is apparent in them is an image of life as a series of fragments. The use of a literary mode recognised as nugatory and minor from Catullus onwards, and the refusal to make of his poems a large and sustained structure in the manner of Renaissance sonneteers, are part of the self-irony by which Donne defeats the romantic humanism of poems like 'The Canonization' and 'The Good-Morrow'. Behind the Renaissance elevation of an occasional form into a major mode through the principle of sequence is the assumption that the emotional life of an individual can be an enduring monument, and the language in which that life is preserved a kind of secular scripture. Behind the anti-sequential and ultimately self-consuming structure of the *Songs and Sonets* is the recognition of the *Second Anniversary*:

> You are both fluid, chang'd since yesterday;
> Next day repaires, (but ill) last daies decay.
> Nor are, (Although the river keep the name)
> Yesterdaies waters, and to daies the same.
> ... whils't you thinke you bee
> Constant, you'are howrely in inconstancee.
>   (ll. 393–400)

From *ELH*, 49 (1982), 805–28.

NOTES

[Rajan's article utilises poststructuralist theory to produce a reading of Donne's love poetry as sceptical and nihilistic. Juxtaposing modern theories of language with their Renaissance counterparts, Rajan argues that the only reality we know is through language and such is language's provisional, metamorphic nature that the reality it constructs is similarly temporary and unstable. Thus for Rajan, the love poems are not so much about love as about 'language itself' (see p. 45 above), and language's inability to mirror any kind of permanent reality. Donne's poem may attempt, through the use of prophetic language, to affirm love as a transcendent reality, but the poems repeatedly leave their readers with the feeling that words have been wittily manipulated, and proved nothing.

Rajan's emphasis upon the self-consuming nature of verbal artifacts is nevertheless balanced by the attention she gives to the realities and independent referents which Donne's lyric poems at least attempt to elevate to the status of transcendent truths. There is, in other words, a recognition of the lyric as a particular kind of (prophetic) communication and project.

Rajan's focus upon Donne's attempts to stabilise the unstable condition of language may be usefully set alongside the different perspectives on the same theme of Belsey, Harvey, Fish and Wright. For further discussion and contextualisation of Rajan's article, see Introduction, pp. 12–13. Ed.]

1. Harold Toliver, *Pastoral Forms and Attitudes* (Berkeley, CA, 1971), pp. 11–12.

2. Rosalie Colie, *Paradoxia Epidemica* (Princeton, NJ, 1966), p. 128.

3. References in the text are to *The Complete Poetry of John Donne*, ed. John T. Shawcross (New York, 1967).

4. Maynard Mack, 'Engagement and Detachment in Shakespeare's Plays', in *Essays on Shakespeare and Elizabethan Drama*, ed. Richard Hosley (Columbia, MO, 1963), p. 277.

5. Arnold Stein, *John Donne's Lyrics* (Minneapolis, 1962), p. 120.

6. Brian Vickers, 'The "Songs and Sonets" and the Rhetoric of Hyperbole', in *John Donne: Essays in Celebration*, ed. A. J. Smith (London, 1972), pp. 132–74.

7. A. E. Malloch, 'The Techniques and Function of the Renaissance Paradox', *Studies in Philology*, 53 (1956), 192, 195.

8. John Donne, *Selected Prose*, chosen by Evelyn Simpson, ed. Helen Gardner and Timothy Healy (Oxford, 1967), p. 111. Letter to Sir Henry Wotton, dated 1600.

9. John Donne, *Selected Prose*, p. 111.

10. Francis Bacon, *Advancement of Learning*, in *The Works of Francis Bacon*, ed. J. Spedding, R. L. Ellis and D. D. Heath (London, 1887), 3: 284–6.

11. Ben Jonson, *Ben Jonson's Conversations with William Drummond of Hawthornden*, ed. R. F. Patterson (London, 1923), p. 18.

12. John Donne, *Sermons*, ed. George R. Potter and Evelyn Simpson (Berkeley, CA, 1953–62), 4:87.

13. J. B. Leishman, *The Monarch of Wit* (London, 1951), p. 193.

14. Donne, *Sermons*, 4:87.

15. Jacques Derrida, *De la grammatologie* (Paris, 1967), pp. 207–8; Paul de Man, *Blindness and Insight* (New York, 1971), p. 123.

16. 'The Funerall' has two addressees: the hypothetical person who comes to shroud Donne, and the beloved. But until the final line the latter is addressed only directly through the former.

17. Paul Ricoeur, *Le conflit des interprétations* (Paris, 1969), pp. 314–15.

18. Donald Guss, *John Donne: Petrarchist* (Detroit, 1966), p. 95.

19. Donne, *Sermons*, 2:200.

20. Paul de Man, 'The Intentional Structure of the Romantic Image', in *Romanticism and Consciousness*, ed. Harold Bloom (New York, 1970), p. 69.

21. Donne, *Sermons*, 5:275.

22. Helen Gardner, ed., *The Elegies and Songs and Sonnets* (Oxford, 1965), pp. lxxxi–lxxxii, lxix.

23. The order of poems in the 1633 edition, according to Gardner, is based on that followed by manuscripts from groups I and II (p. lxxxiii). The group I manuscripts, moreover, derive from a common ancestor,

X, which is thought to have been based on an edition Donne himself was putting together in 1614 (p. lxv).

24. For instance, in both editions 'The Sunne Rising' is followed by 'The Indifferent' and 'Love's Usury', which, in turn, are followed by 'The Canonization'.

25. Richard Hughes, *The Progress of the Soul* (New York, 1968), pp. 87–9.

3

John Donne's Worlds of Desire

CATHERINE BELSEY

I

It is easy to find in the love poems of John Donne in particular the imperatives of empire characteristic of the energetic and optimistic beginnings of English expansionism. Desire is boundless, unrestrained and urgent, and it is formulated in a series of imperatives that do not invite debate: 'Come, madam, come, all rest my powers defie ...'; 'Off with that girdle, like heavens zone glistering / But a farre fairer world encompassing'; 'Unlace your selfe ...'; 'Licence my roving hands ...' (Elegy 'To his Mistris Going to Bed', ll. 1, 5–6, 9, 25). In the Elegy the project is an exploration of the woman's body, an uncovering which reveals a sensual topography of flowery meads and hills (l. 14), an earthly paradise (l. 21), and such joys (l. 33) as explorers commonly found in the landscapes of the new world.[1] But the process of erotic discovery is to precede a new kind of covering that is also and explicitly both a sexual and a social mastery. Among animals, to cover is to inseminate; a feme covert in the period is a married woman who has surrendered her property and her autonomy to her husband. The Elegy 'To his Mistris Going to Bed' concludes its argument with a pun which is in every sense triumphant: 'To teach thee, I am naked first: Why than / What need'st thou have more covering than a man?' (ll. 47–8).

What sort of love is it that persistently finds a meaning for itself in images of discovery and mapping, cosmography and conquest? What is the nature of the worlds of desire which appear so frequently in these love poems of the early seventeenth century? What sexual politics is inscribed in the texts? Historically, this is the moment when intensity of erotic experience is in the process of being regularised and sanctified as the basis of domestic life and family values. The shared, reciprocal desire of the heterosexual couple comes to stand at the heart of society as a source of stability amid the turbulence of politics and the market. What then has love itself to do with territory, property or conquest?

There has been a tendency to identify sexual politics with the cultural analysis of femininity and masculinity, sometimes independently of each other, and to see reading motivated by sexual politics as concerned with the representation of women and (more recently) men. Such a way of reading (and I have no quarrel with it) commonly finds in heterosexual Renaissance love poems by men the characters of a loquacious and predatory man on the one hand, and a wholly silent woman on the other. But in thus placing these figures in opposition to each other, we risk ignoring the relation which, textually at least, binds them together, the very condition, in other words, of their difference within the text. In a love poem this relation consists not only in the differential meanings of man and woman, but also in the desire which assigns the woman who is its object a textual place for the male voice that declares it. Desire in the poems I want to consider is in this sense prior to gender difference, and the condition of its imagined fixing. The sexual politics in question here is the politics of desire itself, and the inscription of a power which includes but also exceeds the difference of gender. Desire, I suggest, has its own political history, and Donne's poems in particular belong on the threshold of its modernity.

Meanwhile, since Foucault, histories of sexuality are increasingly concerned with sexual identities, tracing, for instance, same-sex desire in the documents of other epochs, other cultures, and its exclusion as perversity at a specific moment in the development of the Free West. Heterosexuality, we now know, was produced as a norm, with all a norm's attendant constraints and coercions: it was not so by nature. This project of denaturalising heterosexuality is indispensable, but as the work becomes ever more precise, more attentive to detail, there is a danger of leaving unproblematised our account of the erotic relation between men and women, and thus inadvertently reaffirming its naturalness by another route.

In so far as they dramatise the impediments to true love, the texts of heterosexual desire are commonly read as throwing light not on the sexual relation itself, but on the inadequacy of this or that individual as a lover. And this inadequacy in turn is identified according to an implied standard of sexual correctness, a model of true love which is essentially problem-free, the real thing, because it conforms to the requirements of nature. Early modern love poetry, less certain as yet than the Victorians about the social value of the heterosexual nuclear couple, may perhaps be read as indicating that true love is not, after all, quite so simple.

In *Poetry and Phantasy*, Antony Easthope identifies 'To his Mistris Going to Bed' as an instance of scopophilic male narcissism. His persuasive account of the Elegy draws attention to the way its sexual object is constantly desexualised by reference to knowledges which have no erotic associations: theology, geography, classical mythology ... The woman's body is distanced rather than invoked by the utopian allusions to heaven, paradise and the new world. Meanwhile the male body of the speaker, Easthope points out, is repeatedly made visible in the text, 'standing' (l. 4), 'upright' (l. 24) and finally naked and 'covering' the woman (ll. 47–8). His gaze seems primarily to serve the purpose of installing the subject of the text as the cartographer of an imaginary landscape which mirrors his own ideal image.[2]

> The speaker of the 'Elegy' wants above all to look at the object of his desire, to master it visually as a truth he must see 'reveal'd' so he may 'know' it completely. He desires neither the woman nor sexual satisfaction but rather a transcendent object, one whose perfect atemporal image may return to him an equally perfect reflection of himself.[3]

Easthope's reading is a subtle one, and it goes as far as Freud will take it. Freud does not approve of narcissism. Narcissism is loving what you are, or were, or would like to be. It is an instance of incomplete development. Freud the scientist is no more 'disinterested' than F. R. Leavis when maturity is the issue. Narcissism, Freud says, occurs in people 'whose libidinal development has suffered some disturbance, such as perverts and homosexuals'. True object-love is characteristic of men; it is women who are commonly narcissistic, and all the more fascinating for that, rather like children, cats and large beasts of prey.[4]

But a later psychoanalytic generation acknowledges the inevitability of a narcissistic component of desire. For Lacan, it is one of the tragedies of love that while it is precipitated in the symbolic, it seeks satisfaction in the imaginary. Produced by the inability of the subject to be present to itself in its own utterance, desire seeks reaffirmation of subjectivity in the return to its own image and the assurance of its own singularity: 'the first object of desire is to be recognised by the other'.[5] In Julia Kristeva's version of the Lacanian position, however, the emphasis is on the otherness, the difference, of the other person. While the other offers a mirror to the subject, the lover perceives the other precisely as other. Thus, 'the lover is a narcissist with an *object*'.[6] And the condition of otherness, of difference, is not, of course, anatomy but a Third Party, language, the differentiating practice of signification.

If in the light of this more recent psychoanalysis, the narcissism which is undoubtedly there in the Elegy is an inevitable component of desire, and not necessarily to be classified as perversity, we may perhaps return to the text in the light of Easthope's insights to read it as displaying something of the character of desire itself at this moment in the history of Western culture (probably the 1590s). Easthope points out that the projected uncovering is continually postponed, and is still deferred at the end of the poem. Neither the reader nor the speaker achieves the promised discovery, the mapping of the woman's body: she is still, apparently, in her shift. Easthope compares Ovid's *Amores* I. 5, where the text exclaims over Corinna's arms, her shoulders, her breasts. Donne's poem, by contrast, offers inventive analogies in place of flesh, witty comparisons, not the thing itself. Moreover, Ovid ends with sexual fulfilment; Donne's speaker is still exercising his rhetorical skills when the Elegy ends.[7]

In other words, 'To his Mistris Going to Bed' departs radically from its Ovidian model precisely in so far as it consists of a series of imperatives and not a narrative of an event. Nothing, in short, *happens*: nothing sexual, that is. Even within the fiction which constitutes the poem, the action is all explicitly at the level of fantasy, and it is this above all that characterises the Elegy as a text of desire. Desire is by definition unfulfilled: you want what you don't have. Desire is predicated on absence. Ovid's poem is a text of sexual pleasure, which is not the same thing at all. Desire is thrilling, terrifying, euphoric, but it has no necessary connection with pleasure.

Vision in the Elegy imagines itself as knowledge. The woman's clothes, we are to understood, conceal the mystery of her sexual difference, and it is the lover's privilege that justifies his initiation into this essential secret:

Like pictures, or like bookes gay coverings made
For laymen, are all women thus arraid;
Themselves are mystique bookes, which onely wee
Whom their imputed grace will dignify
Must see reveal'd. Then since I may knowe,
As liberally as to a midwife showe
Thy selfe.

(ll. 39–45)

But at the end of the poem the secret is still not delivered, the privileged knowledge not conferred: the speaker continues to plead, instruct, cajole. In his discussion of the gaze and desire, Lacan argues that to conflate vision with knowledge is always to imagine a full relationship between the subject and the world. Moreover, it is characteristic of the *Cogito* to assume that 'my representations belong to me'. To see, or to see and thereby to know, is thus to take possession, to reaffirm 'this *belong to me* aspect of representations, so reminiscent of property'.[8] But the subject is not where it thinks it is.

> In our relation to things, in so far as this relation is constituted by the way of vision, and ordered in the figures of representation, something slips, passes, is transmitted, from stage to stage, and is always to some degree eluded in it – that is what we call the gaze.[9]

It is as if the gaze itself is a kind of blind spot in the process of perception. Donne's Elegy stages the quest for a completeness of vision as possession, and in the process puts on display the elusive, intervening, distancing and differentiating gaze, which is the condition of perception. What is mapped by the text is not a body at all, not the fullness of a presence, but the unrepresented gaze as the symbol of an absence, the lack that precipitates desire.

Meanwhile, however, all this is to ignore the comedy of 'To his Mistris Going to Bed'. As a characteristically Metaphysical text, the Elegy is a tissue of puns, conceits and outrageous analogies. The mode is consistently mock heroic. At first the encounter with the woman in her bedroom is an epic battle, and the absurdity of this is betrayed by the sexual pun: 'The foe oft-times, having the foe in sight, / Is tir'd with standing, though they never fight' (ll. 3–4) Subsequent comparisons are religious: the bed is a temple (l. 18); the woman brings to it 'A heaven like Mahomets paradise' (l. 21); she wears white, like an angel, and though bad angels also wear white, it is easy to tell the difference between the two: 'They set our hairs, but these the flesh upright' (l. 24). Despite its transcendental allusions, the text does not for a moment allow us to forget that all the argument is a shift and an erection, and it invites us to savour the comedy of the discrepancy within its mode of address. In this sense, what the Elegy reveals is not a body but wit, a claim to mastery of the possibilities of signifying practice.

In Kristeva's account love is addressed to a Third Party. The auto-erotic mother–child dyad becomes love when it is offered to an Other (capital O), who is not, I think, to be confused with the father. In Freudian terms the Third Party is 'the father of individual prehistory', but as Kristeva explains elsewhere, this figure 'is not grasped as a real person by the infant, but like a sort of symbolic instance; something that is here that cannot be here – the possibility of absence, the possibility of love, the possibility of interdiction but also a gift'. And later, 'some sort of archaic occurrence of the symbolic'.[10] Like the semiotic in Kristeva's earlier *Revolution in Poetic Language*, this Third Party is evidently a kind of pre-signifying signification, the beginnings of a difference *avant la lettre*. Love, it follows, is a triangular relationship between a narcissistic couple and a shadowy Third, and this Third Party is a differential formation, a 'ghost' which Kristeva locates 'beyond the mirror'.[11]

> The loving mother, different from the caring and clinging mother, is someone who has an object of desire; beyond that, she has an Other with relation to whom the child will serve as go-between. She will love her child with respect to that Other, and it is through a discourse aimed at that Third Party that the child will be set up as 'loved' for the mother. 'Isn't he beautiful', or 'I am proud of you', and so forth, are statements of maternal love because they involve a Third Party; it is in the eyes of a Third Party that the baby the mother speaks to becomes a *he*, it is with respect to others that 'I am proud of you', and so forth. Against this verbal backdrop or in the silence that presupposes it the bodily exchange of maternal fondness may take on the imaginary burden of representing love in its most characteristic form.[12]

The colonial project is addressed to a Third Party: it offers up the indigenous culture to an Idea: civilisation ... salvation ... God. Its aim is to be able to say to others of the colonial subject, who comes to reflect back the image of the coloniser, 'I am proud of you'. Donne's Elegy is also addressed to a Third Party. 'Isn't she beautiful?', it wants to be able to say, and we are almost convinced that she is, would be, will be, must be. But the text does not prove it. On the contrary, it explicitly withholds the moment of substantiation. It is in this sense that the Elegy is about love and not about the woman who is its object. Meanwhile, beyond the narcissistic mirror, and beyond the vision of the other who is the object of love, desire subsists in what eludes both vision and representation, in what exceeds demand, including the demand for love. It follows that desire is ultimately desire of the Other (the locus of the deployment of speech), to which the subject symbolically belongs, and which is the source of its subjection to desire. The ultimate object of desire is the unmediated, unimagined, unimaginable I Am.

'To his Mistris Going to Bed' is addressed not only to a woman, but also to this capital Other, the place from which one sees and hears, and from which one is seen and heard. This is the significance of the dazzling array of puns and double entendres. This accounts for the brilliant succession of scandalous comparisons and far-fetched arguments. What is affirmed as beautiful is not, in the end, the woman's body, so much as the text itself in its demonstration of mastery of the signifying difference. The Elegy is a display of wit, designed to be heard or read, and offered to a Third Party by a subject who seeks both to placate the Other and to identify with it, to defer to the Other and at the same time to participate in its power to licence the very processes of perception and differentiation.[13] Inscribed in the unsubstantiated affirmation of the woman's beauty, we can hear in the Elegy a bid to be the origin of difference, and not merely its effect.

The poem is not, of course, in the event, an origin at all. Like any signifying practice, it is necessarily intertextually derived, this time quite overtly from Ovid. As an instance of Renaissance imitation, the poem characteristically owes some of its authority to the fact that the Latin text has already been there first. In *Amores* I. 5 it is afternoon; Corinna appears in the poet's bedroom with the belt of her tunic undone; he tears her tunic off; she struggles, like one who does not want to win; he exclaims over the beauty of her body; and finally (in Marlowe's translation):

> Judge you the rest, being tyrde she bad me kisse.
> Jove send me more such afternoones as this.
> ('Elegia' 5, ll. 25–6)[14]

And yet the distance between Ovid's text and Donne's indicates the audacity of the Renaissance poet's project. Where Ovid's is a seemingly transparent narrative of sexual pleasure, Donne presents an intricate, knotty, difficult, dazzling formulation of desire. What fills the gap is history, not least the cultural history of the subject. The Elegy puts on display an emerging subjectivity which is not satisfied with imitation. On the contrary, it insists on its own specificity. The textual density and the baroque wit of 'To his Mistris Going to Bed' are there in order to surpass the tradition to which the poem claims to belong. The Elegy thus dramatises, whether consciously or not, the desire which constitutes the subject's defiance of its own subjection.

II

'The Sunne Rising' is no less overtly patriarchal, and no less explicitly imperialist than the Elegy: 'She'is all States, and all Princes, I' (l. 21). But this time the sexual relationship is marginally more reciprocal, to the extent that the world in question is no longer the world of the woman's body, but a unit formed jointly by the lovers. The Third Party to whom their prince displays the 'India's of spice and Myne' (l. 17) is, in the rhetoric of the poem, the sun, and since its obligations are to warm the world, 'that's done in warming *us*' (my italics, l. 28).

'The Sunne Rising' is also an imitation of Ovid (*Amores* I. 13), and once again with a very considerable difference. This time the specificity of the text is partly the consequence of an intervening medieval European tradition of *aubade* poems, in which the lover conventionally reproaches the dawn for interrupting the pleasures of the night. But the irreverent pose of the speaker and the extravagance of the conceits on which the argument depends are quite without precedent. Once again the poem lays claim both to an intertextual authority and at the same time to a singularity which isolates it from everything that has gone before.

Indeed, the transcendence of the subject-speaker is precisely the theme of 'The Sunne Rising'. The sun, source of life, origin of time and history, is commanded to surrender its sovereignty to the newly emerging sovereign subject of the Free West.

> Thy beames, so reverend, and strong
> Why shouldst thou thinke?
> I could eclipse and cloude them with a winke.
>
> (ll. 11–13)

The subject, which by closing its eyes can shut out the sun, is itself a little world made cunningly of elements, and there is a sense in which, just as in the Elegy, the subject is the real protagonist of 'The Sunne Rising'. The poem is an affirmation of radical subjectivism, where the speaker is 'all Princes' and 'Nothing else is' (ll. 21–2). Moreover, all existing princes are mere players: in an outrageous appropriation of Renaissance Neoplatonism, the text claims that only the lovers represent true reality: 'compar'd to this, / All honour's mimique; All wealth alchimie' (ll. 23–4). Inhabiting a timeless realm beyond the quotidian, the speaker magnificently disdains the trivial world of late schoolboys and reluctant apprentices, sleepy court-huntsmen and busy agricultural labourers (ll. 6–8).

It is love which promises access to this 'zenith of subjectivity'.[15] Western culture, which at this moment is constructing the sovereign subject, is also in the process of producing as the heart of society a private world of intimacy and personal experience, to be distinguished from the world of work, and to be valued above the public and the political. In the poem love, which ensures the enlisting of the whole subjectivity in personal relationship, subordinates honour, wealth and the sun itself. It excludes and keeps at bay work and politics. The ideal and the erotic are united, if indeed there was ever any separation between them: love transcends time and place ('no season knowes, nor clyme ...', l. 9), but it also takes place in bed. In the utopian proposition of 'The Sunne Rising' the earth is contracted to the nuclear couple. The lovers' bed which, like a map, systematically corresponds to the larger world,[16] is to be the centre of the sun's daily revolution, and this moment of reciprocal passion is to have the astonishing effect of putting an end to history.

The argument is as extravagant as it is romantic. The wit of 'The Sunne Rising' depends precisely on the impossibility of what it proposes: that the sun should stop in its course in order to sustain the perfection of the present. Palpably it won't; indeed, it hasn't. Ovid's version concludes by acknowledging the fact that poetic remonstration has not helped at all. In response to the poet's complaint in *Amores* I. 13, Aurora blushes – which only makes things worse. Traditionally, the *aubade* is a lament, and even if the element of comedy is often not far away, these dawn poems commonly recognise the inevitability of parting. 'It is the lark that sings so out of tune, / Straining harsh discords and unpleasing sharps ... /O now be gone! More light and light it grows.'[17] In Donne's text, by contrast, the mood of defiance is sustained to the end, making the poem more intensely romantic – or more absurd.

But which? The hyperbole generates a similar kind of uncertainty. Her eyes blind the sun; his eyes can eclipse it. Are we to believe that love has the power claimed for it? Apparently not. And yet subjectively, perhaps we do … ? Like Wittgenstein's duck-rabbit, which depends on how you look at it, either love in this poem is very exalted, because it is all-powerful, because it transcends the laws of nature, or it is extremely absurd, because it mistakenly supposes that it is all-powerful and can ignore the laws of nature. Or perhaps it is all the more glorious, after all, because it is happy to be absurd and doesn't see that as a problem: love is noble and thrilling exactly in so far as it rejects common sense?

I do not see any way of resolving these uncertainties, nor indeed any very convincing motive for doing so. It is precisely the undecidability of the text, its lack of closure, which sustains the desire of the reader. 'The Sunne Rising' teases and tantalises the reader to the degree that it is at once utopian about love and explicitly witty at the expense of the utopia it depicts. What is proposed as beautiful in this text is not a woman, but love itself. In so far as love evades any final definition, however, and so remains indeterminate, the text not only brings to light, but also stages, puts on show, perhaps even celebrates, the lack which resides in the process of signification. The poem, it seems to say (though it cannot possibly do so), the poem, like love itself, originates in the Other, in the symbolic, and desires to return there. But the problem about identifying with the Other, about seeking to be the origin of difference, is that in the Other there is *only* difference. The Other as the place from which one is seen and heard, hears and sees, is both an indeterminate location and the location of indeterminacy.

III

'The Good-morrow' apparently moves very much closer to portraying the kind of sexual relation that the twentieth century perceives as ideal. In this text imperial and sexual politics diverge radically. Mapping and discovering seem to lead inevitably to territorial possession (ll. 12–14), but love is an altogether more mysterious and mystical affair, in which lovers own a single world of love between them and at the same time constitute a world for each other:

'Let us possesse our worlde, each hath one, and is one' (l. 14).[18]
Either way, these lovers are equal and the relationship is perfectly
reciprocal:

> My face in thine eye, thine in mine appeares,
>> And true plaine hearts doe in the faces rest,
> Where can we finde two better hemispheares
>> Without sharpe North, without declining West?
>>> (ll. 15–18)

Each solicits and finds the gaze of the other: their eyes meet and
they encounter in the depths of the other's pupil a perfect mirror
image of themselves. This jubilant specular recognition entirely
elides the gaze itself: what the lovers see escapes the uncertainty inherent in the process of looking. They know the plain truth, because
each has introjected the eye of the other: her eye is in his head, his
in hers. Like two hemispheres, they merge into a single world, a
perfect sphere, known, mapped, complete in itself.

The auto-erotic dyad is still in practice a triangle, of course: the
lover, the woman, and the poem. But this time the text draws less
attention to itself. The writing is less intricate, less knotty, more
transparent, as befits a celebration of the exchange of true plain
hearts. Such confidence, we are to understand, has no need of esoteric allusions and inventive analogies, no need, in other words, of
rhetoric.

And yet there is a problem of interpretation here more baffling to
editors than any of the conceits in the Elegy or 'The Sunne Rising'.
Immediately after the metaphor of the hemispheres has offered an
image of perfect reciprocity, there follows what Virginia Woolf in a
different context calls 'an awkward break', a significant discontinu-
ity in the text, which in this instance suddenly leads in a slightly un-
expected direction.[19] Up to this point the logic of the argument is
perspicuous: until we met, it proposes, we were like children, or
sleeping, perhaps dreaming; now we wake, and watch, but not out
of fear; what we see with our eyes open is a whole world, the
world of our love. And then suddenly, in the last three lines of the
poem,

> Whatever dyes, was not mixt equally;
>> If our two loves be one, or, thou and I
> Love so alike, that none doe slacken, none can die.
>>> (ll. 19–21)

This is the first mention of dying in a poem where the previous imagery has all been logically linked. The reference is to the belief that if the elements were perfectly mixed in the human body, as they were before the Fall, we should live for ever. Death is the effect of an imbalance of the humours. This is all very well, but what has it to do with anything in the preceding text? And the 'if' of the final assertion is disappointing after the ringing certainty of what has gone before. 'If our two loves be one' seems to call into question the confident image of the hemispheres and the true plain hearts. Helen Gardner examines the textual variants for an improvement, finds none, and decides that the explanation of the alternative readings must be the poet's rewriting of an unsatisfactory line. 'Neither version', she concludes, 'provides a close worthy of the poem's opening. Conditional clauses must always suggest an element of doubt.'

Helen Gardner ignores the additional problem of the word 'slacken'. Her paraphrase reconstructs the syntax so that not slackening is no longer a *consequence* of loving alike, but a *synonym* for it: 'If our two loves are wholly united in one love, or, if they are always alike and *at the same pitch*, neither can perish' (my *emphasis*).[20] It is Theodore Redpath who brings out the difficulty presented by 'slacken'. It makes, in short, for an affirmation of the deepest banality: if our love is perfectly reciprocated (one, alike), so that it does not diminish, it cannot die. This is barely intelligent: *of course* if it doesn't diminish, it can't die. Redpath comments that on this reading 'the mention of slackening would be redundant to the point of absurdity. Donne demands this close kind of reading,' he goes on, 'and his work usually repays it handsomely. In the present case, however, I cannot help feeling that something may have gone wrong, and prevented this otherwise magnificent poem from achieving a truly satisfying ending.' This will clearly not do, and Redpath sets about producing a properly satisfactory conclusion. On his alternative 'none' means no one, neither of us, and the poem asserts that if our love is perfectly reciprocated, so that we do not slacken in our love, *we* cannot die.[21] This is certainly a utopian claim, and lovers are prone empirically to suppose themselves immortal in the intensity of passion. But Redpath's reading would surely reintroduce the kind of indeterminacy which haunts 'The Sunne Rising'. If the speaker of 'The Good-morrow' seriously believes that lovers cannot die, can 'The Good-morrow' possibly be serious about love?

There is, however, another possibility. Every student knows, as presumably did every seventeenth-century reader, that to die is to come. 'The Good-morrow' has already shown itself to be a sexually knowing poem.

> I wonder by my troth, what thou, and I
>   Did, till we lov'd? were we not wean'd till then?
> But suck'd on countrey pleasures, childishly?
>   Or snorted we i'the seaven sleepers den?
> 'Twas so; But this, all pleasures fancies bee.
> If ever any beauty I did see,
> Which I desir'd, and got, 'twas but a dreame of thee.
>
>   (ll. 1–7)

The final lines of this first stanza, invoking women previously desired and possessed, surely reflect back on the sucking and snorting and country pleasures that precede them.[22] Beauties desired and got, however, are no more than fancies: true love is something else. If we take the final 'die' to invoke the familiar pun, the text might be read as urging that if the desire of the lovers is one, perfectly mixed, and thus undying, perpetual, so that detumescence is impossible, so in consequence is orgasm itself. If none is able to slacken, then none by definition can ever 'die'.

Desire is desire to achieve presence, to attain the imaginary plenitude of perfect recognition, of full possession. This longing seeks to make itself perpetual, to preserve its intensity so that desire does not die. There is a direct conflict here with desire's other and equally urgent physical imperative. Understood as sexual impulse, desire fulfilled (got) would be desire in abeyance (dead). On this third reading of 'The Good-morrow' true, ideal, equal lovers are immobilised, frozen like figures on a Grecian urn, in a state of perfect reciprocal excitement which remains ungratified for ever.

IV

In this version of the text the final conceit is after all witty, and it has some connection with the rest of the poem, but it quite punctures the utopian romanticism of the preceding lines, since true love apparently excludes the possibility of sexual satisfaction. The elision of the gaze in reciprocal specular recognition, the merging of two visions into one, then appears in ironic retrospect as precisely imaginary.

Desire, after all, is less optimistic: in Lacan's account of the gaze, 'When, in love, I solicit a look, what is profoundly unsatisfying and always missing is that – *You never look at me from the place from which I see you.*'[23]

The final, authoritative meaning of the text is in my view undecidable. Possibly all three readings, and perhaps others too, were available to Donne's original audience. If so, however, what emerges on the basis of each of the poems I have considered, is the uncertainty of the lover, registered above all in the indeterminacies of the texts. The object of desire is unsure: a woman; a self-image; writing? Its condition is ambiguous: exaltation; absurdity; self-mockery? And its realisation in the subject is indefinite, to the degree that the transcendent union lovers seek is incompatible with sexual satisfaction. No wonder the worlds which were gradually opening up to the gaze of Renaissance explorers and cartographers seemed the appropriate emblem of desire. They were vast, these territories, perhaps limitless, and enticing, rich and beautiful. They were also dangerous, to the degree that they were uncharted both geographically and anthropologically. Desire in Donne's love poetry is a world that remains paradoxically unknown, and that elicits in consequence a corresponding anxiety, which is registered in the texts as undecidability.

We might be tempted to attribute the uncertainty displayed in these poems to an eccentricity, a quirk specific to their author, were it not for the recurrence of similar imagery and a more intense anxiety in the poetry of Andrew Marvell half a century later. In 'The Definition of Love' a whole world turns on two perfect loves, placed as the North and South poles, which cannot 'close':

> Unless the giddy Heaven fall,
> And Earth some new Convulsion tear;
> And, us to joyn, the World should all
> Be cramped into a Planisphere.
> (ll. 21–4)[24]

This text is, of course, both puzzling and plural. But, 'The Definition', read *as* a definition, and not as a narrative, points to a fateful impossibility in the nature of love. If the two poles are to maintain their difference, their otherness, to sustain the structure of the world of love they constitute, they can never collapse into closure. As in my reading of 'The Good-morrow', perfect, parallel loves cannot 'meet' (l. 28). Here anxiety gives way to despair.

And yet, paradoxically, this is the historical moment at which desire becomes the basis of a lifetime of concord. The modern nuclear family is increasingly defined in this period as the centre of society, the place where social values are learned and reproduced. Marriage is no longer a question primarily of property, and the transmission of names, titles, entitlements; and the relation between love and marriage is no longer a matter of indifference. On the contrary, the privileged, intimate world of 'The Sunne Rising' and 'The Good-morrow' is in the process of becoming the foundation of conjugal partnership, where love and consent ensure the harmony of the family and the proper inculcation in the next generation of consensual assumptions, beliefs, meanings.

But, these texts suggest, there is an anxiety at the heart of love itself, an uncertainty about the degree to which it is acceptable or possible to be in possession of the worlds desire makes visible. And it is perhaps to allay this anxiety that notions of property and appropriation reappear in the new model of marriage. In Milton's Paradise wedded love is the 'sole propriety' 'of all things common else', and the word 'propriety' points to the degree of possession – of mind and body, behaviour and disposition – inscribed in the new ideal of marriage.[25] 'For love, all love of other sights controules' ('The Good-morrow', l. 10). True love is a mode of policing the gaze, excluding errant desires, bringing the subject into line. As property, as possession, the object of desire now promises to fill the hollow at the heart of the subject, making a totality in the place of lack. The territorial imagery of the poems is thus not incidental. The nuclear family precisely makes one little room an every where, takes possession of the space it occupies, in order to create and populate a microcosmic private realm, designed to keep at bay the public world of the economy, politics and history.[26]

In its minute attention to the perplexities of desire, Donne's poetry can be read as identifying problems that proponents (then and now) of family values centred on the conjugal couple generally prefer to forget.[27]

From Catherine Belsey, *Desire: Love Stories in Western Culture* (Oxford, 1994), pp. 130–49.

NOTES

[This extract from Catherine Belsey's book makes use of the poststructuralist psychoanalytic theories of Jacques Lacan and Julia Kristeva in order to assign to desire 'its own political history'. According to Belsey, the history of desire precedes other kinds of contingency, for what the speakers in Donne's love poems want is precisely to 'keep at bay the public world of the economy, politics and history' (see pp. 64, 77 above). This public world is the world where the subject is 'subjected' to language, and language, for Belsey (as for Lacan and Kristeva), is the place of lack. Language makes us desire what we cannot have by virtue of its endless postponement and differentiation of meaning, knowledge and subjectivity. It is the subject's desire to overcome 'the lack which resides in the process of signification' which drives the attempts, in Donne's love poems, to locate the I as the 'origin of difference, and not merely its effect' (see pp. 72, 69 above) and return to some imagined prior state of plenitude.

Belsey's essay, which focuses upon emerging divisions between public and private realms, may be usefully contrasted with Guibbory's (which insists upon their interrelationship), and with the differently oriented discussions of subjectivity and/or the formation/existence of autonomous realms in Halpern, Fish, Aers/Kress, Wright and Harvey. For a further example of the use of psychoanalytic perspectives, combined with historicist and feminist insights, see, in particular, Harvey's essay. For further discussion and contextualisation of Belsey's essay, see Introduction, pp. 13–14. References to Donne's poems are to Helen Gardner (ed.), *The Elegies and Songs and Sonnets* (Oxford, 1965). Ed.]

1. See, for example, Andrew Marvell, 'Bermudas'. See also Stephen Greenblatt, *Renaissance Self-Fashioning: From More to Shakespeare* (Chicago, 1980), pp. 180–1. These landscapes were commonly characterised as feminine: see Annette Kolodny, *The Lay of the Land: Metaphor as Experience and History in American Life and Letters* (Chapel Hill, NC, 1975), pp. 4–25.

2. Anthony Easthope, *Poetry and Phantasy* (Cambridge, 1989), pp. 53–60. In Thomas Docherty's rather more blunt formulation, 'What is being sought by the poet is recognition of his maleness, recognition of his phallus, and an acknowledgement of the power its potency is supposed to give him' (*John Donne, Undone* [London, 1986], p. 82).

3. Easthope, *Poetry and Phantasy*, p. 58.

4. Sigmund Freud, 'On Narcissism: An Introduction', *On Metapsychology: The Theory of Psychoanalysis*, ed. Angela Richards, vol. 11 (London, 1984), pp. 59–97, pp. 81–3.

5. Jacques Lacan, *Ecrits*, trans. Alan Sheridan (London, 1977), p. 58.

6. Julia Kristeva, *Tales of Love*, trans. Leon S. Roudiez (New York, 1987), p. 33.

7. Easthope, *Poetry and Phantasy*, pp. 56–7.

8. Lacan, *The Four Fundamental Concepts of Psycho-Analysis*, trans. Alan Sheridan (London, 1979), p. 81.

9. Lacan, *Four Fundamental Concepts*, p. 73. In the Seminar 'Of the Gaze as *Objet Petit a*' the gaze in question is always double: the gaze of the subject, which brings into being the imaginary world of objects, and the gaze of the world, which is constitutive for the subject.

10. 'Julia Kristeva in Conversation with Rosalind Coward', *Desire*, ICA Document 1 (London, 1984), pp. 22, 23.

11. Kristeva, *Tales of Love*, p. 35.

12. Ibid., p. 34.

13. Ibid., p. 36.

14. Fredson Bowers (ed.), *The Complete Works of Christopher Marlowe*, 2nd edn (Cambridge, 1981), vol. 2.

15. Kristeva, *Tales of Love*, p. 5.

16. I owe this point to David Skilton.

17. *Romeo and Juliet* (III.v.27–35), William Shakespeare, *The Complete Works*, ed. Peter Alexander (Glasgow, 1951).

18. Where Helen Gardner gives line 14 as 'Let us possesse our world, each hath one, and is one', most modern editors settle for the version of 1633: 'Let us possesse one world ...' I have not thought it necessary to choose between them.

19. See Mary Jacobus, 'The Difference of View', *The Feminist Reader: Essays in Gender and the Politics of Literary Criticism*, ed. Catherine Belsey and Jane Moore (London, 1989), pp. 49–62, p. 57.

20. Helen Gardner (ed.), *The Elegies and Songs and Sonnets* (Oxford, 1965), p. 199.

21. Theodore Redpath (ed.), *The Songs and Sonets of John Donne* (London, 1983), p. 231.

22. 'The conceit that one's previous mistresses were only shadows or gleams of the lady one addresses is common in Renaissance lyrics, but "desir'd, and got" is not.' A. J. Smith (ed.), *John Donne: The Complete English Poems* (London, 1973), p. 378.

23. Lacan, *Four Fundamental Concepts*, p. 103.

24. H. M. Margoliouth (ed.), *The Poems and Letters of Andrew Marvell*, vol. I (Oxford, 1971).

25. John Milton, *Paradise Lost*, IV. 751–2, *The Poems of John Milton*, ed. John Carey and Alastair Fowler (London, 1968).

26. For a more detailed discussion of these issues, see Catherine Belsey, *The Subject of Tragedy: Identity and Difference in Renaissance Drama* (London, 1985), pp. 129–221; and *John Milton: Language, Gender, Power* (Oxford, 1988), pp. 53–8

[27. I am grateful to Catherine Belsey for her valuable suggestion for a final sentence of this edited version of her chapter. Ed.]

4

Small Change: Defections from Petrarchan and Spenserian Poetics

BARBARA ESTRIN

Perhaps more than ... any other poet, ... the work of John Donne has been critically regarded as misogynistic: 'written by a man whose central theme is his own intense personal mood and whose poetry is composed exclusively, even domineeringly, from the viewpoint of a man'.[1] Accordingly, Donne becomes a poet who (in Janel Mueller's terms) 'perpetuates the prevailing asymmetry of outlook and sexual role that casts the male as persuader and possessor, the female as persuaded and possessed'.[2] His poems and letters thus provide an almost perfect laboratory for feminist critics to explore gender 'asymmetry' as it emerges in the early modern period. But a brief look at the maps of two learned feminist critics, Janet Halley and Ilona Bell, indicates the inherent difficulty of clearly charting the histories of women's lives. Each critic produces a different story, partly because each theorises a very different Donne and a very different woman from the same textual evidence: the poems and letters. The theoretical apparatus of one is cancelled by the historical position of the other, as each attempts to locate the 'real' woman in the 'real sphere' of Donne's life.

On the one hand, Janet Halley maintains that 'the representations of Ann Donne that we have inherited from her husband function no differently in the context of Donne's representations than those of that quintessentially fictional female, the Muse'. In poems and letters,

Donne 'gathered to himself a power he shared whenever he circulated female figures: the masculine power to control the meaning of the feminine'.[3] For Halley, there is a single-layered poet who, imposing what Ann Rosalind Jones calls 'the violent hierarchies that shore up masculine identity',[4] invents the women he writes about, even his real-life wife. In Halley's view, the life Ann Donne lived can be found 'not only by her presence in history but also by acknowledging her absence to us in her husband's discourse' (p. 191).

For Ilona Bell, who on the other hand advocates (in Jones's terms) 'the non-victim status of women' (p. 76), Donne himself is multivalent, spinning out speakers who vary from 'lusty braggadocio, to efficacious rhetorician, to cold avenger, to empathetic understander'.[5] Bell's lady, however, is a composite one whose point of view Donne is 'never able to disregard' (p. 116). 'Unlike his Petrarchan predecessors, Donne writes not of imagined love or exalted beauty but of loving and being loved ... not of ladies seen and admired but of a lady who is highly present, loving and criticising, judging as well as admiring' (p. 129). When, in a later article, Bell turns from the poems to the historical evidence of the letters and concludes that three were written by John Donne to Ann More over a year before their elopement, she also concludes that 'if, as these letters suggest, Donne's love affair with Ann entailed a much wider range of feelings than we thought, it may well have inspired a broader, more various group of poems than we have considered'.[6] According to Bell's logic, the lady listening to the poems must have been Ann.

Bell's 'woman' is independent. Above all she is present in her feelings to poet and man. Created by poet and man, Halley's women are 'absent' in the text and in the life (p. 191). While Bell assumes that Ann More could read the letters she speculates Donne wrote to her, Halley conversely reasons that since no documentary evidence remains 'statistical studies suggest that it is highly unlikely that she was [literate]' (p. 187). Historical argument often proceeds from what Janet Malcolm calls 'the psychological impossibility of a writer's not taking sides' and what Marguerite Waller calls the disinclination of the critic 'to contextualise and relativise – to consider as an ideological construct – the critical ground from which [s]he is arguing'.[7] In this context, the discrepancy between the historical evidence of Bell and Halley can be read as part of their particular 'projects' even if their conclusions 'resist creating presence where none is'.[8]

Halley nevertheless argues cogently that 'if we admit that women in their historical actuality remain the constituency of feminist criticism, we oblige ourselves to keep in mind that the subjective experience and authority of women are, perforce, absent from the representations of them' (p. 191). Halley is right when she says that the subjective experience of women is missing from male representation, if the biographical life is what is meant by subjective experience. But the corollary to that axiom is another question. Can we know the man Ann Donne married from the poetry of John Donne or even from John Donne's letters? Letters, too, can be subject to the conventions of their circulation and to the need, and sometimes even unconscious motivation, for the cover of personae.[9]

But when she speaks of the *authority* of women, Halley enters into yet another sphere – the realm where women might have power – power in the sense of how they materialise in the imagination, either their own or that of the inventing poet. And it is within the realm of multiple identifications that Donne imagines an imagining other with an authority that might make her author of the very representation in which she appears. In such configurations, it is very easy for author and authority to get confused even by the inventing poet who is produced by the original man named John Donne. As 'something imagined, not recalled',[10] a poem suggests that the scales of Halley and Bell are ballasted by ideological projects based on mutually exclusive asymmetries. Neither theory accounts for the 'force' of Lyotard's 'dream-work', or the way in which it refolds and changes experience. When he speaks of condensation as 'a change of state ... or a difference in nature', Lyotard describes the mysterious process of 'producing the imaginary'. That process also produces the authority – or the force – in the 'scenario' of the poem. 'Hiding its other sides', the condensation refigures desire in ways that are not always definable by the biographical self or apparent to the historian.[11] Like the dream-work, the poem presents yet another layer of experience, an opacity that makes it possible to imagine the shifting subjectivities that constitute an anamorphic vision.

If Halley's position results in a feeling that we can never know for certain the 'materiality of women's lives', and Bell's in a feeling that we can never know for certain the 'materiality of poets' lives', then it might be possible to introduce a theory of 'undecidabilities' which functions apart from what Jonathan Goldberg calls 'the single-minded story that some New Historicists have been telling, but also from the ways in which its feminist critics have replied'.[12] To read

Donne with Denise Riley's understanding that individual temporalities are modified by 'the many temporalities of a designation'[13] is to emphasise the complex negotiations between self and other that emerge from an understanding of the many 'alternative possibilities in the writing of gender'.[14] ...

[In the passages omitted here, Estrin draws connections between ideas of poetic creativity and Christian myths of creation. Contrasting Donne's Christmas Day sermon of 1624 with the hierarchical models of creation and replication inscribed in Spenser, Petrarch and sixteenth-century biblical commentaries on Genesis (especially, Miles Coverdale, *The Christen State of Matrimonye* [London, 1552]), Estrin argues that where these latter models 'assert man's invention of the woman he idealises' (*Laura*, p. 159), Donne preaches against the principles of prioritisation and resemblance. The poetic/religious creation of Woman in the image of an 'original', which is God/Man, is subverted by Donne to produce a greater sense of mutuality between the sexes. Ed.]

A HUNDRED LESSER FACES: SPENSERIAN REPLICATION

When, in the Petrarchan tradition, Spenser's Colin Clout of *The Faerie Queene*, book 6, invents Rosalynde, he transforms the resemblances of Genesis into the satisfying – and self-reflective – substitutes that his music provides. His pleasure in the song he *can* make erases his sadness over the woman he *can't* have. If death is what happens to man after the fall, then the artist must deal with it even in his prelapsarian fantasies. The sublimated Rosalyndes he creates from himself replace an experienced loss and perpetuate an established vision. One hundred naked ladies dance to his music, ...

> But that faire one,
> That in the midst was placed parauaunt,
> Was she to whom that shepheard pypt alone,
> That made him pipe so merrily, as neuer none.
>
> She was to weete that iolly Shepheards lasse,
> Which piped there vnto that merry rout,
> That iolly shepheard, which there piped, was
> Poore Colin Clout (who knowes not Colin Clout?)
> He pypt apace, whilest they him daunst about.
> Pype iolly shepheard, pype thou now apace

Vnto thy loue, that made thee low to lout:
Thy loue is present there with thee in place,
Thy loue is there aduaunst to be another Grace.[15]

Colin Clout re-creates Rosalynde from the vacancy fostered by
denial. 'Low-louting' in the flesh fosters his high ambition in the
music. In the Spenserian myth, art imitates nature. The artist produces copies in the same way as nature grows leaves on trees. The
pain of the initial loss is a necessary antecedent for the joy of continual recovery as Colin repeats, in his endless piping, the vision of
the deified Rosalynde who will continue to deny him. ...

Contrastingly, the Donne of 'The Broken Heart' begins – and
remains – in sickness, the irreparable split created by denial. While
Colin produces one hundred beautiful maidens out of his unhappi-
ness, the Donne of 'The Broken Heart' ekes out one hundred lesser
selves. While the Spenser of the Mount Acidale sequence uncriti-
cally multiples, the Donne of 'The Broken Heart' – similarly speaking of numbers – subverts quantification. Spenser spins maidens out
of his creative self. Broken by the single lady of imagination, Donne
replicates only shattered selves. He presents first a sequence of unfolding volume (the increase of hours, days, years) and, then, its
consequential inverse: progressive diminution (the decrease caused
by gunshot wounds, plague, decay). Spenser finds consolation in
replication. Donne finds replication hollow, its impetus merely an
approximation, not an amplification, of feeling. He illustrates the
futility of replication by multiplying parts of his self. While Spenser
invents whole bodies, Donne presents fractured feelings. If Colin
fills the vacuum of his love's denial with images of Rosalynde,
making her physical absence the emotional presence of his vision,
Donne, writing a poem about the creation of a vacuum, fails to fill it
with his beloved. Instead of praising the woman's parts, he multiplies parts of himself. In his reproduction of Rosalynde, Spenser's
Colin imitates the creative power of Venus and Genius by remaining
isolated and disconnected. His self-sufficiency allows him to function like the goddess of love: 'Syre and mother ... her selfe alone,
Begets and eke conceiues, ne needeth other none' (*TFQ*, 4.10.41).
To be like Venus, 'alone', Colin must be denied. If Venus is a
woman who incorporates the man, Colin (alone) is the man who incorporates the woman. 'Beget[ing] and eke conceiu[ing]' the sequential vision of unfolding Rosalyndes, Colin ... 'needeth other none'.
In contrast, 'The Broken Heart' explores the extended loneliness of

the denied self. Donne's poem is about need and what happens when needs are not met. Like his Venus, Spenser's Colin endlessly replaces the nature he avoids. Donne's 'I' denies the poetry that makes an art of the self in the first two stanzas and satirises the poetry that reveals the self in art in the last two. Where Rosalynde's rejection encourages Colin to create the other as he pipes merrily alone, Donne's losses result in a self who sings – gloomily – of his fractured heart. Alone, Colin invents his unique song of the woman. Injured, Donne hollows out only the song of the self. The poetry Donne denies in the first two stanzas is trivial; it cannot imitate nature. The poetry of the last two stanzas is egocentric; it cannot produce a lady.

Like the Petrarch of *Rime sparse* 105, Donne incorporates the critical other and belittles the persistent lover, the one who – wounded by love – continues loving:

> He is starke mad, who ever sayes,
> That he hath beene in love an houre,
> Yet not that love so soone decayes,
> But that it can tenne in lesse space devour;
> Who will beleeve mee, if I sweare
> That I have had the plague a yeare?
> Who would not laugh at mee, if I should say,
> I saw a flaske of *powder burne a day*?
>
> Ah, what a trifle is a heart,
> If once into loves hands it come!
> All other griefes allow a part
> To other griefes, and aske themselves but some;
> They come to us, but us Love draws,
> Hee swallows us, and never chawes:
> By him, as by chain-shot, whole rankes doe dye,
> He is the tyran Pike, our hearts the Frye.
>
> (p. 51)

There are two links between the first and second stanzas: the first, the image of love the devourer (completed in the tyrant pike of the second stanza); the second, the image of poets devoured (resolved in the 'our hearts' of the second stanza). The stanzas are alike in their representation of massive suffering (the eaten ten of the first stanza, the several 'fry' of the second). When he compares himself to other poets in a 'school' that seems Spenserian, the speaker explains why all such poets are prey to mockery. The intricate series of containers he sets up places his poetry – and that of other Spenserians – in the centre. Contained by the rhyming 'hour' and 'devour' is the little 'our' of the first stanza; contained by the rhyming 'heart' and 'part' of the second stanza is the tiny 'art'. 'Our art' is immediately absorbed by the larger truth that love destroys the poet totally. As his swearing is out-shouted, his art is overcome, trivialised by the larger power of love.

As the remover, Love allows no partial discourse. In the realm of Love, in the belly of the whale, art (human endeavour and measure) is defeated. The lover who claims that his passion lasts into hours, days, and years is enveloped by decay, the plague, or gunshot. All undermine the prolongation he extols. The poet is outwardly pressured by voluminous Time and inwardly emptied by devouring decay. The increasing numbers of time weaken the poet. The increasing numbers of poets (the ten of stanza one, the whole ranks of stanza two) deny his originality. In the Spenserian ethos, the artist allies himself, as self-sufficient creator, with the strength of the androgynous Venus. The 'I' of 'The Broken Heart' is overcome in the first two stanzas by the increasing avalanche of decay and the reductive impact of numbers that Spenser (through Colin in book 6) escapes. Like Venus, Colin guarantees his immunity from the pull of love by replacing the fleshly Rosalynde with successive musical imitations. But the 'I' of 'The Broken Heart' cannot prevent his absorption into the 'tyrant' Time. Surrounded by the feeling *heart*, his *art* is absorbed by the larger forces Spenser escapes. Donne's 'I' lives in the long aftermath of denial. Capitalising on its immediate impact, Spenser's Colin protects himself by a ring of naked bodies. The encircling Rosalyndes of his imagination sequester, feed, and so strengthen his pipe. But the circle depends on his initiative. Its movement reflects his energy even as its dependency encourages him to keep on piping. Surrounded by the destructive critics in stanza one, joined by other poets in stanza two, the 'I' of 'The Broken Heart' is finally devoured by the crippling pike. His instrument is sterilised. It brings forth no life.

If the strategy of the first two stanzas is to reduce the 'I' as the world enlarges, the strategy of the last two is to make more of less. In the first two stanzas, the 'I' is the size of a heart, small enough for the pike to swallow it, as the whale engulfed Jonah and Cronos – the father – ate his children. In the last two stanzas, the heart is replicated and enlarged. In response to the fact that Rosalynde made him low to lout, Colin produces many Rosalyndes. But Donne subtly questions the replication of the Spenserian solution. Instead of reproducing many fully formed ladies, he projects many hollowed-out selves. Reliving his initial confrontation with the 'thee', the 'I' calls her (as he did the pike in stanza 2) a devourer of men. Taking the lady's theft seriously, the 'I' investigates heartlessness; unlike Petrarch's, his heart-robbed Battus doesn't automatically go on singing. Where Petrarch survives his robbery and Spenser rises from his low louting to reinvent music, Donne cannot continue writing: 'I brought a heart into the roome,/But from the roome, I carried none with mee' (p. 51). If the first two stanzas present Love as Cronos-the-father eating his children by drawing them back into the self, the last two, going back further in chronology, depict Love, as Cronos-the-child, shivering his parent's member, and rendering him (as he says at the end) unable to love. In answer to the woman's objection to the initial disclaimer that the 'I' lacks a believable self, the poet counters with yet another disclaimer: broken in pieces, the 'I' contains too many selves. Diffuse, he loses his potency.

Cronos's dismemberment of his father produced the goddess Aphrodite, who, as in Spenser, contains syre and dame in one. But whatever happened to the dismembered father? Donne takes the mutilation literally. No member, no remembrance. Castrated, the 'I' reproduces versions of his castrated self, weak remnants of his scattered parts. In the revisionist history of stanza 3, Donne places the blame for his impotence on the woman's initial failure to accept his love:

> If it had gone to thee, I know
> Mine would have taught thy heart to show
> More pitty unto mee: but Love, alas,
> At one first blow did shiver it as glasse.
>
> (p. 51)

Piping merrily alone, Spenser produces the sequential vision of Colin's dancing ladies. Donne's shivered 'I' reproduces many shivering selves. The shivered heart is, by implication, a cold heart and that coldness, Donne also implies, is the true source of Spenserian replication.

The glassy selves Donne proliferates reflect the icy self of the lady. Instead of assembling a complete body out of his broken self, Donne multiplies the broken pieces. The shivered heart thus enables the 'I' both to revenge the lady and to defend his silence. If, as Rosalie Colie argues, postulating a vacuum was sinful,[16] Donne's woman is the sinner. The postulation is hers. After he confronts her, his *one* heart is *none* and *gone*. She is the source of his cancellation even if Love at the end delivers the fatal blow. In stanza 3 he says of his heart: 'I carried none with mee.' The 'I' speaks of himself as empty, the *vide* of the vacuum Pascal was later philosophically to corroborate.[17] He has no heart. It is gone. But, in stanza 4, he quickly retracts that statement:

> Yet nothing can to nothing fall,
> Nor any place be empty quite,
> Therefore I thinke my breast hath all
> Those peeces still, though they be not unite.
> (p. 51)

When he denies the heterodoxy of the previous stanza, Donne substitutes an emotional for a physical emptiness.[18] Like Adam and Eve expelled from Eden, his heart continues to function after the fall, albeit in a diminished state.[19]

Stanza 3 speaks of three forms of simplicity, the zero of emptiness, the oneness of initiation, and the first blow. Stanza 4 speaks of multiplicity and multiplication, a heart replicated endlessly:

> And now as broken glasses show
> A hundred lesser faces, so
> My ragges of heart can like, wish, and adore,
> But after one such love, can love no more.
> (p. 52)

As the broken glass 'shows' (both displays and reveals) a hundred copies of the same originating image, so the broken heart performs the hundred lesser acts of the unsatisfied 'I'. All three verbs – liking, wishing, adoring – turn backward to the self rather than forward to the other. The 'lesser faces' reflected in the multiplying glasses are the poet's diminished selves not the lady's idealised likenesses. They stem from the poet, are his *littler* emotions. All three verbs suggest – in the comparison of metaphor (liking), the expression of desire (wishing), and the act of worship (adoring) – variations on nothingness. The source of this distorted replication is the injured and uncreative self, giving off an afterglow of energy – liking, wishing, adoring – that reflects his emptiness. Manifold variations on a theme without a centre, the remnants of a heart, like the shards of broken glass, produce fractions of what once was but now is disembodied. The liked, wished for, and adored 'you' doesn't exist in her own right. She is simply carved out of the 'I's' inadequacy. Donne refuses to make from himself the Spenserian other. Denied, he offers instead one hundred sequential versions – liking, wishing, adoring – of his injured 'I'.

When, in *The Winter's Tale*, Florizel tells Perdita that 'all [her] acts are queens', he describes her in a social context, 'speak[ing], sing[ing], buy[ing], sell[ing], pray[ing], ord'ring, danc[ing]' (IV.iv.30), of a diurnal, even a mundane, existence. In its cataloguing technique, his list is similar to Donne's 'liking, wishing, adoring', but Florizel describes communal acts, Donne private feelings. Florizel's community of action leads to a communion with nature. With the oxymoron 'move still, still so' (IV.iv.42). Florizel seeks to make Perdita a wave of the sea, part of an eternally recurring cycle. As the wave is defined by the shore, so the image of Perdita depends on contact. The sequential acts Donne describes (liking, wishing, adoring) result from the remoteness, the insularity, of separation. Like Colin to the Spenserian maidens dancing in a ring, Donne remains at a distance. But that position is unsatisfying to him and, he implies, unrewarding to the lady. Unlike Perdita who lives through her function in the world, the 'liked', 'wished-for', and 'adored' lady of Donne's broken self exists apart from the world. She is a product of his lack. The injured 'I' can hobble through with the poetics of absence – liking, wishing, and adoring – but the poetics of fullness, the re-creation of regeneration, demand a partner, a fleshly other. Like Florizel's wave coming back to the shore, Donne's ideal vision of love … includes the fertility of procreation, rather than the androgyny of succession. For a brief moment in *Rime sparse* 129, Petrarch admits that his 'thought shadows [Laura] forth', that his attempts at re-creation produce imitations that are self-deceiving.[20] In 'The Broken Heart', Donne elaborates the shadow. His ragged heart is the remnant of a vacant body, his evaporation into ineffectuality an extension of Petrarch's depressed moments in *Rime sparse* 129.

Liking, wishing, and adoring are the linguistic manifestations of the shadow self, voices that echo (as the images look like) what they mirror. Love produces poems. Liking produces shadow poems. The voice is empty, the image vacant. Unlike Colin Clout, the injured 'I' of 'The Broken Heart' cannot substitute a lesser feeling for the initial impact of love. While Colin pipes merrily alone, the speaker of 'The Broken Heart' is joyless. Out of an 'I' who can 'love no more', Donne cannot re-create (as Spenser does) more lovely 'yous'. Deprived of the energetic instigation of love, Donne is unable to generate consequentially idealised versions of the beloved. Unmanned by Love, Donne produces only shrinking replicas of the shivered self. No Venus arises, like Colin's Rosalynde, from the broken member. Castration does not augur the phallic re-emergence of the sublimating poem. A lessened self produces lesser versions of its own image rather than progressive images of the idealised lady.

ON DIVERS SHORES: PETRARCHAN SEPARATION

The 'Of Weeping' speaker is similarly unable to recover from the blow of denial. But if, in 'The Broken Heart', the poet-lover makes himself into the many-faceted singer of emptiness, here the poet-lover turns the lady into the multiply originating man. That conversion comments on the Petrarchan model. Petrarch uses the woman to create an art where the man is at the centre. In 'Of Weeping', the speaker creates a world where the woman emerges as the potential poet presiding over a dismembered world. Rendering to the woman the power which Petrarch only *claims* to give her and spreading to the world a disorientation in the self, Donne questions the healing power of sublimation. For the Donne of 'The Broken Heart', no alternative feeling can substitute for love. For the Donne of 'Of Weeping', no other presence can replace the beloved.[21]

In 'The Broken Heart', Donne refers to a past failure to praise the denying beloved; here he anticipates his future silence. In 'The Broken Heart', it is her remembered refusal (whatever happened in that room); in 'Of Weeping', it is her imminent excess (whatever will happen after she sighs). In both poems, *she* becomes the deadening, rather than inspiring, force. If 'The Broken Heart' reappraises the origins of Spenser's Petrarchan replication, 'Of Weeping' questions the sources of Petrarch's reflex deification. 'Of Weeping' begins where *Rime sparse* 23 ends: in separation. Petrarch recovers from the devastating Lauras of 23 (who first as Mercury paralyse, then as Diana dismember, him). He reinvents a moving (even a flying) and a remembering (even an apotheosising) 'I'. Such an emergence into eminence can only come from the divergence into difference Petrarch forges in the remarkable last stanza of *Rime sparse* 23 where all the previous annihilations seem miraculously not to have happened. In the light of such a second reading, Petrarch's initial laurelisation (his conversion into a womanly shape) leads ultimately into a reaffirmation of his manliness.

At the end of *Rime sparse* 23, Petrarch defines the process whereby he achieves the separation essential to poetic articulation:

> Song, I was never the cloud of gold that once descended in a precious rain so that it partly quenched the fire of Jove; but I have certainly been a flame lit by a lovely glance and I have been the bird that rises highest in the air raising her whom in my words I honor; nor for any new shape could I leave the first laurel, for still its sweet shade turns away from my heart any less beautiful pleasure.
>
> (p. 68)

In the final telling he details the stages of the process: his history before he met Laura (he never was a cloud of gold); what he became when he met her (the first laurel); and what that becoming enabled him to be (a flame and an eagle). Petrarch alters the chronology of his encounter with Laura to describe those states. There are three stages in the Petrarchan transformation: first, the poet's absorption by the woman; second, the poet's separation from her; third, the poet's deification of her. At the end of *Rime sparse* 23, Petrarch catalogues what he never could have been, what he did become, and *then* the laurel that facilitated the second stage. The laurelisation should come second not third. But it is told last because it suggests his final resting place – the sweet shade of an eternal laurel *under* which Petrarch presently composes. In that shade, the laurel emerges at last the poetic crown he sought before Laura's injunction in the Battus episode. ... Though the familiar shapes of Ovidian metamorphosis form the flora and fauna of *Rime sparse 23*, the final figure is that of the incontrovertible poetic 'I'. Separate from the woman he absorbed, Petrarch defines her renewed otherness and ... his consolidated originality. As crown, Laura is the culminating adornment, rather than the rooting fixture, of the poet's identity. She is what he projects. His energy renders her divine. But it is only *within* his discourse that she reigns.

That self-conscious 'I' is what Donne stands to lose in 'Of Weeping'. Whereas Petrarch remains in coolness, protected by the shade of the laurel, Donne (all emotion) emerges vulnerable to the forces of nature he sought to control. When he emphasises his victimisation, Donne also adumbrates the limits of Petrarchan consolidation. Petrarch creates Laura in the gap between imminence and distance. He is reborn when he pushes her out of himself and into the heavens while he remains autonomous in the cooling distance of shade. In Laura's physical absence, Petrarch celebrates her presence

as artifact. It is the absence Donne fears. At the end of 'Of
Weeping', Donne's 'you' is painfully earthbound, blasted with the
sighs and tears of conventional poetry. Petrarch's Laura inspires
even in her remoteness. Donne's 'I' argues that his 'you' can only
inspire in the temporal present of his physical presence. Through
his woman poet, the 'I' of Donne's 'Of Weeping' demonstrates the
deadening impact of Petrarchan separation. It kills in its excessiveness.[22] If the Coverdale Adam rejoices in his doubly creative capacity as inventor (through the mind) and parent (through the rib) of
Eve, Donne tosses that creative and procreative doubleness to and
from the woman of the poem. In the first stanza, he builds her up by
making her into the artist-man. In the second stanza, he retracts her
power and attempts (by his own force) to restore his world. When
that fails, he makes her an artist-god again in the third stanza where,
totally dependent on her sighs, he anticipates the death of the
reduced self he initially had. Twice through the lady and once
through himself, Donne rejects prioritisation, the 'derogation' of
firstness. Through his woman-artist, Donne argues that loving connection, not separation, is necessary to art. Through his woman-
coiner, Donne demonstrates that hierarchy has little to do with
poetry.

The first and second stanzas ridicule the separation and the third
stanza undermines the deification that Petrarch effects at the end of
Rime sparse 23. The reduction is apparent from the outset:

> Let me powre forth
> My teares before thy face, whil'st I stay here,
> For thy face coines them, and thy stampe they beare,
> And by this Mintage they are something worth,
> > For thus they bee
> > Pregnant of thee;
> Fruits of much griefe they are, emblems of more,
> When a tear falls, that thou falls which it bore,
> So thou and I are nothing then, when on a divers shore.
>
> > (p. 69)

Like Juliet, who calls parting a 'sweet sorrow', Donne attempts
both to stay, to remain in place as long as possible, and to create a
stay, a prop against the ensuing annihilation: he will say 'good
night till it be morrow' (*Romeo and Juliet*, II.ii.186). As long as he
is able to pour forth in her presence the tears which re-create her
image, so long can he ward off the nothingness of separation. If

Colin re-created Rosalynde in the absence of low-louting, so Donne re-creates his woman in the presence of equality. The tears must be at the level of her face. They depend upon her presence. Like the Petrarch who returns to the moment before Laura's heart-robbery in *Rime sparse* 129, Donne sets up a peculiar set of antecedents where the tears both precede her face and her face in turn produces more. Nothing has happened; all will still happen. The speaker has not yet wept, but his tears are ready to fall. He has not yet left, but he is about to leave. They are not yet nothing, yet they will soon be undone. By creating an anterior present and by putting off the act which can only take place before departure, Donne further postpones that departure and relegates it to the future. The more actively he weeps, the richer life he will conceive in the first half of stanza 1; the more tears she inspires, the better able he is to postpone death in the second part of stanza 1.

In order for the mirror of his tears to become her, she must be 'before' him. Her chronological place as originator of his being is tied to her physical space as origin of his reflection. He must give her an antecedent rationale as well as a formulating presence. He establishes her prior existence and creative potential by pulling her into first place. As originator, she coins and stamps the tears so that they emerge, by this mintage and through the present stamping, round. Without her stamp, the tears are empty. With it, they both contain her (are pregnant *with* her) and are instigated by her (are pregnant *of* her). Without the mirrors of identity, there is no artistic recognition. She emerges, like Petrarch, the substance and originator of the poem and, the inventor and parent of her partner. But the reflection is dependent for its substance on constant presence. In order to be, she needs the tears that contain her. Though she is the originator of the poet, he provides the cylindrical mirror that proves her materiality. Without his reflection, she doesn't exist. Like Mieke Bal's Eve, Donne is the 'other character indispensable for [her] to be a character at all'.[23] Her material body is crucial to the body of his idealisation. If she moves away and rejects him, then he must cancel the terms of her idealisation.

Petrarch brings Laura to her apotheosis through the separation of birth; in this poem, the 'diversity' of separation signifies death. Once the tear falls beneath his face, the lady falls too. The poet must continually weep in her presence in order to produce a new supply of vessels to contain her. In diversity, he cannot continue to create vehicles that signify her value. She is nothing without the vehicle; he is nothing when he cannot contain her. As mirror-producer, he needs the emotion to create the mirror. As mirrored originator, she needs him to feel the emotion. Closeness produces the stimulation that feeds desire. Desire produces the void that necessitates closeness. The circles encircle each other. Petrarch finds his strength by separating himself from the being – the laurel – that possessed him. Once separated, he can make more of her. In 'Of Weeping', Donne refuses to accept the consolation of separation. He argues instead that even a moment of sadness together is worth more than something recollected in the shade of distance.[24] Separated from Laura, Petrarch rests comfortably beneath her. Donne denies the inspiration of absence.

In the second stanza, Donne renders himself the artist, the woman the artifact. But the result is the same. As Bal writes about Eve: 'they mutually create each other, differently in a different act' (p. 336). In the first stanza, as coiner, she is the maker of him. In the second, as workman, he is the maker of her. Without her frame of containment and without the difference of her difference, his art dissolves. As she needed the mirror to contain her in the first stanza, he needs her frame to support his art in the second. Without her sustaining wrapper, the globe falls apart. Without his originating presence, there is no initial circle which will subsequently grow. That reversal back of roles (he as impresser in stanza 2, she as coiner in stanza 1) illustrates the necessity of physical presence and the futility of poetic substitution. The validity of impression results not from an identity where each is the same but from a sharing where each retains the original and joins with the other. Yet if diversity causes the nothingness in the first stanza, mixing causes the dissolution in the second. If, like him, the lady becomes all tears, then the result is a flood. In both stanzas Donne stipulates that the first two Petrarchan stages – the originally inspiring woman and the powerfully re-creative man – can exist only in a state of physical equality. Whereas Petrarch recognises the first stage through the lady's denial and the second through his absorption into her, Donne demonstrates how both stages undercut the poetic impetus. His first stanza ends in the nothingness of difference, the second in the vagueness of similarity. If she pulls apart from him, then there is too much distance. If she becomes totally like him, then there is too much of the same. Poems depend, he argues, on the demarcation of formal boundaries her nearness and difference provide. Absence yields nothing for both sexes. To remain the creative generator in stanza 1, she needs the mirror he holds. To fulfil the creative mandate of stanza 2, he needs the wrapping she lends. In the first two stanzas Donne subverts the productivity of Petrarchan separation.

In the last stanza, he undercuts the piety of Petrarchan apotheosis. There the recovered 'I' invents the woman's godliness, her superiority to nature:

> O more then Moone,
> Draw not up seas to drowne me in thy spheare,
> Weepe me not dead, in thine armes, but forebeare
> To teach the sea, what it may doe too soone;
>   Let not the winde
>   Example finde,
> To doe me more harme, then it purposeth;
> Since thou and I sigh one anothers breath,
> Who e'r sighes most, is cruellest, and hasts the others death.
>   (pp. 70–1)

Donne's moon and waters are dependent upon each other for their cyclical and recurrent being. To be more than the moon is to be greater than nature, to have both the power (as magnet) to pull the man to her and the force (as wind) to push him totally away. When she pulls him to her, he becomes the dead baby, smothered in her arms. When she pushes him away, he becomes the dead man, lost at sea. By destroying the balance, she creates either the diversity of the first stanza (as wind) or the dissolution of the second (as water). To be more than moon is to be more than full – no longer the pregnant woman of the first stanza. But her 'more' makes less of him. As larger container, she exceeds the potential of fullness (realising Petrarchan separation). As greater power, she presses beyond the dimensions of nature (achieving Petrarchan deification). The full moon (the more than moon) causes his annihilation. For him to be her child cradled in her arms is for her to be physically overwhelming. For her to be his child and made a goddess by his design is for her to become creatively overbearing: the ruler of the sea, the example for the wind, and the cause of his end.

If the first stanza begins by asking for permission – 'Let me', which operates to preserve the balance of wholeness – the last stanza ends by imposing an injunction – 'Let not', which attempts to avoid the pitfalls of idolatry. If the first stanza begins with waters, the last ends with the wind upon the waters, the spirit of inspiration. As tears are the microcosm of amorphous waters, sighs are the microcosm of

potential winds, winds humanised. Winds cause separation. They
push the sails of the ship. In the first stanza, equal tears preserve
their union. In the last stanza, equal sighs preserve their lives. The
preserving quality is equality not distance: 'Since thou and I sigh
one another's breath.' The interanimation, sighing each other's
breath, is both a plea for balance ('don't be more than the moon')
and a plea for union. ('If you blow too hard, you will blow me
away, into the fall of stanza 1.') He asks her just to breathe enough
to maintain the parity of mutual goodwill and the proximity of
mutual support. 'If you sigh too much you become (like Petrarch)
the annihilator of my earthly being. You become the Petrarchan
poet who hastens my death.' When he casts the woman as the
sighing poet in the end, Donne places the onus of separation on her.
If she sighs too much, she will push him away. In the distance, he
will emerge the absent beloved, and she, the sad suitor, of the
poetry of separation. Too much sighing – too much Petrarchism –
leads to too much dying: the end of the poem. He leaves her where
he found her, in the 'coining', or originating, position. While
Petrarch recoups an energetic self through psychic distance, Donne
underlines the speciousness of such a spaciousness.

In 'The Broken Heart', Donne demonstrates the limits of Spenserian duplication via the empty mirror of his replicated self. In 'Of
Weeping', he denies Petrarchan distance through the destructive
potential of the deified beloved. 'The Broken Heart' reproduces
only a broken poet. 'Of Weeping' turns the woman into another
version of an empty self. By refusing to write a Petrarchan tribute
in these two poems, Donne challenges the poet's kinship to the
biblically inherited Adam who, finding Eve in his own likeness,
claimed her for his own. His poems move away from Acidale and
Eden and into the long aftermath of the initial confrontation. Still
injured, his 'I' refuses the recovery his poetic models found.
Through that refusal, he must deal with the world beyond Adam's
'now'. In terms of time, that means remembering the difficulty of
the long year after in 'The Broken Heart', and anticipating the
perils of the imminent separation in 'Of Weeping'. In terms of the
psyche, it means more than Shakespeare's saying 'granted I never
saw a goddess go' when he refuses to deify his lady. It means
dealing with her expectation that he would do so and his own
feeling that perhaps he should do so. Donne turns his rejection of
the Petrarchan and Spenserian models, so culturally available, into
a disquisition about the futility of denial in 'The Broken Heart' and

the anguish of separation in 'A Valediction: Of Weeping'. His refusal to accept the solace of art and insistence on maximising his injuries are, in their ways, homages to the woman's power. Each poem is a rhetorical argument, saying 'see what an actual broken heart yields and a literal physical separation means', in order presumably to find a way to avert the denial and postpone the departure Petrarch and Spenser celebrate. ...

Through the unravelled disguise of *Rime sparse* 23, Laura-Mercury demonstrates that the audience Petrarch has in mind is not necessarily the woman.[25] It may be anyone who extends the sympathetic pity of empathy or the poetic laurel of fame. Petrarch's bonding is fraternal. He appeals to those who understand the man's experience. Laura-Mercury's outrage is directed at Petrarch's having rendered her the specular pin-up girl other men ogle. Her punishment is for the misrepresentation such tellings incur. For Donne, the primary audience is the imagined lady. In 'The Broken Heart' and 'Of Weeping' he suggests that she has control of future tellings. Her reflection, in the broken glass of the former and production of the cylindrical mirror in the latter, depends on the image she commands. To render the anamorphic vision whole, the lady must intervene with something that will inspire a better picture. That 'device' is nothing less (or more) than her assent to the wholeness Donne withholds. To round out the picture, she need only say 'yes'. Petrarch's Laura is a projection of the poet. Donne's lady in the next poem has the opportunity to project herself in an image she is persuaded to choose. Her reinvention of herself will produce another poet. By reasserting her importance to the productions of her life and by implying that she can change the poem she hears, Donne acknowledges the woman's formulative capacity and her real difference. She is the only reader that matters. In such a configuration – the woman feeding his love, he feeding her words – inspiration emerges a continuous revitalisation that triumphs over the first and last of Petrarchan hierarchy and the false mothers and fathers of male poetic dominance. Love and words mutually nourish.

Who is the Silvia-Laura of these poems? Is she a biographical woman or is she (as Proteus suggests in *Two Gentlemen of Verona*) a thing 'all swains commend', her beauty validated only within the coterie of the 'swains'' imagination? The distinction between the biographical and poetic woman is made in the opening line of the play's most famous song: 'Who is Silvia? What is she ...' In the play, everyone knows *who*

Silvia is. She is the daughter of the duke who, in the Folio dramatis personae, is listed as 'Father to Silvia'. But *what* is Silvia? In the song, she is the daughter of her wooer, Proteus, who engenders her idealisation so that she becomes the common property of what Eve Sedgwick calls the homosocial group.[26] She is the 'swains' creation', a construction evolved by, and then circulated among, male image-makers. The transference from earthly body to heavenly orbit is the result of a song which self-consciously proclaims its parenthood:

> Then to Silvia let us sing
> That Silvia is excelling.
> She excels each mortal thing
> Upon the dull earth dwelling
> To her let us garlands bring.
> (IV.ii.48–52)

When the audience observes the idealising process through the eyes and ears of the betrayed Julia, it retreats with her from swain to Proteus. (She quickly shifts from song to singer. 'The music likes you not.' 'You mistake: the musician likes me not', IV.ii.54–5.) Julia reads beyond the excellent Silvia of the song. She sees the musician who betrayed her. In the drama, art is framed by life. There is always a listening *who*. In the song, life is generated by art. There is always an invented *what*. Like Colin's exalted Rosalynde, the excelling Silvia is assembled out of denial.

In 'The Broken Heart' and 'Of Weeping' Donne suggests that the rejected and absent self can neither invent a song out of his brokenness nor fabricate an ideal out of the lady's absence. Though the lady in the Petrarchan dyad is always a constructed 'what' and the man in the Petrarchan dyad is always an invented 'swain', Donne's contribution to the lyric form changes the poetic power structure. ... His *whats* have more agency, an agency he fleshes out in the poems where the lady's gesture initiates the poetry-making cycle. There is no univocal reading woman for Donne existing somewhere outside the poem. Inside the poem, she is what the poet is, an imagined creation who – with the poet – might experience yet another incarnation inside yet another poem. The overhearing Julia of *Two Gentlemen* suggests that there is, even for the confident swain, a sense in which the woman's reaction to a poem may change its impact, may in fact reveal how little authority poets have in shaping their world. Sometimes even a controlling swain can become an object lesson. When Donne brings the imagined woman into the poetry-making complex, he assumes a still more complex reading woman. Consequently, his swains have less agency and emerge less artful. His empty self in 'The Broken Heart' spits out a likeness of poems. His submerged self in 'Of Weeping' pours out an excess of lines.

When he shifts poetic initiation to the imagined woman, Donne makes her responsible for the poet's imagination and the imagined poet. He becomes her *what* – a self produced by the construct she determines. Imagining the woman's agency, Donne begins to see her (as he will absolutely in 'The Dreame') as a writing subject. In 'The Broken Heart' and 'Of Weeping', Donne takes literally the idea that the force of the woman is implicated in the representing man. If she chooses to be destructive or excessive, the result is a broken or inundated poem. The cracked mirror and the flooding poem are the result of her flawed or overbearing brush stroke. In this vision, poet and woman are products of the dream-work, where experience is unfolded and refolded to provoke a 'change in nature'. Within yet another spiral the scrambled signs might, in some future poem, produce a change in art. Donne invents that future poem in 'The Dreame' where the woman's originary and shining light inspires his belatedly reflective glorification. Rekindling Laura-Eve's generosity as the origin of the poem, Donne calls the woman the source of his giftedness.

From Barbara Estrin, *Laura: Uncovering Gender and Genre in Wyatt, Donne, and Marvell* (Durham, NC, 1994), pp. 149–79.

NOTES

[This extract from Barbara Estrin's book reconsiders feminist perceptions of Donne as a misogynistic poet who effectively writes female experience and female subjectivity out of existence. Estrin is interested in the way lyric poetry, as a form of dream-work, 'refolds and changes experience' (see p. 83 above), and in doing so, disturbs existing or inherited gender hierarchies. Amongst these hierarchies is the potent figure of the male poet who compensates for a usually absent or unavailable female by inscribing her as his own poetic creation. Contrastingly, in Donne's love poems, Estrin argues that speaker and beloved, self and other, male and female, exist in a state of mutual dependence.

Estrin's essay is worth comparing and contrasting with the alternative feminist perspectives of Elizabeth Harvey and Stanley Fish: Harvey and Fish both argue that Donne empties female subjects of their own substance and specificity, by egotistically supplanting them with his own verbal appropriations of them. Estrin's counter-perspective is still based upon the idea that Donne's verbal universes create their own reality, but this is positively endorsed by Estrin, on two counts: first, because she sees the lyric (similarly to the way Aers and Kress see literature [see p. 133 below]) as a utopian space of alternative possibility, including alternative masculine and feminine selves; and, secondly, because the invented universe of the lyric is the creation of two, male and female, and not one. For further discussion and contextualisation of Estrin's essay, see Introduction, pp. 14–15.

Unless otherwise specified, citations from Donne's poems are taken from *The Elegies and Songs and Sonnets*, ed. Helen Gardner (Oxford, 1965). Ed.]

1. Patrick Crutwell, 'The Love Poetry of John Donne: Pedantique Weedes or Fresh Invention?' in *Metaphysical Poetry*, ed. Malcolm Bradbury and David Palmer (Bloomington, IN, 1977), p. 22.

2. Janel Mueller, 'Women among the Metaphysicals: A Case, Mostly of Being Donne For', *Modern Philology*, 87 (1989), 147.

3. Janet Halley, 'Textual Intercourse: Ann Donne, John Donne, and the Sexual Politics of Textual Exchange', in *Seeking the Woman in Late Medieval and Renaissance Writings*, ed. Sheila Fisher and Janet Halley (Knoxville, TN, 1990), pp. 199, 202. [Further references are cited within the text. Ed.]

4. Ann Rosalind Jones, 'Imaginary Gardens with Real Frogs', in *Changing Subjects: The Making of Feminist Literary Criticism*, ed. Gayle Greene and Coppélia Kahn (New York, 1993), p. 76. [Further references are cited within the text. Ed.]

5. Ilona Bell, 'The Role of the Lady in Donne's Songs and Sonnets', *Studies in English Literature*, 23 (1983), 116, 124. [Further references are cited within the text. Ed.]

6. Ilona Bell, 'Under ye Rage of a Hott Sonn & Yr Eyes: John Donne's Love Letters to Ann More', in *The Eagle and the Dove: Reassessing John Donne*, ed. Claude Summers and Ted-Larry Pebworth (Columbia, MO, 1986), p. 27.

7. Janet Malcolm, 'The Annals of Biography', *The New Yorker*, 23–30 August 1993; Marguerite Waller, 'The Empire's New Clothes', in *Seeking the Woman*, ed. Fisher and Halley, p. 167.

8. Sheila Fisher and Janet E. Halley, 'Introduction', in *Seeking the Woman*, ed. Fisher and Halley, pp. 13–14.

9. Annabel Patterson, for example, maintains that it is 'one of the paradoxes of language that in the personal letters the spontaneity of self-expression meets certain conventions of privatisation; and never more so than in the seventeenth century'. See 'Misinterpretable Donne: The Testimony of the Love Letters', *John Donne Journal*, 1–2 (1982), 40–1.

10. Robert Lowell, 'Epilogue', in *Day by Day* (New York, 1977), p. 127.

11. Jean-François Lyotard, 'The Dream-Work Does Not Think', in *The Lyotard Reader*, ed. Andrew Benjamin (Oxford, 1989), p. 24.

12. Jonathan Goldberg, *Sodometries: Renaissance Texts, Modern Sexualities* (Stanford, CA, 1992), p. 61.

13. Denise Riley, *'Am I That Name': Feminism and the Category of 'Women' in History* (Basingstoke, 1988), p. 98.

14. Jonathan Goldberg, *Sodometries*, p. 61.

15. Edmund Spenser, *Poetical Works*, ed. J. C. Smith and E. de Selincourt (London, 1932), p. 381. [Further references, abbreviated to *TFQ*, for *The Faerie Queene*, are cited by book, canto and stanza numbers within the text. Ed.]

16. Rosalie Colie, *Paradoxia Epidemica: The Renaissance Tradition of Paradox* (Princeton, NJ, 1966). See her discussion on the reactions to Pascal's experiments, pp. 252–72.

17. Ibid., pp. 256–72.

18. On infinity as a formless imperfection, see Joseph E. Grennan, 'John Donne on the Growth and Infiniteness of Love', *John Donne Journal*, 3 (1984), 34.

19. David A. Hedrich Hirsch reads these lines more positively: 'Despite being shattered by love's plague-like decay, ['The Broken Heart'] possesses an integrity still potentially salvageable because "nothing can to nothing fall".' See 'Donne's Atomies and anatomies: Deconstructed Bodies and the Resurrection of Atomic Theory', *Studies in English Literature*, 31 (1991), 76.

[20. Quotations from Petrarch are from *Petrarch's Lyric Poems*, trans. and ed. Robert Durling (Cambridge, 1976). Further references are cited within the text. Ed.]

21. James S. Baumlin argues that the failure of poetry to assuage the loss of absence is a theme for Donne. 'Writing provides but a weak compensation and surely no antidote for absence, becoming a *pharmakon* or drug – or more precisely, a compulsive action that seeks to allay (though it never can cure) the anxiety of separation.' See *John Donne and the Rhetorics of Renaissance Discourse* (Columbia, MO, 1991), p. 190.

22. William Empson writes of the difference between this poem and those in which Donne consoles the woman, 'There is none of the Platonic pretence Donne keeps up elsewhere that their love is independent of being together; he can find no satisfaction in his hopelessness but to make as much of the actual situation of parting as possible.' *Seven Types of Ambiguity* (New York, 1968), p. 139.

23. Mieke Bal, 'Sexuality, Sin, and the Emergence of Female Character', in *The Female Body in Western Culture*, ed. Susan Rubin Suleiman (Cambridge, 1985), p. 336. [Further references are cited within the text. Ed.]

24. Tilottama Rajan speaks of the poem as a commentary on the insufficiency of substitution: 'As an attempt to restore the presence of the beloved [the poem] is aware of itself as growing from an experience of loss and absence and therefore as an enterprise whose compensatory nature only serves to heighten the realities that it fights off.' '"Nothing Sooner Broke": Donne's *Songs and Sonets* as Self-Consuming Artifact', *ELH*, 49 (1982), 816. [Reprinted in this volume. Ed.]

[25. In her introduction, Estrin distinguishes between three contrasting mythological manifestations of the Laura of Petrarch's love poems (Laura-Daphne, Laura-Eve, and Laura-Mercury), Laura-Mercury being that 'unknowable' figure who denies the poet's 'power to circumscribe her' (*Laura*, p. 13). Ed.]

26. See Eve Sedgwick, *Between Men: English Literature and Male Homosocial Desire* (New York, 1985). Jonathan Goldberg similarly writes of Silvia's artificial being: 'The song inserts Silvia within a poetic economy, Ovidian metamorphosis as her end. Poets have always affirmed that they confer immortality, as Sidney among others, might remind us. Silvia's excellence is textual; her "being", literally, is figurative. No wonder then that she ends up in the forest, voiceless.' (*Voice Terminal Echo: Postmodernism and English Renaissance Texts* [New York, 1986], p. 69).

5

The Lyric in the Field of Information: Autopoiesis and History in Donne's *Songs and Sonnets*

RICHARD HALPERN

[In the opening sections of his article, omitted here, Halpern explains the theory, developed from the natural and social sciences, of 'autopoiesis'. In brief, this theory proposes that biological and social organisms/organisations form their own informationally closed and independent systems. As employed by the sociologist Niklas Luhmann, the theory of autopoiesis conceives of modernity as the evolution of society into an array of increasingly autonomous, specialised, and non-communicating systems.[1] For Halpern, Luhmann's theory offers a way of accounting for the often deconstructed, but less often historicised, autonomy and formal closure of the lyric. Ed.]

In the critical reception of John Donne's poetry one can trace the rise and decline of modernist aesthetics. Praised by T. S. Eliot for their difficulty, which he saw as prefiguring that of modernist poets, Donne's *Songs and Sonnets* later served Cleanth Brooks as a test case for the thesis that poetic meaning inhered entirely in a poem's total immanent structure.[2] More recently, and partly in reaction to his enshrinement by critical modernism, Donne has also attracted attention from poststructuralist and new historical critics. Arthur Marotti's important book, *John Donne: Coterie Poet*, helped inspire a spate of historical readings by focusing on what he calls Donne's 'context-bound verse' and by announcing his intention 'to view Donne's poems as coterie social transactions, rather than as literary icons'.[3] Restoring Donne's *Songs and Sonnets* to their original positions within the poet's total *oeuvre* and its socioliterary contexts, Marotti clearly enriches both their historical and literary meanings. My procedure in what follows differs so strongly from Marotti's that it may wrongly be construed as a critique of his work and of more recent historical studies by Annabel Patterson, David Norbrook, and others.[4] I want to insist at the outset, then, that there is no contradiction between a poem's being at once self-referring and context-bound. Autopoiesis and allopoiesis, autonomy and heteronomy, are not contradictory states but simply inhabit different descriptive domains. Far from being an impediment to historical criticism, the thesis of lyric autonomy can reveal different modes of historical labour and significance.

Part of his appeal to a critic like Brooks doubtless arose from Donne's strong and explicit claims, in several of the *Songs and Sonnets*, to have created a poetic space or domain sealed off from the rest of society. 'We'll build in sonnets pretty rooms' is perhaps the most famous line in 'The Canonization', a poem which vigorously insists on poetic and erotic autonomy.[5] Yet if such claims tend to obscure the social and institutional forces which shape much of Donne's verse, they also offer historical evidence of a different kind. For in declaring the birth of a literary space distinct from other social spaces, Donne's poem attests indirectly to a more general if incipient process of social differentiation which, for Luhmann, characterises modernity in its broadest sense. In constructing a world which blocks out others, Donne registers the epistemic fragmentation that results from the modernising process. My thesis, then, is that Donne's 'pretty rooms' ultimately signify neither a utopian withdrawal from society nor a pseudo-aristocratic refusal to engage in business.[6] Or rather, even if they do both or either of these things, they also bear witness to a growth of social complexity which they help to produce. The autonomy of lyric is thus itself a form of historical and social testimony – and in Donne's case it is explicitly so.

It would be misleading, however, to suggest that Donne's 'pretty rooms' are exclusively aesthetic spaces. For they are also spaces of love and sexuality. Love, after all, is what 'makes one little room an every where', as Donne puts it in 'The Good Morrow'. It is for love or sexual passion that Donne claims, in 'The Canonization' and elsewhere, to sacrifice wealth and worldly power. And finally, it is love that, at least occasionally in Donne's verse, provides a utopian realm of mutuality among persons, contrasting with the litigiousness of civil society and the tyranny of the political realm. Thematically, at least, the autonomy of Renaissance lyric is strongly bound up with the autonomy of love and sexuality. Some recent new historical work has challenged both halves of this relation by claiming that the rhetoric of love in the Elizabethan lyric is primarily a way of encoding political discourse. Thus Arthur Marotti entitles his influential essay on the politics of Elizabethan sonnet sequences 'Love is Not Love'.[7] By demonstrating how Elizabethan love poetry provided an acceptable expression for political and social criticism, Marotti attacks the notion of poetic autonomy precisely by undercutting the autonomy of love; and thus he demonstrates, in a negative fashion, how closely these two issues are tied together. In what follows I will be arguing, somewhat tautologically, that love *is* in fact love, and I will employ this (now strangely controversial) idea to offer an anti-Foucauldian reading of Donne's place within the history of sexuality.

The basis for such a reading is supplied by Niklas Luhmann's book *Love as Passion*, the argument of which I will summarise here because it provides an illuminating context for Renaissance love poetry in general. Luhmann situates his treatment of love within his larger narrative of modernity and its effects on the individual person. The evolving differentiation of social systems, Luhmann argues, inhibits the ability of any given system to select information from others. Social systems become less receptive to their environments, leading to a breakdown of communication unless institutional countermeasures are taken.[8] What Luhmann calls 'generalised symbolic media' attempt to make improbable communications between social systems possible.[9] Such media attempt, in effect, to create a common world or semantic space through which self-referring systems can communicate.

Among other distinctions produced by the transition from stratified to functional differentiation of society, argues Luhmann, is that between personal and social systems. 'This is the case because with the adoption of functional differentiation individual persons can no longer be firmly located in one single subsystem of society, but rather must be regarded a priori as fundamentally displaced.'[10] As increasingly isolated and dislocated systems, individual persons suffer the general fate of decreasing receptivity to one another and to the other social systems that constitute their environments. Love, argues Luhmann, is a compensatory mechanism which surmounts mutual indifference among persons. In his view, love is a generalised symbolic medium of communication; its role is to establish a personal sphere of mutual receptivity in contrast with a public world which to the individual appears increasingly indifferent and incomprehensible.

In the seventeenth century, argues Luhmann, love is codified in a way which renders it at once more unified and more strictly differentiated from other systems. It develops a ramifying set of differences which are meaningful only within its own field and thus approaches a condition of autopoiesis or self-reference even though, paradoxically, its function is to bridge the space between other closed systems. Love's temporality, for example, increasingly detaches itself from other kinds. Earlier Renaissance love poetry tended to assert the eternity of love, thus protecting it from the mutability and decay of mundane things. Donne often follows suit, but sometimes, as in 'The Broken Heart' or 'Farewell to Love', he claims that love is, by contrast, an ephemeral, even momentary state. Commenting on this latter notion, Luhmann writes: 'Love inevitably ends, *and indeed faster than does beauty*, in other words, *faster than nature*; its end is not accorded a place in the general decline of the cosmos, but is self-determined.'[11] In Donne, the ephemerality of love is thus a sign of fragility but also of strength. Only love can kill love; love dies according to its own temporality, and its absolute power is the power to dispose of itself. In this way the ephemerality of love is identical to its eternity; though opposed in content, both render love immune to external or mundane temporalities. The paradoxical incorporation of suffering into the experience of love – another recurrent theme of Renaissance lyric – also feeds the self-reference of the code. 'Even its negative value is part of love in such a way that it cannot be outbid by values of a different order.'[12] If love is suffering rather than pleasure, it cannot enter into a calculus with other pleasures or values but determines its own value.

But it is above all in the discourse of *passion* that this autonomising labour is carried out. As its etymology suggests, 'passion' indicates a subjection to something outside of oneself, 'something unalterable and for which one cannot be held accountable'.[13] Descriptions of love as disease, folly, madness, miracle, or religious ecstasy, all common in Renaissance love lyric, participate in this discourse. Donne's lyric 'The Canonization' is typical in portraying passion as that which transgresses social convention. The demands of civil society – demands that one earn a living, that one meet one's obligations, that one find a vocation or course in life – give way to an all-consuming demand which negates all the others. Passion manifests itself precisely in the violation of other social norms. Its very excessiveness, as Luhmann points out, abrogates the older medieval conception of love as feudal contract, with its attendant services, duties, rewards, and so forth. 'Love only comes into being when one exceeds what can be demanded and prevents a legal entitlement to love from ever coming about.'[14] In Donne's lyrics as in Shakespeare's, juridical language paradoxically insists on the incompatibility of passion with any social contract – above all, with the contract of marriage. In Donne, as in the Renaissance love lyric generally, the female partner occupies the position of mistress, not wife; even those lyrics which Donne seems to have written for Ann More after their marriage – including 'The Canonization' – contain no hint of domesticity or any indication that the addressee of the poem might be the writer's spouse. The 'pretty rooms' of Donne's songs and sonnets are most definitely not part of a household; they require neither dusting nor duty. They are, rather, the space of a seemingly autonomous eros which resists institutionalisation.[15] In the discourse of passion, lovers are no longer defined by their places in the social order; they are in effect rebaptised as lovers and enclosed in a quasi-religious state of seclusion from the secular world.

In 'The Canonization', love claims to establish just such a private, autonomous domain predicated on the abandonment of civil society, however real or effective we may judge this domain to be. In fact, the poem's opening stanzas describe the public realm not as a unified field but as a plurality of alternative professions and institutions: commerce, the arts, law, the court, the church.

> For God's sake hold your tongue, and let me love,
>   Or chide my palsy, or my gout,
> My five grey hairs, or ruined fortune flout,
>   With wealth your state, your mind with arts improve,
>   Take you a course, get you a place,
>   Observe his honour, or his Grace,
>   Or the King's real, or his stamped face
>   Contemplate; what you will, approve,
>   So you will let me love.
>
>   (ll. 1–9)

Offering an array of options at once bewildering and unappealing, the exterior world seems to answer to Luhmann's vision of differentiating social systems whose dislocating effect pushes Donne into yet another, private system – that of love, which establishes at once mystical unity between the lovers and their complete separation from the world. Love is not a reaction to this or that social system but to the ramifying distinctions among them. In 'The Good Morrow', Donne writes: 'Let sea-discoverers to new worlds have gone, / Let maps to others, worlds on worlds have shown, / Let us possess one world, each hath one, and is one' (ll. 12–14). Here again the opposition is not between two worlds – public and private – but between a dizzying multiplication of worlds on the one hand, and a single, unifying world on the other. This multiplicity renders the social environment as a whole unmappable; but by withdrawing into its own space, love attempts to bestow on its environment a kind of negative unity, in that everything else can now be grasped under the rubric of 'not-love'. This early attempt at what Fredric Jameson has called 'cognitive mapping'[16] bears its fruits in the final stanza of 'The Canonization', where the external world in all its immensity and multiplicity is reduced and epitomised in the mutually gazing eyes of the two lovers. Love masters that from which it previously fled, and assimilates that which it previously expelled. Withdrawing from the social world, love then seemingly reproduces it as a manageable microcosm.

'The Canonization' thus figures love as a generalised symbolic medium of communication, one which by means of its own self-reference attempts to overcome or compensate for the differentiated closure of other social systems and the resulting dislocation of the individual subject. Yet this project is always necessarily paradoxical. Because its presumed capacity to map its environment depends on its self-referential closure, the code of love is just one more autopoietic system added to the others. Love does not occupy an Archimedean point from which it can grasp the whole of a social terrain; rather, its attempt to produce an exterior domain simply extends the chain of subsystems, because autonomy is not the same as exteriority. Even religious hermitage, which 'The Canonization' takes for its model, does not really renounce the social world but occupies a well-defined space within the Church and its system of religious observances. The language of paradox which suffuses 'The Canonization' may thus be regarded as a local instance or symptom of the larger cognitive paradox which governs the poem's utterance.

To say all this, of course, involves accepting the fictional premises of Renaissance love poetry; and it seems to result in a commentary which looks less like a critical analysis than a rather credulous re-statement. The antidomestic autonomy of Donne's eros, one might reasonably argue, cannot be taken at face value; it at once encodes a recognisably gendered fantasy and at the same time denies the historical fact that love and sexuality were deeply embedded in – indeed, deployed by – a social system of class, property, and political alliance. Donne's pretty rooms enact at best a utopian denial of the fact that love and marriage are socially determined; and they mask their resistance by coding action as passion or passivity, freedom as subjection to desire.[17] Such objections, while legitimate, seem to me to pose the issue misleadingly. For the dichotomy 'fictive-real' obscures the fact that the literary system and its semantics are as 'real' as any other. The autonomy of the sexual emerges at first in the literary realm, and its effects are no more utopian than those produced by social differentiation in general. Donne's lyric poems generate a real politics even if we entertain their arguments instead of immediately puncturing them. Hence I choose to take Donne at his word; and in doing so I am simply adopting the anti-hermeneutic stance which, in Foucault's view, should govern the description of any discourse.[18] ...

To ask, 'How did sexuality become autopoietic?' is no small question, for it is in effect to ask, 'When does the history of sexuality begin? When, that is, does sexuality gain *its own history*, which is not merely an effect of some other history – of the economy, say? How is it that sexuality came to define an apparently independent domain, so that, for instance, a science of psychoanalysis developed which took sexuality as its distinctive field?' Michel Foucault, of course, has done the most to transform our way of posing questions about the history of sexuality. Like Luhmann, Foucault looks to the seventeenth century as a crucial period of transformation. But while Foucault has insisted that the history of sexuality cannot be grasped as a mere effect or reflex of other histories – say, that of the modes of economic production – his approach is nevertheless opposed to any conception of sexuality as a closed or self-referring domain.[19]

An alternative history to Foucault's, I believe, can be derived from within psychoanalysis itself – specifically, from the work of Jean Laplanche. Laplanche's book *Life and Death in Psychoanalysis* does in fact offer a compelling 'history of sexuality', even though this history is strictly ontogenetic.[20] Laplanche, moreover, is concerned precisely with those mechanisms through which sexuality detaches itself from the vital order and becomes autopoietic, thus establishing, at one stroke, an independent topology which also defines the scientific boundaries of psychoanalysis. Laplanche's exposition begins with the Freudian concept of anaclisis or 'propping', wherein sexuality initially emerges as dependent on the self-preservative instincts. In the infant, sexual pleasure begins as a marginal phenomenon attendant on nursing; but sexuality as such arises in what Laplanche calls a 'derivation from the vital order'. Only when the aim of the instinct is metaphorised (here, when the nutritive ingestion of food is replaced by fantasmatic introjection) and the object of instinct is metonymised (here, when milk is displaced by the breast as part-object) does sexuality begin to define an independent domain separate from the instincts of self-preservation. 'Sexuality appears as a drive that can be isolated and observed only at the moment at which nonsexual activity, the vital function, becomes detached from its natural object or loses it. For sexuality, it is the reflexive (*selbst* or *auto*-) moment that is constitutive: the moment of a turning back towards self, or "autoeroticism" in which the object has been replaced by a fantasy, by an object *reflected* within the subject.'[21] Once the sexual object has become fantasmatic, its significance is determined by its place within the subject's own system of representations, and not by the objective characteristics of the real object that corresponds to it. 'Insofar as the object is that "in which" the aim finds its realisation, the specificity or individuality of the object is, after all, of minimal concern; it is enough for it to possess certain *traits* which trigger the satisfying action; in itself, it remains relatively indifferent and contingent.'[22] What Laplanche describes here, in virtually so many words, is the relation between an autopoietic system and its environment. External objects can trigger, but not specify, a reaction within the sexual field; they are a source of deformation, not information. Likewise, in the Renaissance love sonnet, the mistress as loved object tends to become a mere triggering device whose specific characteristics are increasingly irrelevant. For Laplanche – and, if we accept his argument, for Freud as well – sexuality is constitutively autopoietic, and its (ontogenetic) history is thus necessarily the history of its self-reference.

Through a 'metaphorico-metonymic displacement' of the kind he describes, Laplanche's own reading of Freud can, I believe, be usefully mapped onto the field of history in its larger, social sense. For sexuality in the early modern period emerges from a state of what might be called social anaclisis, embedded not in a vital order but in an economic, social, and political one. Love and sexuality, in other words, 'prop up' and – even more fundamentally – are in turn propped up by a varied set of social functions: property transfer, political alliance, the reproduction of kinship and domestic relations. ...

'The Canonization' enacts in an unusually dense yet lucid way the movement whereby sexuality detaches itself from a condition of social anaclisis or propping and achieves a state of autopoietic closure. It does so, moreover, not only in its thematic and semantic registers but in its figural and rhetorical work. The poem, it has plausibly been argued, was composed around 1603, following the catastrophic consequences of Donne's secret marriage to Anne More.[23] I don't believe that an interpretation of the poem necessarily hinges on this dating or its biographical significance; yet Donne's ill-fated marriage strikingly illustrates the penalty someone of his social class might pay for placing love and sexuality above considerations of property and patronage. John and Anne Donne did indeed 'at their own cost die', as the sexual pun in stanza 3 of 'The Canonization' suggests; but it is from the ashes of their social death that the phoenix known as sexuality is born.

'The Canonization' stages the social unpropping of sexuality in two phases, in a kind of protonarrative. The first phase occurs in stanza 2:

> Alas, alas, who's injured by my love?
>   What merchant ships have my sighs drowned?
> Who says my tears have overflowed his ground?
>   When did my colds a forward spring remove?
>   When did the heats which my veins fill
>   Add one more to the plaguy bill?
> Soldiers find wars, and lawyers find out still
>   Litigious men, which quarrels move,
> Though she and I do love.
>
>   (ll. 10–18)

Here Donne's irony grants love a utopian force. The poet claims merely that loving does not *harm* civil society by interfering with its work; but he clearly suggests that the aggressive competitiveness and litigiousness of that society would *benefit* from contamination by love. In this sense, then, Donne's love *does* injure the world by withdrawing from it. Yet this is true not only in the utopian sense which underwrites the stanza's irony. Donne's marriage to Ann More, for example, may not literally have sunk merchant ships or flooded ground, but it *did* interfere with the workings of commerce and landed property by denying George More his accepted right to dispose of his daughter's hand in an economically and politically expedient manner. Thus Donne's and Ann More's sexual desires *did in fact* upset the business of the world; and in this respect the stanza is disingenuous.

Donne obscures the social transgression of his love, however, by converting a causal or metonymic relation into a merely reflective or metaphoric one. Sexual desire no longer plays a role of 'propping' with regard to an economic and political order; but in abandoning its productive contiguity with civil society, love then substitutes for this a metaphoric resemblance. At the very moment that sexuality ceases actually to be a form of cargo or wares, its sighs become *like* the winds that propel (or sink) a merchant's ship. The Petrarchan metaphors that ramify in this stanza mark the absence of the metonymic ties for which they now substitute. Sexuality detaches itself from a state of social anaclisis or 'propping' by undergoing at once a metonymic contraction and a metaphoric exfoliation.

We have now arrived at one of the leading paradoxes of Donne's work: at the level of argument, his erotic poems define a private space set off from the social world. Yet his metaphors often reintroduce the very world he claims to want to exclude. The languages of law, mercantile exploration, and monarchy inhabit the figural register of the poems, thus apparently undercutting or ironising the movement towards privacy, exclusion, or detachment. Yet this seeming contradiction dissolves once we grasp the fact that for Donne, resemblance is a way of negating causality, metaphor a way of fending off metonymy or continuity. Dr Johnson's famous description of the metaphysical conceit as 'the most heterogeneous ideas ... yoked by violence together' captures the precise dynamic of Donne's metaphors, in which the conjunction of vehicle and tenor serves to drive the two apart, generating the semantic equivalent of a repulsive force. The Donnean conceit is a structure of absolute difference or separation generated paradoxically through the medium of resemblance.

What is probably Donne's best-known conceit perfectly illustrates this mechanism. In 'A Valediction: Forbidding Mourning', Donne famously compares the lovers' two souls with 'stiff twin compasses'. This simile generates as many differences as it does resemblances:

differences between the incorporeality of souls and the rigid materiality of the compasses, between the elevation of the spiritual realm and the banality of a mechanical instrument, and not least between the internalised privacy of the lovers' world and the exterior, public world of navigation, exploration, and commerce represented by the compasses. The twin compasses, moreover, comprise a kind of meta-conceit, because they represent not only the poem's two lovers but also Donne's manner with metaphor. Connecting at one end solely to ensure their constant separation at the other, Donne's twin compasses are like the two terms of his conceits. In Donne the metaphoric vehicle is held at a rigid distance from the tenor, troping around it but never actually approaching it. Indeed, it inscribes a kind of protective circle around the tenor, which never partakes of its orbit but can only be inferred as a kind of virtual point, at once central yet invisible. And if we now recall that Donne's conceits in the *Songs and Sonnets* invariably pertain to love or eros, we can see that the protective circle of the compasses defines the boundaries of love's autopoiesis, cutting it off from the public world as social environment. Metaphor, in other words, does not work here as a window which allows us to peer voyeuristically into love's pretty rooms; it is, rather, a mirrored surface which simply reflects the public world back onto itself. Or again, it resembles the eye in the last stanza of 'The Canonization' which 'epitomises' the world in the tiny reflective mirror of the pupil. Once it becomes autopoietic, sexuality involutes; once the metonymic accessibility of *linkage* is broken, only the play of environmental surfaces remains. The emergence of sexuality is thus at one with its disappearance.

Drawing a firm boundary between sexuality as autopoietic or self-referring system and its social 'environment' might seem to foreclose any possibility for a political reading of Donne's verse. Yet it does not in fact do so, any more than the autopoietic nature of the neurological system forbids us to speak of perception, memory, or communication. The point is simply that sexuality's linkage with other social systems cannot be conceived of in terms of direct exchange or transfer but rather as a kind of adaptive coupling carried out through the autopoiesis of each system. Questions of gender, for instance, manifest themselves within the poems' internal system of differences. Indeed, women are threatening to Donne insofar as they represent a possible blurring of the lines of difference; that is to say, insofar as they represent the Kristevan 'abject' or the collapse of a firm symbolic grid.[24] Conversely, homosexuality – both male and female – is represented in the verse by a principle of identity or consonance among terms, which is now coded not as abjection but rather as purity, transparency, or cleanliness.

The broadest political reading of Donne's erotic verse, however, would seem to develop along Foucauldian lines. For what is the Renaissance love lyric if not a form of confessional discourse? What does it do if not implant sexuality as the truth of the subject, which seems of its own will to seek expression in language? Indeed, the Renaissance love lyric seems to reflect what is, for Foucault, a crucial shift in confessional practice, whereby emphasis on particular sexual *acts* is replaced by an interest in accompanying states of mind: thoughts, desires, fantasies, delectations, appetites, etc.[25] Support for a Foucauldian reading can be found in Donne himself – for instance, in his 'Valediction: Of My Name in a Window', in which he writes: "Tis much that glass should be / As all-confessing and through-shine as I' (ll. 7–8). In his elegy on Donne, affixed to the 1633 edition of the poems, Sir Thomas Browne tries to defuse the embarrassingly 'promiscuous' mixture of erotic and religious verse in that collection by explaining the former as acts of confession.[26] Donne's *Songs and Sonnets* seem to fit comfortably within Foucault's history of sexuality, and to respond most readily to an analysis based on the politics of surveillance.

The theory of autopoietic systems, and particularly the work of Luhmann, allows us to forestall, or at least question, such a reading by pointing to what we might call a 'cybernetic hypothesis' in Foucault's work. For Foucault, power is frequently predicated upon information and transmitted or circulated as data. Sexuality, for instance, emerges as a confessional practice whose results are transferred among, and routed through, various mechanisms of surveillance and discipline. Yet the capacity for linkage (*agencement*) among the various micromechanisms of power relies silently on the assumption of cybernetic transparency: it assumes, in other words, that the information produced by one social agency will be legible or useful to another. More fundamentally, it assumes that something like a transfer of information occurs in the first place. A theory of autopoietic systems will, by contrast, postulate a fundamental limit to informational linkage, because as social mechanisms become increasingly complex and differentiated, their principles of selectivity will render them increasingly closed to one another. The discourse of sexuality, for instance, will become less and less legible to other systems as its own semantics becomes more fully developed and differentiated. Or rather sexuality actually becomes more and less legible at once. More, when a form of psychoanalytic listening develops whose specialised function is to 'hear' and decode sexuality; less, because the increasing complexity and differentiation of psychoanalysis renders its results more opaque to other social systems, such as the law.[27] This is not, I should add, the result of any kind of resistance to, or struggle against, surveillance; it is, rather, an inevitable systemic necessity which nevertheless produces the happy result of limiting coordination among mechanisms of social power.

If John Donne's poetry seems to participate in the ominous history of sexuality described by Foucault, it also resists this history and questions some of the assumptions that underlie it. First of all, the *Songs and Sonnets* do not implant sexuality as the latent truth of the subject because, as I argued above, Donne's erotic space does *not* coincide with that of subjectivity; it is, rather, a social sphere or domain to which the subject tries to repair in a paradoxical and ultimately self-frustrating attempt to escape the effects of social differentiation. Second, and more important, the emergence of sexuality as an autonomous and self-referring domain renders its semantics increasingly opaque. In Donne's *Songs and Sonnets*, the opacity of the sexual is a persistent thematic refrain. Donne repeatedly portrays love as mystical, esoteric, impenetrable, uncommunicative. In 'The Ecstasy', for instance, he writes:

> This ecstasy doth unperplex
> (We said) and tell us what we love,
> We see by this it was not sex,
> *We see, we saw not what did move.*
> (ll. 29–32)

Even for the lovers themselves, passion can be obscure, inarticulate. Luhmann argues that the code of love is transformed in the seventeenth century through the incorporation of sexual passion into it. Yet passion and pleasure fit awkwardly into Luhmann's conception of love as communicative medium. As he admits: 'taken on its own, *plaisir* is not actually a medium of communication because it is not affected by the problem of acceptance or rejection.'[28] Figured in the Renaissance as a kind of death or loss of self, sexual climax resists the transmission of meaning.

Yet informational poverty or semantic closure is less striking as a thematic concern in Donne's work than as a textual effect. From the beginning, Donne's critical reception has largely been governed by the issue of his *difficulty*. Ben Jonson complained to Drummond that 'Donne himself for not being understood would perish', and in the eighteenth century Lewis Theobald called Donne's poems 'a continued Heap of Riddles'.[29] Donne does not simply portray eros as incomprehensible; he produces it as such. In 'The Canonization', this fact is represented somewhat emblematically in the movement between the poem's second and third stanzas. If stanza 2 represents the poem's metonymic contraction from the world, stanza 3 represents its metaphoric exfoliation:

> Call us what you will, we are made such by love;
>   Call her one, me another fly,
> We are tapers too, and at our own cost die,
>   And we in us find the eagle and the dove,
>   The phoenix riddle hath more wit
>   By us; we two being one, are it.
> So to one neutral thing both sexes fit
>   We die and rise the same, and prove
>   Mysterious by this love.
>
>   (ll. 19–27)

Arthur Marotti surveys the critical commentaries on this notoriously complex stanza and concludes: 'Religious, Neoplatonic, alchemical, as well as Petrarchan and other literary sources are possible aids to interpretation, but it would seem that for the coterie reader these metaphors, finally, would have been multivalent, ambiguous, and fundamentally *resistant* to interpretation.'[30] Donne's poetry instals sexuality in an inaccessible domain, either by adopting an esoteric closure, or by assuming a transparency which allows one to look *through* sexuality but not *into* it, or else by mirroring the public world back onto itself. Yet paradoxically, difficulty is conjoined in Donne's verse with a kind of intimacy. Donne's love lyrics often invite the reader into the bedchamber or other private space, but then cancel this gesture of admission by generating a fog of obscurity.[31] We might vary Luhmann's phrasing and say that Donne's *Songs and Sonnets* are voyeuristically open but informationally closed. Yet it is this contradictory double-coding, this apparent clash of form and content, which constitutes sexuality as a self-referring domain. Donne's erotic poetry does its historical work not only by participating in a confessional discourse, then, but by frustrating it as well.

Literary history has ironically reversed Ben Jonson's prediction that Donne would perish for not being understood. For the

difficulty of Donne and the other metaphysical poets was what attracted figures such as Cleanth Brooks and T. S. Eliot, who saw in
Donne an important precursor of the modernist aesthetic. In his
essay entitled 'The Metaphysical Poets', Eliot writes: 'Our civilisation comprehends a great variety and complexity, and this variety
and complexity, playing upon a refined sensibility, must produce
various and complex results. The poet must become more compre-
hensive, more allusive, more indirect, in order to force, to dislocate
if necessary, language into his meaning. ... Hence we get something
which looks very much like the conceit – we get, in fact, a method
curiously similar to that of the "metaphysical poets", similar also in
its use of obscure words and simple phrasing.'[32] For Eliot, as for
Luhmann, modernity is marked by 'great variety and complexity'.
And the difficulty of the modernist poem arises from trying to con-
dense this discursive variety within a single form. Something like the
metaphysical conceit arises when the modernist poet attempts to
bridge distinct epistemic regions, to combine or bind together closed
autopoietic domains. This project is rendered paradoxical, moreover, because the literary sphere which envisions this binding is
itself a specialised cultural system. Hence the modernist poetic
idiom increasingly becomes closed to all but a relatively small elite
of academics and connoisseurs. It is suggestive that Northrop Frye,
himself a pillar of Anglo-American critical modernism, chooses to
render *melos*, the Greek word for lyric poem, as 'babble'.[33] 'Babble'
suggests a kind of pleasantly meaningless utterance; it comports as
well with extreme simplicity as with difficulty, but it alludes with
special force to the discursive closure of the modern lyric. Roland
Barthes betrays a similarly modernist bias in claiming that the essential aim of literature is to 'inexpress the expressible'.[34] But his
phrasing suggests that literature, in the modern period, may play a
role precisely opposed to Luhmann's concept of a 'generalised symbolic medium of communication'. Rather than attempting to relink
closed autopoietic domains in a common semantic field, literature –
and above all the lyric – may serve to express in an especially vivid
way the discursive fragmentation of modern society. Reversing
Luhmann, we may say that lyric poetry makes improbable communications still less probable, and thereby comes to represent the cybernetic barrier *as such*. Or again, inverting Heinz von Foerster's
famous principle of 'order from noise', we may suggest that the
modern lyric tends to produce noise from order.[35] Donne's literary
significance, judged correctly by the modernists, thus consists largely

in his creation of *difficult* poems, full of cybernetic noise. And his role in helping to produce sexuality as a closed discursive domain results from a kind of constructive interference with his more 'proper' labour as lyric poet. In Donne, the discursive walls of lyric enclose the 'pretty rooms' of eros.

[In the concluding section of his article, also omitted here, Halpern discusses the political consequences of Luhmann's approach to autopoiesis and considers its implications for Marxist theories of lyric poetry. Ed.][36]

From *The Yale School of Criticism*, 6 (1993), 185–215.

NOTES

[Richard Halpern's article rehabilitates and revises the notion, questioned by numerous modern theorists, of literature's autonomy. Halpern's argument, like that of many of the other contributors, is still historically oriented, but Halpern's version of the history of the Renaissance period emphasises the increasingly closed and independent nature of such categories as love, law, politics and poetry. This contrasts significantly with the approach of those other contributors, like Guibbory, for example, who put into question the boundaries separating one kind of discourse from another.

Halpern's essay is not totally dismissive of the interdisciplinary and intertextual trajectory of modern theory. Neither is modern theory blind to the kinds of insight offered by Halpern. The other contributors to this volume may variously resist or question the notion of autonomy, but they nevertheless recognise the gravitation in Donne towards autonomy and/or the attendant concepts of transcendence, essentialism, incommensurability and boundaried space. Thus Halpern's points about the autonomisation of passion bear comparison with Catherine Belsey's similar argument that desire 'has its own political history' (see p. 64 above). Further continuities and dicontinuities between historical approaches to Donne may be productively illuminated by reading Halpern's contribution alongside the essays of Guibbory, and Aers/Kress. For further discussion and contextualisation of Halpern's essay, see Introduction, pp. 15–16. Ed.]

[1. Amongst the several books cited in the omitted section of the article on the theory of autopoiesis, Halpern gives particular attention to Niklas Luhmann, *Essays on Self-Reference* (New York, 1990). Ed.]

2. Cleanth Brooks, *The Well Wrought Urn: Studies in the Structure of Poetry* (New York, 1974), pp. 3–21.

3. Arthur F. Marotti, *John Donne, Coterie Poet* (Madison, WI, 1986), pp. 3, 19.

4. David Norbrook, 'The Monarchy of Wit and the Republic of Letters: Donne's Politics', in Elizabeth D. Harvey and Katharine Eisaman Maus (eds), *Soliciting Interpretation: Literary Theory and Seventeenth-Century English Poetry* (Chicago, 1990), pp. 3–36; Annabel Patterson, 'All Donne', in Harvey and Maus, pp. 37–67.

5. All quotations of Donne's verse are taken from *John Donne: The Complete English Poems*, ed. A. J. Smith (Harmondsworth, 1971).

6. These are, respectively, Empson's and Marotti's positions. See Norbrook, 'The Monarchy of Wit', p. 15.

7. Arthur F. Marotti, '"Love is Not Love": Elizabethan Sonnet Sequences and the Social Order', *ELH*, 49 (1982), 396, 428.

8. Niklas Luhmann, *Essays on Self-Reference* (New York, 1990), p. 33.

9. Niklas Luhmann, *Love as Passion: The Codification of Intimacy*, trans. Jeremy Gaines and Doris L. Jones (Cambridge, 1986), p. 18.

10. Ibid., p. 15.

11. Ibid., p. 70.

12. Ibid., p. 65.

13. Ibid., p. 26.

14. Ibid., pp. 67–8.

15. The depiction of marriage in Donne's *Epithalamion Made at Lincoln's Inn* is suggestive. The poem nervously deflects all economic motives onto the 'Daughters of London' in stanza 2 and avoids any suggestion that the bride is a token to be exchanged in an economic and political network; rather, it portrays the wedding as the culmination of the bride's own sexual maturity: 'Today put on perfection, and a woman's name', runs the refrain. Focusing on autotelic development, rather than paternal law, the poem struggles to disentangle sexuality from its social environment.

16. Fredric Jameson, 'Cognitive Mapping', in Cary Nelson and Lawrence Grossberg (eds), *Marxism and the Interpretation of Culture* (Urbana, IL, 1988), pp. 347–57.

17. Luhmann, *Love as Passion*, p. 60.

18. Michel Foucault, *The Archaeology of Knowledge*, trans. A. M. Sheridan-Smith (New York, 1972), esp. pp. 21–30, 118–25.

19. Michel Foucault, *The History of Sexuality, Volume I: An Introduction*, trans. Robert Hurley (New York, 1980).

20. Jean Laplanche, *Life and Death in Psychoanalysis*, trans. Jeffrey Mehlman (Baltimore, MD, 1976).

21. Ibid., p. 88.

22. Ibid., p. 12.

23. Marotti, *Coterie*, pp. 137, 138, 147.

24. See Julia Kristeva, *Powers of Horror: An Essay in Abjection*, trans. Leon S. Roudiez (New York, 1982). For Donne's most outrageous portrayal of women as embodying the abject, see his elegy 'The Comparison'. For more on the symbolic destabilisation effected by women in Donne's poems, see Stanley Fish, 'Masculine Persuasive Force: Donne and Verbal Power', in Harvey and Maus, pp. 223–52 [reprinted in this volume – Ed.]; and Thomas Docherty, *John Donne, Undone* (London and New York, 1986), pp. 51–87.

25. Foucault, *The History of Sexuality*, p. 63.

26. Arthur Marotti, 'John Donne, Author', *Journal of Medieval and Renaissance Studies*, 19 (1989), 74.

27. See Gunther Teubner, 'How the Law Thinks: Towards a Constructivist Epistemology of Law', in Wolfgang Krohn, Günter Küppers, and Helga Nowotny (eds), *Selforganization: Portrait of a Scientific Revolution* (Dordrecht and Boston, 1990).

28. Luhmann, *Love as Passion*, p. 89.

29. Quoted in Marotti, *Coterie*, p. 20.

30. Ibid., p. 163. Author's emphasis.

31. Writing on Donne's elegy, 'To his Mistress Going to Bed', Marotti comments on Donne's transformation of his Ovidian model: 'Ovid focuses entirely on the erotic space, but Donne fills his poem with metaphoric distractions, using the mistress's clothes and body as occasions for witty metaphors' (*Coterie*, pp. 83–4).

32. *Selected Prose Works of T. S. Eliot*, ed. Frank Kermode (New York, 1975), p. 65.

33. Northrop Frye, *Anatomy of Criticism: Four Essays* (Princeton, NJ, 1957), p. 275.

34. *Essais Critiques* (Paris, 1964), p. 15. Quoted in Christopher S. Braider, 'Chekhov's Letter: Linguistic System and its Discontents', in Krohn *et al.*, *Selforganization*, p. 156.

35. Heinz von Foerster, 'On Self-Organizing Systems and their Environments', in *Observing Systems* (Seaside, CA, 1984), pp. 2–22.

[36. I am grateful to Richard Halpern for his contributions to the summaries of the omitted sections of his article. Ed.]

6

'Darke texts need notes': Versions of Self in Donne's Verse Epistles

DAVID AERS AND GUNTHER KRESS

Donne's verse epistles have not received much notice from the awesome critical industry centred on his work. Any explanation of this surprising fact might make reference to an assumed lack of poetic richness in these poems, the assumption that patronage poetry is too conventional to merit serious critical attention, and perhaps even some embarrassment at a deification of living patronesses.[1] But we believe that the most significant factor is unrecognised: namely the lack of a descriptive and theoretical framework within which the real interest of these poems can be perceived and analysed. In this chapter we attempt to establish such a framework and carry out an analysis which will locate, describe, and account for versions of the self emerging within these verse letters. In the course of our critical inquiry we shall build on John Danby's hints about the explicitly social basis of so much that seems, on first sight, to be purely metaphysical speculation.[2] We hope to develop an approach which, through its very attention to the minute movements of a particular text, reveals how these become intelligible only when inserted in a wider context which includes the writer's precise social situation.

In 1608 Donne wrote a poem beginning, 'You have refin'd mee', a verse epistle to his new patroness Lucy, Countess of Bedford, in what seems to have been the most personally testing period of his life.[3]

Although Donne himself includes the comment that 'darke texts need notes', his editors and critics do not seem to have found this a particularly interesting poem. However, we think it both demands and rewards scrutiny. These are the first two stanzas:

> MADAME,
> You have refin'd mee, and to worthyest things
>   (Vertue, Art, Beauty, Fortune,) now I see
> Rarenesse, or use, not nature value brings;
> And such, as they are circumstanc'd, they bee.
>   Two ills can ne're perplexe us, sinne to'excuse;
>   But of two good things, we may leave and chuse.
>
> Therefore at Court, which is not vertues clime,
>   (Where a transcendent height, (as, lownesse mee)
> Makes her not be, or not show) all my rime
> Your vertues challenge, which there rarest bee;
>   For, as darke texts need notes: there some must bee
>   To usher vertue, and say, *This is shee*.[4]

Editorial glosses on these stanzas treat them as fairly unproblematic. Grierson finds Donne's introduction of himself in 'as, lownesse mee' (stanza two), 'quite irrelevant' (and is more unsettled than Milgate), yet he assumes that he has solved any minor enigmas, and the lines seem not to need extended commentary.[5] However, there are important and unresolved tensions in these lines. The countess is alchemist, a near creator (as lines 21–2 of the poem make explicit) through whose agency the poet can now perceive things as they *really* are. This sets up a dichotomy between things as he perceives them now and things as he perceived them before. *Now* he sees that value is the product of contingent social relationships. Already there may be hints, which are clarified later in the poem, that value, being generated by rareness or use, is an aspect of market transactions. Even seemingly transcendent, platonic forms, Vertue, Art, Beauty, 'worthyest things' indeed, get their worth in this way and so have to be placed in the same category as the thoroughly contingent sublunar abstraction, Fortune. But before his 'refinement' the poet had assumed, in good idealist (platonic or stoic) fashion, that value transcended the contingent placings of social practice; he had assumed that value was a reflection of the object or person's intrinsic nature – that, in his own words, 'nature value brings'.

Such relativising attitudes, which are of course quite appropriate to a 'market-society', may not surprise readers today. But when we recall that the poem is addressed to Lucy, and that Donne is overtly talking about her, the worthiest thing whom he is both worshipping and elegantly asking for patronage, it is, at the very least, a strange and rather risky compliment. After all, the poem implies that she is not inherently valuable, that her worthiness is a product of contingent social circumstances, and that her refining has given him perceptions of this kind. (The second stanza is connected to the first by the logical connector 'Therefore', thus removing any lingering doubts that the first stanza is also about Lucy.) The countess's value as one of the 'worthyest things' paradoxically *depends* on her being 'circumstanc'd' in a social situation where her attributes (virtues, it so happens) are most valuable precisely because they are rare, the court rather conspicuously not being the 'clime' of virtue.

This does have a rationale and can be resolved once we see the structure of Donne's argument. He is actually working with a model which assumes the existence of two worlds or 'climes'. One is a platonic clime in which Lucy exists with platonic forms, and which her usher-exegete has knowledge of. (This world of essences transcends all contingency and relativity, and so supersedes all notions of value deployed by social man.) A second clime is the present historical world, the world of the court, of Mitcham and of Donne's frustrated daily existence, a world where value is a function of contingent market relations, supply and demand, mere 'circumstance'. It is in this second world that the countess is 'worthyest', most valuable, and it is here that Donne so desperately wishes to find employment as the official usher of the valued one. His role is to introduce the myopic courtiers to the rare (and useful?) worthy one. In this he himself gains value as the indispensable spectacles through which courtiers can perceive the rare and hidden riches of that dark text, Lucy. The 'alienated intellectual' overcomes his alienation, finds community, wins employment and use as an essential mediator between the two climes.[6] However, Donne fails to show us why the lower climes should value virtue, why this particular rare commodity should be desired by courtiers at all. The unexamined gap in his argument here is simply leapt over as he assumes, optimistically, that the second clime must find use and market value for representatives of the higher world.

Donne does not resolve the paradox in the way we have been doing, but wisely leaves it in its highly compressed form, with only hints that the very absence of virtue at the court makes the countess 'worthyest' and endows both her and her usher-exegete with value.

It is understandable enough that Donne should not have wanted to express these views in such plain form, so we already have sound reasons for his wish to darken the text. Of course Donne need not have introduced the double-edged paradoxical compliment to the countess, and could have avoided the danger of relativising the countess's virtue. But this would not have permitted him to introduce the important self-reference, so well worked into a complex image of the relations between poet, patroness, society and ethical idealism. Here we have a non-trivial explanation for his desire to keep the text dark, one which offers an account of verbal processes and of relevant social and psychological motivations.

We mentioned the significant degree of self-reference in the poem; this invites some further consideration, especially in the light of Donne's 'egocentricity', widely commented on by critics.[7] The expression of this egocentricity is inevitably more complex here than in many of the *Songs and Sonnets*, where the poet-lover focuses on himself and his relations with a lover. This poem, however, is focused on the patroness, and since he delicately seeks patronage the relationship is one which needs most careful handling; not the time, one would think, for an overt display of egocentricity. And yet the poem begins with a reference to himself. It certainly bestows credit on the countess – she, as alchemist, has succeeded in refining him. But the image turns Donne into the central object of attention, just as the alchemist's attention focuses on the materials he desires to transform. And as the success of the alchemist is defined by his success in refining the material, so the countess's success is defined in terms of her effectiveness in working on the present material, the poet. Thus at the very opening of the poem the overt focus on the patroness has been inverted and become part of a rather complicated self-referring process. Lines two and eight (the self-mentioning, which Grierson found 'irrelevant') again refer to him; so do lines nine, eleven and twelve. Without doubt there is a large enough amount of self-reference in the opening stanzas at least to attract one's curiosity.

In addition there are some peculiarities of reference, predominantly in the pronouns. Line one contains the two pronouns, 'you' and 'mee': in the same line there is the 'pronoun' 'worthyest things'. Its reference is ambiguous: Donne has just been refined, so that one possible reference is 'mee'. If he is included in the category of 'worthyest things', then he belongs to the same class as Lucy ('you'), another possible referent of this phrase. 'Worthyest things' is plural in number, and so it can indeed refer to both Lucy and the poet. Presumably Donne intended the reference to be ambiguous; at any rate it is not immediately clear, and in searching for an appropriate and permitted referent, the reference to the poet will arise and need to be assessed, and decided on. The fact that in the next line Donne glosses 'worthyest things' as 'Vertue, Art, Beauty, Fortune' shows that he acknowledged the need to provide a gloss. As we pointed out above, this list collapses platonic categories into the social and contingent clime of 'Fortune', relativising and undercutting the platonic model. By the time we reach the end of the second line 'worthyest things' has accumulated a wide range of possible references: 'you', 'mee', 'you and mee', 'Vertue, Art, Beauty, Fortune'. All of these lead into 'Fortune' and are placed in the same category as Fortune, so that the relativising tendency has become thoroughly pervasive.

The fourth line of the poem continues to draw on this multiple ambiguity: 'And such, as they are circumstanc'd, they bee'. Here 'they' may refer to all the referents mentioned. Another pronoun, 'such', is introduced. It in turn may refer to all three and to 'they'; or it may pick up just one of these. If the latter, then we have at least the following readings: (1) Lucy (such → worthiest things → You), the countess, such as she is circumstanced so she is – as she is placed in the contingent social market of fortune, so she is valued, worthiest. (2) Donne (such → worthiest thing → me → refined), the poet, such as he is circumstanced so he is – as he is placed in Lucy's platonic world, as a new creature, so he is valued, worthiest. As he is placed in the contingent social market, so he is valued, as nothing. His appeal to Lucy is therefore that she should 'translate' his worth in her platonic world, into a recognised use and hence value in the market, in the appropriate place; as an indispensable usher. The countess is well able to do this. So the reading as it stands is: I, as I am circumstanced so I am, as I am *now* placed in the social market of fortune so I am currently valued – as nothing.[8] At this point the paradox, deploying the model of two climes, functions to give line four another, Donne's real, though covert, reading: I am (not as I *am*, but) as I am *circumstanced*. The paradox enables Donne to present simultaneously two versions of the self here: one, the platonic one covertly (I am as I am regardless of social valuation and placing); the other, the one constructed according to market values overtly (I am as I am circumstanced). He puts one against the other in a most complex and rather disturbing form, and asks Lucy to realise his worth in one 'clime', the platonic, as 'value through use' in the other 'clime', that of contingent social situation and of fortune.

On the surface the statement is of course less complicated: the countess has refined him and now he sees that either rareness or use (being used by or of use to someone) brings value. It is precisely the patronage relationship which makes the poet useful to someone who can use him, and therefore valuable. Until he is used his identity is bestowed by his circumstances and, through no fault of his, or of nature, he is circumstanced such that he has no value.

Stanza two now becomes clearer. It refers to the countess but it also refers to Donne. At court he does not appear (either he is physically absent through having no position, or, if there, is not noticed) because he currently has no value. He places himself in a revealing structural relationship with the countess: her value does not appear at court owing to transcendent height, while his does not appear at court owing to *lownesse*. So the structural opposition links him firmly with her, in a link which comes close to an equation. This provides a perfect explanation for the difficulty Grierson recorded, and indeed it would be most odd if such a phrase appeared in one of Donne's patronage poems without precise significance and motivation. The concluding couplet gives us a final confirmation: this is about her and about him. She is the 'darke text' (as is the poem, as is his motivation) and 'darke texts need notes'.

We should ask what or whose need this is. As we noticed earlier, it is most obviously a need of the potential audience of the text, the benighted courtiers. It is also the countess's need; she who is the 'darke text' needs to be explicated if she is to be truly valued in the lower 'clime'. She needs an exegete, like Donne. Lastly, it is Donne's need: exegetes need 'darke texts', and above all Donne needs to be an exegete, he needs to be of specific use to the countess and the community. Just as the 'need' has to be explained, so too with the 'must' in the same line. 'Some must bee' refers to the exegete, implicitly Donne himself, so that this 'must bee' seemingly has the force of an existential imperative, and it echoes the 'not be' of line nine. That 'not be' takes in both Lucy and Donne; how does the non-existent poet of line nine come into existence as the necessary exegete-usher of line eleven? By being employed: and this employment not only brings him into existence, creates him indeed (as lines 21–2 make explicit),[9] but also brings the countess's virtue into the social world, thus indirectly giving her existence and, as we saw earlier, value. This is an astonishingly delicate combination of begging and self-assertion, and the relations hinted at are very complex. Donne is the created creature, she the creator; he low, she high; he patronised, she patron; he exegete, she dark text; he usher, she virtue; he excluded, she included. Yet she too is excluded until he realises her social potential and value for her. Structurally Lucy and Donne are opposed and yet equated, transforms of each other creating each other from shared invisibility into apparent existence and social value.

We have by now accounted for the text's darkness. It lies in the double-layered model Donne uses to understand his complex relationship with the patroness and their mutual relations to the social world and to value. But we need to go further. On this level the explanation has entailed an account of the supplicant's perception of himself, and we now wish to explore this perception in more depth. We have made clear the way the first two stanzas offer distinct and contrasting versions of the self. To recapitulate. One version of self refers an autonomous self to inherent values which would doubtless be recognised in a platonic utopia or by stoic and platonic individuals who have detached themselves from existing societies and are strong enough to pursue a Crusoe-like existence (without dog or man Friday of course). The other version of self sees it as socially constructed and dependent, either through equal relationships (as those between friends) or through the social relations of the market based on rareness, use and contingency. It is not difficult to believe that Donne could see these two versions of the self as competing and contradictory. But then, it is also plausible to see them as complementary, so that only those who do have inherent worth, participating in the platonic forms, *ought* to be usable, find employment and value. Such, however, is obviously not the case in the world which Donne strove so hard to convince about his marketable potential and use. For Donne these competing versions of self-identity became highly problematic and a constant, often agonised, preoccupation, in the period before his ordination.

The two stanzas with which we opened our discussion are thus legitimately seen as explorations of the self. The question of the poet's consciousness of this exploration is one which we have not treated here. Nor do we exclude a range of other possible readings of these stanzas, or for the rest of the patronage poems. But we are suggesting that this reading goes to the heart of these poems and points up their place in Donne's central preoccupations and problems. We believe these neglected poems have much to teach us about these preoccupations and the poetic and intellectual strategies with which Donne confronted them.

The double version of self certainly connects most of the verse epistles, for they are attempts to work out self-identity, polarising or clustering around one or other of these two basic stances. Above all, it invites us to link abstract metaphysical problems with the concrete reality and pressures of the poet's existence.

One important feature that we have touched on in our depiction of the versions of the self in 'You have refin'd mee' can now be brought into prominence. We noted that in presenting contrary versions of self-identity and evaluation Donne envisaged his own level of being in a necessarily equivocal way. He does exist in some mode, but he needs refining, and even creation, by a patroness-alchemist; he does not exist or is not visible (ll. 7–12) at court, yet he, or some, 'must bee To usher vertue'. Later in the poem he defines himself as one of Lucy's 'new creatures', part of a 'new world' created by her (ll. 21–2). In other poems to patronesses this tendency becomes an overt assertion by Donne: that he is nothing. In 'T'have written then' he says (again to the Countess of Bedford), '*nothings*, as I am, may / Pay all they have, and yet have all to pay' (ll. 7–8). Of course, line seven is paradoxical: the 'am' asserts existence, 'I am'; and syntactically the verb *to be* functions to relate entities to other entities or to qualities. That second function is prominent here: the classification of an individual, though he exists, as *a nothing*. Classifications are culturally and socially given, conventional and subject to historical change. But for an individual they tend to assume the force of external, changeless forms. This is particularly so as the syntactic form X is Y is used to make classifications which are established by changing cultures and conventions (e.g. 'I am a ratepayer'), as well as those relating to the impersonal, natural order (e.g. 'The sun is a star'). In this way language blurs the distinction between the two kinds of statements and their reality-status. But over and above that, any member of a society is socialised into sets of value systems which become 'reality'. In other words, if we look at Donne's 'actual' situation, even at this, his worst time, we cannot by any stretch of the imagination see him as nothing: a reasonably comfortable house in Mitcham, one or two servants, frequent trips to London, to influential friends who remain loyal and help in a host of ways, access to books, writing poetry which has an appreciative audience, no hunger ... To the landless labourer in Mitcham Donne would have seemed the opposite of 'nothing'. But this only confirms the strength of the conventionally given perception, which meant in Donne's case that not being of the court group was not being at all. For Donne therefore these lines do not have the force of paradox: *being* is defined in terms of membership of the group to which he aspires: creation is therefore a social act, the act of admitting, drawing in the individual to the group.

Nevertheless, no sooner has Donne offered a negative version of self reflecting his present social situation than he proposes a contrary version of the self as having a transcendental and valuable identity:

> Yet since rich mines in barren grounds are showne
> May not I yeeld (not gold) but coale or stone?
> > (ll. 11–12)

Donne is certainly barren ground at the moment, in so far as he is anything at all. Yet in the same breath he *assumes* that he is also a rich mine. This draws, precisely in the ways we have shown before, on the versions of the self as having intrinsic value, whatever the social market value. But the image is most subtly chosen, for it also informs the patron of the self's potential market value, however hidden that may be. The intrinsically valuable platonic, private and independent self turns out to be as much the property of the patron as the public social self. In specifying the kind of rich mine (l. 12) it may be that Donne loses confidence, moving from coal to stone. But whatever the exact market value, this hidden self is certainly cashable. Indeed, he suggests the most valuable kind of mine: a gold mine (negation being the permissible way of articulating the nearly forbidden). Still, however high his self-estimation, however much he feels he has a self beyond the *nothing* which he is socially, the clash between secret hidden core and apparent social identity forces him to invoke an external agent to strip away this surface (where before it was to burn away impurities), to dig up the riches, so that he may 'yeeld' the riches to someone else. Syntactically *yield* always occurs in forms such as '*yielded* something for/to someone', where the *someone* is never *I*. Thus the image and the syntax are tied absolutely into *use*, commerce and markets. The social creator is revealed as a potential and willing social user and exploiter, while creation turns out to be the discovery of market value in the human being. Conversely, the sense of nothingness, negation, has a social origin – namely the absence of such exploitive use. Again, the metaphysics of annihilation, of being and of nothingness, the fundamental questions of identity raised in these poems, find very tangible social explanation.

'Creation' becomes a specific term here, meaning admission to the desired social group. Some present members of such groups had membership from the beginning and did not need creation. But the process is a general one and may apply to any individual at any social level in relation to any coveted group. The only exception to this is the king – hardly surprising in the time of James I, Donne's ultimate patron – who proclaimed that kings 'are not onely Gods Lieutenants vpon earth, and sit vpon Gods throne, but even by God himselfe they are called Gods'.[10] In the poem 'To Sir H. W. at his going Ambassador to *Venice*', the king fulfils the role of creator for Wotton:

> And (how he may) makes you almost the same,
> A Taper of his Torch, a copie writ
> From his originall ...
>
> (ll. 4–6)

This view of the individual and society encourages one to ask whether it was a common mode of perception at that time, or especially found in any specific group; or whether, for example, Donne's origins in an institutionally excluded group – the community of Roman Catholics – disposed him to view self in this way. Much more work on the lines we are suggesting will be necessary before satisfactory answers can be given.

The source of the creator's credentials could become problematic for anyone who is not totally content to accept the social order and the processes maintaining it. This is in fact a constant concern in the epistles, and is the obverse of his anxiety about his own lack of being, his own lack of credentials. In the light of this consideration, lines such as these from the opening of 'You have refin'd mee' take on a peculiarly bitter and ironic tone:

> now I see
> Rareness, or use, not nature value brings;
> And such, as they are circumstanc'd, they bee.

It is the removal of his blindness which makes him see this unpalatable truth; the countess is indeed creator, though not because of her inherent virtues or nature but because this is how she happens to be circumstanced. The removal of his own blindness makes him see the more massive blindness of the social system to which he seeks admission. Donne's reiteration of the theme that the countess's virtue might go unrecognised (and so her value diminish) except for his good offices takes on a somewhat darker note in this context; Donne covertly assumes for himself the role of creator. The situation is complex enough for Donne to see himself as nothing, as inherently valuable, and possibly as creator, all simultaneously. All these involved shifts are firmly related to a highly specific set of social relationships. Discussions which perpetually divorce the literary language, the psychological, and the social, will inevitably introduce grave distortions and prove limiting in disabling ways.

We have space to glance at only one more patroness poem, 'To the Countess of Salisbury' in 1614. The first half of this poem ('Faire, great, and good') uses material from 'A nocturnall upon S. Lucies day' and the two Anniversaries for Elizabeth Drury. Donne argues that 'all is withered, shrunke, and dri'd / All Vertues ebb'd out to a dead low tyde', with all striving for universal annihilation, 'to draw to lesse, / even that nothing, which at first we were' (ll. 1–21). In this state the patroness, like the Countess of Bedford or Elizabeth Drury, is the female creative deity: 'you come to repaire / Gods booke of creatures' (ll. 7–8).[11] And as we saw in 'You have refin'd mee', however much Donne may negate his being in response to the social situation, he simultaneously presents himself as an intrinsically valuable self, as her seer and exegete (ll. 31–6, 65–74). Yet, once more, this stage is superseded as he acknowledges that it is the countess herself who (like God here too) illuminates the dark text he is able to study. The poem concludes with a similar movement worked out in terms of a socially given blindness (ll. 75–84) which is contrasted with an intuitive angel-like vision, transcending the lack of 'social eyes' through inner illumination. Characteristically, Donne does not leave the matter there. Just as the angelic intuition is actually dependent on a higher power, so Donne's illumination depends on a higher power – the Countess of Salisbury – within the profane, social world (ll. 71–4, 79–82). Again Donne uses metaphysical language and imagery to mediate and transform specific social relationships. To understand and describe this process is not reductive of Donne's art or his metaphysical stratagems: quite the reverse, we follow the full implications and subtlety of the art and metaphysics Donne is using to manage, under grave difficulties, the social situation which was central to his psychic, intellectual and poetic development. ...

From David Aers, Bob Hodge and Gunther Kress, *Literature, Language and Society in England 1580–1680* (Dublin, 1981), pp. 23–48.

NOTES

[The book from which this extract is taken begins by exploring the relationship of what the authors call 'significant art' to the culture in which it is produced (*Literature, Language and Society*, p. vii). Drawing on the work of Herbert Marcuse, the authors argue, with qualifications, that significant art negates its host culture, and affirms the possibility of other realities. Thus an appeal, albeit from a Marxist perspective, is made to a traditional, and essentialist, conception of art as transcendent. The introduction outlining the book's methodology commits itself to the task of analysing specific historical discourses in order to show how art transforms them.

The poems upon which the extract included here focuses seem unlikely candidates for the status of 'significant art': Donne's flattering verse letters to patronesses might be more appropriately thought of as the seventeenth-century equivalent of job applications. And yet, the close analysis which is undertaken by Aers and Kress and which is usually reserved for more conventionally literary texts, reveals Donne's struggle to transcend, and transform through writing, the historically contingent self embedded in the market relations of the patronage system.

This approach, affirming the relative autonomy, and de-contextualising capacity, of literature, whilst analysing the precise nature of the context it transgresses, might be usefully compared/contrasted with the alternative perceptions of literature's relationship to history in the essays of Halpern and Guibbory. For further discussion and contextualisation of this essay, see Introduction, pp. 16–17. Ed.]

1. J. F. Danby, *Elizabethan and Jacobean Poets* (London, 1964; originally published as *Poets on Fortune's Hill*, 1962), ch. 1.

2. 'Donne's assumption is the relationship of a poet to patron as of nothing to everything, and out of this he spins his conceits direct. He makes metaphysics out of the poet and patron relations, and a poet–patron relation out of metaphysics' (*Elizabethan and Jacobean Poets*, p. 39).

3. See R. C. Bald on this period in *John Donne: A Life* (Oxford, 1970), ch. 8; see too Donne himself in his letters: *Life and Letters of John Donne*, ed. E. Gosse, 2 vols (1899; rpt. London, 1959), especially 1:114–15, 166, 181, 185–7, 191.

4. All quotations are from *Donne's Poetical Works*, 2 vols, ed. H. J. C. Grierson (1912; rpt. Oxford, 1966), referred to hereafter as Grierson. This quotation is from vol. 1. We have also used W. Milgate's edition of *The Satires, Epigrams and Verse Letters* (Oxford, 1967).

5. Grierson, *Donne*, 2:156–7: cf. Milgate, *Satires*, pp. 256–7.

6. See M. H. Curtis, 'The Alienated Intellectuals of Early Stuart England', *Past and Present*, 23 (1962), reprinted in *Crisis in Europe*, ed. T. Aston (London, 1965). On Donne's desperate wish for 'incorporation', see the letter to Goodyer in Gosse, *Life and Letters*, 1:191–2.

7. One of the best studies of this issue is by R. Ellrodt, *L'inspiration personnelle et l'esprit du temps chez les poètes metaphysiques anglais*, 3 vols (Paris, 1960). See vol. 1, especially chs 3–4.

8. As Danby suggested, Donne is obsessed with his nothingness (note 2, above). For examples of the explicit social causes of his sense of being *nothing*, and its remedies, see especially prose letters in Gosse, *Life and Letters*, 1:181, 167, 191–2, and on loss of employment as death, for example, 291; also 2:28, 42; and the verse epistles to the Countess of Bedford and the Countess of Salisbury.

9. See previous note.

10. James I, 1609 speech to Parliament, in *The Political Works of James I*, ed. C. H. McIlwain (1918; rpt. Cambridge, MA, 1966), p. 307.

11. There remain important connections to be examined with the political Petrarchianism cultivated under Queen Elizabeth and discussed in L. Forster, *The Icy Fire* (Cambridge, 1969). The theological vocabulary in patron poems has also been studied by B. K. Lewalski in *Donne's Anniversaries* (Princeton, NJ, 1973); relevant here are chapters 1 and 2: her approach (well illustrated in comments on p. 46) tends to isolate the metaphysical and the social in a way which we think distorts both areas.

7

Matrix as Metaphor: Midwifery and the Conception of Voice

ELIZABETH HARVEY

I

How do authors image their own voice in poetry in order to guaran-
tee its recognisability and hence its survival as their product? Emile
Benveniste and Roland Barthes have argued that the 'person' of the
author dissolves into the linguistic subject of the text (the one who
says 'I'), and is, according to Barthes, given life only by the reader,
and Foucault has pointed to the ideological and historical construction of the author-function;[1] drawing on both of these theoretical
positions, I will be examining how the 'I' of a text fashions itself and
is shaped both by the immediate cultural circumstances of its production and by the history of its readership. The construction of
John Donne's poetic voice provides us with a particularly clear
example of this problem. Until very recently, critics have tended to
read Donne's voice through the authoritative legacy bequeathed to
us by T. S. Eliot and the New Critics; in his celebrated essay on the
Metaphysical poets, Eliot situates Donne before the 'dissociation of
sensibility', so that thought and feeling, expression and experience
were unified for the seventeenth-century mind in a way that became
impossible for the twentieth-century poet. Where Eliot saw the
Donnean text as the pure medium of expression, 'a direct sensuous
apprehension of thought, or a recreation of thought into feeling',

subsequent critics tended to locate the purity or accessibility of Donne less in the process of poetry than in the presence of the poet.[2] As Thomas Docherty has recently characterised this tradition of reading, 'in stressing the purity or instantaneity of Donne's medium, Eliot inaugurated the critical process of restitution of Donne's body, starting not from the cerebral cortex, but from the voice'.[3]

Not only has this critical tradition of assuming that the authorial voice is present and clearly identifiable dominated Donne studies, but the voice that marked the outrageous rhythms and compelling diction of his poetry as his was also, according to his critics, definitively gendered as male. This brings me to the second half of the problem I will be exploring, then, the gender of the voice that speaks. Following the speaker's characterisation of his own rhetoric's 'masculine persuasive force' in Elegy 16, contemporaries of Donne have applied that epithet to Donne's poetry as a whole. Ben Jonson's censure of Donne's verse 'for not keeping of accent' correlates with Jonson's gendering of style in his *Discoveries*, in which the so-called 'women's poets' write 'a verse, as smooth, as soft, as cream', but in sounding the wits of this verse, one discovers them to be but 'cream-bowl' or 'puddle deep'.[4] The masculine style distinguishes itself by its eschewing of these effeminising impulses and its substitution of a muscular power that avoids mere mellifluousness and metrical ornamentation. Thomas Carew's 1633 'Elegie upon the Death of John Donne' furnishes a similarly gendered depiction of Donne's poetic bequest. Apostrophising the dead poet, he claims that 'Thou hast redeem'd, and open'd Us a Mine / Of rich and pregnant phansie, drawne a line / Of masculine expression'.[5] Samuel Johnson's famous definition of metaphysical wit incorporates the ingredients of mastery and violence (nature and art are 'ransacked for illustrations, comparisons, and allusions'),[6] and C. S. Lewis's more recent dichotomisation of style into two distinct strains reiterates Ben Jonson's categories, associating Donne not with the luxurious style of Spenser's *Amoretti*, but with the 'abrupt, familiar, and consciously "manly" style' of Wyatt's lyrics.[7]

Yet this confined description of voice in Donne criticism – even when it has expanded to consider his use of personae – has been largely unable to account for Donne's perplexing and shifting treatment of woman. By focusing on a unitary voice emanating from a contained authorial figure, traditional criticism has paid little attention to the issue of poetic inspiration as it is imaged both culturally and in Donne's poetry. Although my interest in voice derives partly from current feminist debates, there is in recent feminist theory a strong emphasis on the recovery of an authentic female voice, a refrain that has in some cases had the effect of reifying and essentialising voice, as if it emerged from a gendered body and remained thereafter perennially tethered to it.[8] I will question this assumption by arguing that voice is, first, a construction that takes place within a cultural and historical matrix, and, second, that it is often ambiguously and complicatedly gendered, crossing the boundaries between sexes with a freedom largely unacknowledged by current theoretical treatments of voice.[9] For instance, even in the lines I have just cited from Thomas Carew's 'Elegy', the 'masculine expression' that he claims stamps Donne's verse is modified by what he calls the 'Mine / Of rich and pregnant phansie' that provides the source of subsequent poetic inspiration. Why should this aggressively masculine poetic tradition be seen as springing from an image typically associated in Donne's poetry with the female body and the body of the earth that is pregnant with treasure, waiting to be ransacked? To attempt to answer that question, I will concentrate on the way voice as a construct coheres in a particular constellation of metaphors that is frequently found in Renaissance poetry: the image of the pregnant male poet giving birth to voice, being impregnated or impregnating his muse, or serving as a midwife to poetic birth. ...

My claim is that poetic use of birth metaphors registers a cultural preoccupation with birth as a new territory, which, like the human body generally, was being explored by science and medicine in ways that were to have profound political, religious, and economic repercussions. What makes (physiological) childbirth particularly interesting for my purposes is that it is gender coded; birth, as a function specific to women, was traditionally set within a feminine space and supervised by female midwives, but this architectural and epistemological space was increasingly encroached upon by men in the late sixteenth and early seventeenth century in England. One element of this encroachment – which was both a vehicle for it and a symptom of it – was the publication of midwifery books translated into the vernacular for the first time during this period. The books disseminated information about pregnancy and birth and provided illustrations both of the inside of birthing chambers and also of the womb's interior. These images provide evidence of the medical curiosity about gestation and birth, they point the way toward the economic and scientific dimension of the struggle to control childbirth, and

they also reflect the interpenetration of medical and literary discourses. The midwifery texts, too, employ the familiar metaphor –
which is as old as Plato's *Theaetetus* – of book as child, they ground
language and creativity in the female body and its reproductive
processes, and they re-enact in their rhetorical strategies the appropriation both of the female body and the poetic voice that putatively
springs from it. We can read a poetic text like Donne's *Anniversaries*
in relation to the medical discourses that subtend so much of his
metaphorical language, just as we can read the medical texts both
for what they tell us about the historical context and for their figuration of language. Put together, these texts allow us to begin to understand the historicist dimension of the strange transvestism of the
male poet giving birth to his own voice, as well as to recognise the
complexity of the construction of gender in the early modern
period. ...

II

In his discussion of prophecy in *The Discoverie of Witchcraft* (1584),
Reginald Scot offers an etymological interpretation of the Hebrew
word 'Ob', commonly translated as 'Pytho', 'Pythonicus spiritus',
or, less properly, as 'Magus'.[10] 'Ob' literally means bottle, and it is
associated with oracular utterance because 'the *Pythonists* spake
hollowe; as in the bottom of their bellies, whereby they are aptlie in
Latin called *Ventriloqui*'.[11] Ventriloquism, literally the act of appearing to speak from the abdomen or belly, is for Scot closely linked to
prophecy, for in both cases the voice proceeds from a locus other
than the organs of speech, since the ventriloquised voice originates
in another place (the stomach) or being (a deity or evil spirit). We
have already seen that woman's putatively unlimited capacity for
speech associates her with the power of voice, and, in the case of
prophecy, her ability to be a receptacle or mouthpiece for discourse
other than her own is closely tied to cultural constructions of gender
and, specifically, to female physiology. Voice or language appears
to emerge from her body in a process analogous to birth; the
woman is impregnated or filled with voice (as, in Christian tradition, Mary becomes the receptacle of the Word); she produces what
issues from the belly. I now turn to a series of poems and texts that
associate ventriloquism, poetic inspiration, and the origin of the
voice with pregnancy and childbirth, for, as I will claim, the use of

the metaphor derives both from an established tradition and also from the particular historical and cultural circumstances of the early modern period.

The *locus classicus* for this metaphor is Plato's *Theaetetus*, a dialogue whose very structure is informed by the trope of midwifery. As Socrates himself reminds Theaetetus, his mother, Phaenarete, was a midwife, and, by his own admission, he professes to practise the same art.[12] By claiming to follow in his mother's footsteps, he not only constructs a maternal origin for his skill, but encroaches on a traditionally female arena of knowledge and expertise. The difference is that his patients are men, not women, and where female midwives deal with the body, Socrates is concerned 'with the soul that is in travail of birth' (Plato, 1961: p. 855). In the transvestism of this transgression, the real art of midwifery is converted into a vehicle for a higher purpose; its function is not material (the birth of human bodies) but transcends that 'lower' physical function in order to facilitate the delivery of true knowledge. The experience of conceptual birth is represented simultaneously as exactly the same as a woman's labour and also more intense in terms of the experience of pain. Those who seek Socrates's company, then, 'have the same experience as a woman with child; they suffer the pains of labour, and by night and day, are full of distress far greater than a woman's' (Plato, 1961: pp. 855–6). The main instrument of his skill in assisting the birth of wisdom in others is the dialogic process, a process of questioning and insistent probing that often engenders the pains of labour, with surprising results.

> Those who frequent my company at first appear, some of them, quite unintelligent, but, as we go further with our discussions, all who are favoured by heaven make progress at a rate that seems surprising to others as well as to themselves, although it is clear that they have never learned anything from me. The many admirable truths they bring to birth have been discovered by themselves from within. But the delivery is heaven's work and mine. The proof of this is that many who have not been conscious of my assistance ... suffered miscarriage of their thoughts through falling into bad company, and they have lost children of whom I had delivered them by bringing them up badly, caring more for false phantoms than for true.
>
> (Plato, 1961: p. 855)

It is Socrates's calling, one that humbly seeks to efface itself but that is a position of extraordinary potency, 'to bring on these pangs or to allay them' (Plato, 1961: p. 856). Like a midwife, Socrates assists at the births of others but claims that he himself is constrained from giving birth: 'of myself I have no sort of wisdom, nor has any discovery ever been born to me as the child of my soul' (Plato, 1961: p. 855). Yet, despite his disclaimers, he aligns his skill in midwifery with divine power, for, while he may create no direct offspring, he controls conceptual fertility or barrenness, the safe delivery of ideas, and the survival and health of intellectual progeny: in short, the life of the mind itself. ...

III

If the body of the woman who dies in childbed is the metaphorical source of the poetic voice for Milton, the speaker of Donne's 'Elegy 19: To His Mistress Going to Bed' figures himself *as* a woman in the throes of childbirth at the opening of the poem. He then compares himself to a midwife in the closing lines, so that the elegy is framed by references to childbirth. That the poem is generated rhetorically by the metaphor of labour is registered in the tautological structure of the second line, 'Until I labour, I in labour lie', where the chiasmic formulation replicates the sense of suspense characteristic of the poem's situation and of labour. The male speaker can be released only through a process that is not entirely within his control, for until he 'labours' (archaic sense of pounding or beating) in the act of love, he lies in discomfort, as a woman does who seeks relief through giving birth. By usurping the role of midwife in the final section of the elegy ('Then since I may know, / As liberally, as to a midwife, show / Thyself'), the speaker also seeks the privileges of vision and knowledge that were in the Renaissance properly the province of the midwife. Men were explicitly excluded from this knowledge, as is made clear by the taboo against the man-midwife gazing upon the woman's body. ...

The speaker of Donne's poem desires to bring his mistress to the labour of love, to look upon the privacy of her body revealed to the gaze normally only in such circumstances as childbirth. This vision and the subsequent carnal 'knowledge' he will have proleptically invokes the literal sense of generation: the act of love may beget a child and thus ultimately necessitate the attendance of a midwife. The woman is imaged as a 'mystic book', a phrase that divides knowers into laypeople and initiates, and that may function as an oblique reference to the knowledge of the female body that was being circulated in obstetrical handbooks. Between the two allusions to childbirth that frame Elegy 19 lies the body of the poem itself which, like Sidney's sonnet No. 1, is analogically generated by these references to birth. The image of the elegy's central section alludes, of course, to a double colonisation; on the one hand, to the lands England was exploring and claiming in the early seventeenth century ('O my America, my new found land'), and, on the other, to the body of the mistress the lover seeks to make his own ('My kingdom, safeliest when with one man manned, / My mine of precious stones, my empery'). Medical colonisation of the human body, like geographic exploration, 'claims' the territories it discovers by naming them after the explorer. The human body is thus imprinted with the history of its own discovery, registered in the names given to particular organs or bodily processes (e.g. Fallopian tubes). The apostrophic 'O' in 'O my America' and the image of the mine (which also functions as a double possessive – 'My mine') refer specifically to the female genitalia that the lover desires to conquer, a conjunction of colonisation metaphors that points towards the historical transition from midwifery as a specifically female area of knowledge and specialisation to its metamorphosis into a branch of distinctively male medicine.

Where Elegy 19 borrows the trope of childbirth to frame its voyeuristic exploration of the female body, the power of the imagination to shape an unborn child (a power that is often cited in midwifery books with respect to monstrous births) becomes the basis for Donne's elaborate conceit in 'A Valediction: of Weeping'. Here the lover's tears are impregnated with the image of the beloved:

> Let me pour forth
> My tears before thy face, whilst I stay here,
> For thy face coins them, and thy stamp they bear,
> And by this mintage they are something worth,
>   For thus they be
>   Pregnant of thee;
>
>   (ll. 1–6)

What the speaker sees (the beloved) is imprinted upon the tears that issue from his body, as if he were a pregnant woman giving birth to a child that had been influenced by the vision of what she saw. The effect is strangely bisexual; because the speaker is self-conscious about the imminence of his departure ('whilst I stay here') and because he projects the dangers he may encounter in a hostile world, he figures himself as male. Yet his assumption of feminine physiology effects a crossing, a transvestism, in which his empathy for the pain of the addressed woman metaphorically places him in the position of a woman giving birth. He occupies the relatively passive role of supplying matter (tears), which is stamped with her image, while she appears to act upon him, generating replications of her own image. The simile for the lovers' parting is, in keeping with the conceit, parturition: 'When a tear falls, that thou falls which it bore, / So thou and I are nothing then, when on a divers shore' (ll. 8–9). Even as the speaker seems to give himself over to grief, vicariously placing himself in the position of the woman who is abandoned by her lover or by the child who leaves her body at birth, he distances himself from that position through the intellectual intricacy of the poem. In other words, the poem foregrounds its own metaphoricity, creating a linkage of sympathy and similitude between lover and beloved, but the nature of similitude also posits difference (two things are like one another because they are not the same as one another). Docherty has asserted that, whereas '[m]ale lovers look into the mirror of their lover's eye, or womb, and see a reflection of themselves (or of their sons as representations of themselves), thus supposedly guaranteeing a stable, transhistorical identity' (1986: p. 200), woman is the prior condition that guarantees both the product of poetry and the writer's masculinity. While Donne certainly repudiates the feminine in some of his poetry, and where some lines suggest the danger and shame of becoming a woman, as in Elegy 4, where the speaker says that 'the greatest stain to man's estate / Falls on us, to be called effeminate' (ll. 61–2), he is elsewhere (as in 'A Valediction: of Weeping') extraordinarily self-reflexive about his relation to gender, about his naming the feminine as his source, even about his willingness to occupy – however provisionally – the place to which he assigns women.

Readers of Donne's poetry have often remarked on the plenitude of images that represent the merging of lovers: the compass and the 'gold to aery thinness beat' of 'A Valediction: forbidding Mourning', the interinanimated souls of 'The Ecstasy', or the phoenix in 'The Canonization', but the psychic union of the lovers in 'A Valediction: of Weeping' is represented in a conceit of pregnancy and birth. The poem seems to figure what Julia Kristeva – borrowing from Plato's *Timaeus* – has called the *chora*, the utopian space occupied by the mother and child before the child enters the Symbolic, language, or the Law of the Father.[13] The paradigmatic expression of the chora is pregnancy itself, where the child is still enclosed within the womb, and where the body of the mother and child are contiguous. This space, which Kristeva describes as an '"enceint" separating (the pregnant woman) from the world of everyone else', is thus a kind of protective enclosure that encompasses both mother and child, even though it also always contains an inevitable separation or division between mother and child.[14] Donne's poems are, of course, full of these choric spaces – the 'little room' that is the womb in the Holy Sonnet 'Annunciation', the 'one little room, an every where' in 'The Good Morrow' or the bedroom of 'The Sun Rising' – images of a merging that would defy change and separation. The pregnant tears of 'A Valediction: of Weeping' give way to (or birth to) the blank round globe of the second stanza, a world that is peopled solely by the lovers and affected only by their (Petrarchan) storms of emotion. Yet this world is also, as the New Critics so memorably demonstrated, the poem itself, a work born of and inspired by the grief the speaker expresses; like the tear impregnated with the beloved's image, so, too, is the poem a reflection (carried emblematically in the sorrow that issues from the poet) of the lovers, an enclosed space that preserves their union even as they face inevitable separation. Elaine Scarry has suggestively said that Donne repetitively materialises language and interiorises it within the body, seeking, especially in the Valediction poems, to establish a way of representing the body during absence.[15] As Kristeva has reminded us in 'Stabat Mater', the body of the Virgin Mary is only synecdochically available, accessible in the ear (which signifies listening and compassion), the breast (which stands for maternity and nourishment), and tears (the privileged sign of sorrow). Tears and milk are, she says, 'metaphors of nonspeech, of a "semiotics" that linguistic communication does not account for'.[16] In a sense then, Donne's tears are a kind of doubling, expressing, on the one hand, the semiotics of sorrow, feminine (and maternal) silence, and the unrepresentability of grief, and, on the other, the carefully fashioned male appropriation of that semiotics of silence in the language of the poem.

If pregnancy and generation are tropes that (apotropaically) shield the lovers from change and separation, they also serve as a metaphor for the generation of the text. Donne is especially self-reflexive about the inspiration and conception of poetry in the verse letters, where his Muse is frequently invoked in terms of her sexual status – her barrenness, her fecundity, her chastity, her progeny. In a letter to Mr B. B., Donne urges his addressee to marry his Muse, and 'multiply'; he, himself, is divorced from his Muse, 'the cause being in me, / That I can take no new in bigamy' (ll. 20–1), and therefore both his 'will' and his 'power' are crippled.

> Hence comes it, that these rhymes which never had
> Mother, want matter, and they only have
> A little form, the which their father gave;
> They are profane, imperfect, oh, too bad
> To be counted children of poetry
> Except confirmed and bishoped by thee.
>
> (ll. 23–8)

Reiterating the Aristotelian dichotomy that sees matter as feminine and form as masculine, the poet designates his poetic offspring as lacking content (matter) because they are without a feminine source (*mater*); although the paternal influence yields some form, they are sickly and imperfect. Renaissance physiology privileged the connection between women and the imagination because of the uterus, which was putatively susceptible to the influence of both the moon and the imagination. While this impressionability meant that pregnant women were vulnerable to the image-making capacity of the imagination, as we have seen, it also gendered the imagination as feminine, so that, although women themselves did not have access to or control over the power their physiology bestowed on them, they were nevertheless the locus of imaginative creativity. It was the uterus – which was sometimes characterised as having a life of its own – that produced the female qualities of insatiable sexual desire and garrulity, and it was woman's combination of moist and cold humours that disposed her to changeability, inventiveness, and to the special retentiveness of her memory.[17] This may help to explain Donne's obsession with female changeability, which he both fears and desires (as Docherty has argued [1986: pp. 51–87]), his fascination with the sexual status of his Muse, and his interest in the pregnant female body. Perhaps no other of Donne's poems so explicitly express this ligature of speech, sexuality, and pregnancy than his two elegies written to commemorate the death of Elizabeth Drury.

The imbrication of poetic voice and the representation of the feminine in the *First* and *Second Anniversaries* of 1611 and 1612 is both rich and relatively unexplored.[18] As virtual set pieces articulating the sense of epistemological crisis of the early seventeenth century ('The new philosophy calls all in doubt'), the *Anniversaries* stand at the beginning of the English tradition of funeral elegy,[19] and their preoccupation with voice – with the distinctive voice of the elegiac poet, whose emerging reputation depends upon his skill in the art of lamentation, and with the now voiceless, deceased subject of elegy, whose continued life in the memories of the bereaved depends upon the surrogate voice of the poet – is complicated by gender. That is, where in an elegy like 'Lycidas' the act of mourning Edward King's lost promise also celebrates Milton's emergent poetic ability, Donne's elegiac voice is empowered by the ghostly muse of Elizabeth Drury in an act of appropriation that relies simultaneously (and paradoxically) on her virginity and her maternal qualities. The *Anniversaries* are full of metaphors of her sexuality and fecundity, but, because they are also preoccupied with bodies, disease, and explicit medical terminology, I claim that Donne's references to pregnancy and birth are contiguous with the discourses of theology and physiology, which themselves furnish a linkage between pregnancy and voice.

The *Anniversaries* have been the subject of critical controversy since they were published, primarily because of the perceived gap between the extravagant hyperbole of their expression and the relative insignificance of their occasion, the death of a young girl Donne probably never even met.[20] Ben Jonson summed up this outrage in his judgement that the *First Anniversarie* was 'profane and full of Blasphemies', and he told Donne that 'if it had been written of the Virgin Marie it had been something', to which Donne supposedly replied 'that he described the Idea of a Woman, not as she was'.[21] Jonson's insight, if not his criticism, is apt, however, for the iconography of the Virgin suffuses both poems, in their linkage of maternity and virginity, in their explicit fascination with Mary, 'the blessed mother-maid', and in their simultaneous obsession with physical procreation or conception and the desire to transcend it. (Although Jonson chastises Donne for his blasphemy, he was not above using the comparison himself on appropriate occasions; his 1630 'Epigram to the Queen, then Lying In', begins by citing the Angel Gabriel's address to Mary, 'Hail Mary, full of grace', and argues that the words are as fittingly addressed by the poet to the 'mother of our prince'.[22] The linkage between the Virgin Mary and Elizabeth Drury is, in fact, crucial to Donne's representation of the relationship between Elizabeth Drury and himself, which is figured in the emergence of the poetic voice from her simultaneously pure and maternal body. This focus provides a way of understanding how the poet constructs her as his own discursive origin, a source that he simultaneously acknowledges, appropriates, and also obliquely denigrates, an ambivalence toward female sexuality and power that is manifested throughout his poetry. Even in the *Anniversaries*, which celebrate the transcendent purity of Elizabeth Drury, there is a prevalent strain of misogyny, as in the conventional sentiment that the 'first marriage was our funeral: / One woman at one blow killed us all, / And singly, one by one, they kill us all' (1: ll. 105–7). Purified and exonerated from the charge levelled against ordinary women, Elizabeth Drury, like the Virgin, 'could drive, / The poisonous tincture, and the stain of Eve, / Out of her thoughts, and deeds; and purify / All, by a true religious alchemy' (1: ll. 179–82). Donne's figuration of his relationship to the dead girl he celebrates, in fact, displays some of the symptoms of paranoia and empowerment described by Kristeva in 'Stabat Mater', a text that is particularly pertinent to my discussion.

Kristeva's juxtaposition of the semiotic and cultural history of the Virgin and psychoanalytic theories of language and the maternal in 'Stabat Mater' is enacted theoretically and visually. Like a ventriloquised text (and I will argue that the *Anniversaries* are ventriloquised in their appropriation and use of the feminine voice), 'Stabat Mater' is double-voiced; the text is divided into two columns that are distinguished from one another by typeface and discursive style. While the right-hand column appears to be a historical, analytic account of the Virgin (one that draws on Marina Warner's *Alone of All Her Sex: The Myth and Cult of the Virgin Mary*), the left-hand column seems initially to be a rhapsodic, lyrical record of Kristeva's own experience of childbirth.[23] The doubleness of the text replicates both the split between theoretical discourse and poetic expression, and also the split of the maternal body, which is divided within itself (even as it at once expresses and represents itself as text). This neat dichotomy is continually ruptured, however, by the intrusions of the analytic into the poetic column, and the irruption of the poetic in the theoretical text, as if the discourses were bounded by a permeable membrane that could not sustain their separateness. 'Stabat Mater' thus figures itself as a kind of maternal body that encompasses the Freudian silence on maternity and the myth of the Virgin, both discourses that support from opposite perspectives the power of the imaginary, preverbal mother that provides a fantasy of plenitude designed 'to compensate for the actual poverty of language and its inability to situate or articulate the (maternal) speaking subject'.[24] While Kristeva's account moves towards the transhistorical (even as it refers to Warner's historical study), elements of her psychoanalytic analysis seem nevertheless to offer insight into Donne's specific historical circumstances.

If, as Kristeva asserts, a 'mother is a continuous separation, a division of the very flesh' (1987: p. 254), evoking the separation from the mother in primary narcissism, or the division of language itself, her analysis of the myth of the Virgin must also confront the division of death. One of the most attractive aspects of the myth, according to her, is its homologisation with the life of Christ: where Christ suffered, died, and was resurrected, Mary 'experiences a fate more radiant than her son's: she undergoes no calvary, she has no tomb, she doesn't die and hence has no need to rise from the dead' (1987: p. 242). Where for the seventeenth century, the maternal, as epitomised by childbirth, stood for mortality and the inevitability of death, the Virgin fulfils the paranoid fantasy of being exempt from time or death because of the Assumption, which allows her to be translated directly to Heaven. On the one hand, physical birth signifies death for Donne; as he says in the *First Anniversarie* and in his Holy Sonnet 'Annunciation', the womb is a prison of flesh, and the body is 'a poor inn, / A province packed up in two yards of skin' (ll. 175–6), threatened by sickness and its 'true mother, age'. On the other hand, death itself becomes a birth or liberation from the shackles of the flesh, and it is this translation, or elegiac conversion of death into life, that Donne seeks to effect. In this process, he not only links Elizabeth Drury to the Virgin, but he models himself on the mother-maid as well, borrowing her capacity to act as intermediary between the carnal and the spiritual, her consolatory qualities (and her capacity for sorrow), and her maternity that is not subject to death. Paranoia is a protective mechanism, whereby projection shields the subject by replacing what is threatening with a megalomaniacal fantasy of power (or by displacing a threat to an other not the subject). The relationship of men and women to the myth of the Virgin is complementary but not symmetrical; it subtended and supported the connection between the sexes by providing a means of satisfying feminine paranoia (through the fantasy of power) and male paranoia about women (by bifurcating femininity and maternity). Given its capacity to isolate maternity from female sexuality in general and to separate maternity from mortality, we can begin to see both how the myth of the Virgin satisfied certain cultural needs and also why the representation of Elizabeth Drury is imbricated with that of the Virgin.

The *Anniversaries* are, after all, elegies, and their subject is ostensibly death; more specifically, they are elegies written for the parents
of a dead child. Elizabeth Drury functions as a kind of counter in the
monetary sense, an object which can be endowed with value and exchanged. She is lost to her parents through death, but returned to life
through the poetic resurrection Donne effects in the *Anniversaries*.
The poetic rebirth that Donne engineers is designed in turn to secure
him the patronage of the Drury family, so that the dead girl serves as
a kind of intermediary. Kristeva argues that the body of the Virgin is
synecdochised in the ear, which associates her with hearing and voice
(1987: p. 248), signifying her capacity to intercede on behalf of
petitioners. In this way, in her association with art and patronage
(p. 250), and with her maternal and liminal status, she becomes a
go-between, an intermediary between mortal and immortal life ('this
commerce 'twixt heaven and earth' [I: p. 399]), between poets and
patrons. In the *Second Anniversarie*, Donne apostrophises his soul,
speaking of his 'new ear' that will hear the angels' song when his
soul sees the 'blessed mother-maid' (II: l. 339). The exchange
implied by the patronage system was, however, complicated by
Donne's personal circumstances; he had captured the interest of
Sir Robert and Lady Drury with his shorter 'Funerall Elegie', which
contained the animating idea for the *Anniversaries*, and so, when
Sir Robert asked Donne to accompany him on an extended journey
to the continent, it was difficult for Donne to refuse, even though it
meant a long separation from his wife and family.[25] According to
Walton's admittedly imprecise rendition, Ann Donne 'was then with
child and otherways under so dangerous a habit of body as to her
health that she professed an unwillingness to allow him any absence
from her, saying "her divining soul boded her some ill in his
absence", and therefore desired him not to leave her'. (Her premo-
nitions were grounded in experience; she was pregnant twelve times
in sixteen years of marriage, and she died in 1617, just five days
after giving birth to a still-born child.) Nevertheless, Donne made
plans for his wife and children to stay with her younger sister on the
Isle of Wight, and readied himself for departure. It was apparently
during this interlude, when he was in London waiting to leave, that
he composed *An Anatomy of the World*, and it was almost certainly
in print when he and the Drurys at last journeyed to the continent
in November, 1611 (Bald, 1970: p. 244). He must have begun work
on *Of the Progres of the Soule* soon after he arrived in Amiens, and
it was published early in 1612. According to Walton's account, it

was at this time that Donne's 'ecstasy' occurred, the vision in which he saw his 'dear wife pass twice by me through this room with her hair hanging about her shoulders and a dead child in her arms'. As he learned twelve days later from the urgent messenger he dispatched, his wife had indeed been delivered of a still-born child 'after a long and dangerous labour', on the same day and 'about the very hour' that Donne saw the apparition. Although it is difficult to reconcile Walton's account with the chronology of Donne's letters,[26] it is clear that Donne left with the Drurys when his wife was both pregnant and also fearful about her health and that of the child she carried, and Donne's correspondence does suggest a preoccupation with her condition. Where Walton's recounting of the episode implies a sympathy so powerful that it was capable of generating visions, we can at least see a kind of parallel, in which Ann's pregnancy produced a still-birth child, whereas Donne's sympathy delivered two elegies laced with references to pregnancy and birth.[27]

The metaphoric framework of the *First Anniversarie* is given to us by its subtitle, 'An Anatomy of the World'. Although the anatomy was a fashionable kind of writing in the Renaissance that referred as much to a systematic analysis or satiric exposure as an actual dissection, Donne registers its literal sense both in his obsessive concentration on bodies and decay and also in his witty reminder near the end of the poem that the carcass he is anatomising will putrefy and smell if he is not selective in his dissection.[28] The function of an anatomy is, of course, to make visible to the eye what could otherwise not be seen (as William Harvey puts it, to make available to light, ocular inspection, and reason the hidden secrets of nature).[29] The body that he examines in the *First Anniversarie* is ostensibly that of the world, and, yet, there is a complex overlapping with the figure of Elizabeth Drury. Most obviously, according to the conceit of the poem, she is the balm or preservative of the earth; with her death, the world decays. The radical loss of coherence both in the physical and social worlds is attributed to her death, for she had the capacity to reunite the fragments by magnetic force, but with that power no longer accessible, the world has become increasingly chaotic and dispersed. Yet her physical body is conflated with the world's, and synecdochised, it continues to inform Donne's description of it, as in the lines 'she whose rich eyes, and breast, / Gilt the West Indies, and perfumed the East' (1: ll. 229–30). As the animating spirit of the world, she is also matter or *mater*, the nourishing mother, and her departure from the world compromises its ability to produce life:

> The clouds conceive not rain, or do not pour
> In the due birth time, down the balmy shower.
> Th'air doth not motherly sit on the earth,
> To hatch her seasons, and give all things birth.
> Spring-times were common cradles, but are tombs;
> And false conceptions fill the general wombs.
>
> (1: ll. 381–6)

No longer the nurturing life of the earth, she becomes instead the animating spirit of the anatomised world of the poem. In 'A Funeral Elegy' the anatomised body is the poem itself, the 'carcase verses' (l. 14) that cannot contain her soul. Anatomy is, after all, a partitioning of the body, and the division of the poem into parts by means of the reiterated lament, 'she, she is dead; she's dead', as well as the wordplay on 'part'/'partake' (l. 434), become ways of propagating or increasing the text, just as birth is a way of propagating the self. What is lost to the macrocosmic world, then, is displaced into the poem, where Donne draws on and shapes its generative properties.

The *Anniversaries* do not celebrate Elizabeth Drury's maternity, however, but her virginity, and, paradoxically, her ability to propagate texts is dependent upon that sexual purity. Like the Virgin, her fecundity is a-sexual. While the hymen is itself a figure of partition, and virginity is thus aligned with textual dilation or increase, it is also true that, for Donne, poetry is only produced by a chaste muse. His figuring the dead girl as his poetic source can thus only be accomplished by a kind of transsexual exchange, in which the spirit of Elizabeth Drury impregnates Donne's muse:

> Immortal Maid, who though thou would'st refuse
> The name of mother, be unto my Muse
> A father, since her chaste ambition is,
> Yearly to bring forth such a child as this.
> These hymns may work on future wits, and so
> May great grandchildren of thy praises grow.
>
> (2: ll. 33–8)

Elizabeth Drury becomes the male, inseminating principle, which by analogy makes Donne's muse the bearer of these annually produced progeny. The anniversary poems that he promises are likened to life returning after the deluge, a Lethe flood that has caused the world to forget the name of its departed soul: Donne dedicates his life to remedying that amnesia, but his motives are not unselfish. As he tells us, 'my life shall be, / To be hereafter praised, for praising thee'. As at least one critic has pointed out, the poem is obsessed with nomination, with naming Elizabeth Drury (Docherty, 1986: p. 228); yet despite the repetitions of 'she' and the lavish periphrastic descriptions, she is never named directly. The question of whose fame or name verse enrols is not a simple one for the *Anniversaries*, or, for that matter, for elegy in general. Where funeral elegy conventionally laments a dead person, the name that is commemorated is as often that of the mourner or elegist rather than the mourned. Grief never subordinates Donne's fierce sense of ego or his awareness of the patronage system. Claiming that she died too young to speak (at age 14), while yet *infans* (without speech), Donne seems to assume a kind of prophetic stance, allowing her to speak through him. Far from becoming a transparent medium, however, Donne functions as the privileged translator, relaying a voice that only he can hear and only he can interpret:

> Nor could incomprehensibleness deter
> Me, from thus trying to imprison her.
> Which when I saw what a strict grave could do,
> I saw not why verse might not do so too.
> Verse hath a middle nature: heaven keeps souls,
> The grave keeps bodies, verse the fame enrols.
> (1: ll. 469–74)

Like a patron herself, albeit a ghostly one, Elizabeth Drury becomes a kind of muse, who, like the mother of the muses, Mnemosyne, presides over a commemoration, a recreation through the action of memory. If the governing metaphor of the *First Anniversarie* is the anatomy of the body, the progress is the organising principle of the *Second Anniversarie*, where the speaker follows Elizabeth Drury in her progress to heaven, to becoming at the end of the poem 'the trumpet, at whose voice the people came' (2: l. 528), the embodiment of voice. She is the proclamation (the speaking before – *proclamare)*, the text, and he is the mouthpiece, the voice who articulates her muteness. In an apostrophe to his soul, the speaker berates his soul for its ignorance, for knowing neither how it will die or how it was 'begot' (2: l. 256). The puzzle in the catalogue of ignorance that follows is the relationship between inside and outside; how the stone enters 'the bladder's cave' without breaking the skin, how the blood flows from one ventricle to the other, and how putrid matter gathers in the lungs (2: ll. 270–80). The paradigm for the link between inside and outside is the body–soul relationship, which is the conundrum not only of life and death, but also of subjectivity. The speaker places himself in a privileged position with respect to these questions, for, like the anatomist, he has a specialised access; not through the 'lattices of eyes' or the 'labyrinths of ears' (2: ll. 296–7) does he know, but directly, as is possible only in heaven. Elizabeth Drury is the embodiment of knowledge, she 'who all libraries had thoroughly read' (2: l. 303), and who is imaged as 'written rolls / Where eyes might read upon the outward skin, / As strong records for God, as minds within' (ll. 504–5). And it is this figure of knowledge, whose inside, or invisibility, can be read by eyes, that the speaker claims to translate.

That Donne never knew the person he was elegising and that this depiction of her remains so idealised as to lack any human specificity at all enhances his ability to usurp her speechlessness, her absence, and to colonise her dead spirit, as it were. He apostrophises her, employing the trope that is the figure of voice and that animates the dead or inanimate.[30]

> blessed maid,
> Of whom is meant whatever hath been said,
> Or shall be spoken well by any tongue,
> Whose name refines coarse lines, and makes prose song,
> Accept this tribute, and his first year's rent,
> Who till his dark short taper's end be spent,
> As oft as thy feast sees this widowed earth,
> Will yearly celebrate thy second birth,
> That is, thy death.
>
> (1: ll. 443–51)

The lines invert the conventional definition of life and death, producing a familiar religious paradox where death engenders the new life of the soul. This paradox also illuminates the operations of patronage; it is Elizabeth Drury's death, after all, that occasions the poems, which in turn secure him the potentially regenerating favour of the Drurys. Yet Donne's use of the inversion provides a new context: 'Our body's as the womb, / And as a midwife death directs it home' (1: ll. 453–4). What is specific to woman (the womb) is generalised to all humanity; anyone who has a body also has a womb, from which Death, as the midwife, delivers new life. In the same way, Donne, as poetic midwife, delivers life from death, serving as what he calls that 'middle nature', which makes manifest what has been hidden from other human eyes, the interpreter figure between life and death. All bodies become wombs, and the midwife, Death, oversees a process of spiritual birth, in which the poet is complicit. Like Kristeva's Virgin Mary, whose power depends on her overcoming her own death and on the separation of the maternal function from ordinary female sexuality, the poet is linked to a maternity that has no repercussions of mortality, no contamination of the feminine. He, too, becomes a midwife, an intermediary, and liminal figure, who stands poised between this world and the next, impregnated with the ghostly voice of Elizabeth Drury.

From Elizabeth Harvey, *Ventriloquized Voices: Feminist Theory and English Renaissance Texts* (London, 1992), pp. 76–115.

NOTES

[This extract from Elizabeth Harvey's book focuses upon Donne's ventriloquising, in *The Anniversaries* and elsewhere, of a feminine voice through his appropriation of metaphors of midwifery and pregnancy. Harvey argues that because Donne never knew Elizabeth Drury, the subject of *The Anniversaries* who died at the age of 14, he is able to 'usurp her speechlessness', take on the role of 'poetic midwife' (see p. 152 above), and give voice to an idealised version of Woman, as simultaneously fecund, virginal and spiritual. Elizabeth Drury is, in other words, a vacuum, and Donne the filler of that vacuum, exploiting a version of the feminine to fashion an image of his own poetic creativity.

The analysis forms part of the book's overarching concern with the way feminist, and other critics, have (mis)understood the concept of 'voice'. It would be tempting to think that there is an authentically feminine voice, linked to the female body, which Donne, as a man, inevitably misconstrues. In her introduction, however, Harvey argues against the existence of an essential feminine voice issuing from the 'facts' of female physiology. Harvey's alternative emphasis, upon the *constructed* nature of subjectivity, suggests that there is no easy passage, as some forms of feminism have implied, from ventriloquism/constructed voice to physiological 'truth'. Even as the 'constructed voices within the texts' considered by Harvey 'vigorously reassert their (feminine) bodily origins', those origins remain elusive to the (male) voices seeking to represent them. This is because language in general (and not just male language in particular) is always a construction, a version of (physiological) truth, rather than the truth itself. This poststructuralist perspective is balanced, however, by a 'tactical essentialism', which holds to a conviction that 'women and men (and their respective voices) are not politically interchangeable' (*Ventriloquized Voices*, pp. 4, 13).

Harvey's approach might be usefully compared with that of Stanley Fish, for both essays discuss Donne's ventriloquistic powers of appropriation. These two essays might in turn be contrasted with Barbara Estrin's piece, which argues the alternative perspective of a mutual dependency existing between male and female in Donne's poetry. For further discussion and contextualisation of Harvey's essay, see Introduction, pp. 17–18. References to Donne's poems are to A. J. Smith (ed.), *The Complete English Poems* (Harmondsworth, 1971). Ed.]

1. Roland Barthes, *A Lover's Discourse: Fragments*, trans. Richard Howard (New York, 1978); Emile Benveniste, *Problems in General Linguistics*, trans. Mary Elizabeth Meek (Coral Gables, FL, 1971); Michel Foucault, 'What is An Author?' in *The Foucault Reader*, ed. Paul Rabinow (New York, 1984), pp. 101–20.

2. T. S. Eliot, 'The Metaphysical Poets', in *Selected Prose of T. S. Eliot*, ed. Frank Kermode (London, 1975), p. 63.

3. Thomas Docherty, *John Donne, Undone* (London, 1986), p. 3. [Further references are cited within the text. Ed.]

4. Ben Jonson, *Complete Poems*, ed. George Parfitt (New Haven, CT, 1975), pp. 462, 396.

5. *The Poems of Thomas Carew*, ed. Arthur Vincent (New York, 1989).

6. Samuel Johnson, *The Lives of the Poets*, ed. George Birkbeck Hill (1905; rpt. New York, 1967), 1:20.

7. C. S Lewis, 'Donne and Love Poetry in the Seventeenth Century', in *John Donne's Poetry*, ed. A. L. Clements (New York, 1966), p. 144.

8. Elaine Showalter's distinction between 'feminist critique' and 'gynocritics' operates on an implicit definition of voice and authorship as stable categories. Where Anglo-American critiques of French feminist writing have accused theorists like Hélène Cixous and Luce Irigaray of essentialism, of describing an *écriture feminine* that emerges from a biologically female body, in fact, as Alice Jardine has argued, French feminism has tended to be preoccupied with subjectivity and enunciation in ways that should modify this charge. (Elaine Showalter, 'Toward A Feminist Poetics', in *The New Feminist Criticism*, ed. Elaine Showalter [New York, 1979], pp. 125–43; Elaine Showalter, 'Feminist Criticism in the Wilderness', in *The New Feminist Criticism*, ed. Elaine Showalter [New York, 1981], pp. 243–70; Alice Jardine, *Gynesis: Configurations of Woman and Modernity* [Ithaca, NY, 1985]. See Ann Rosalind Jones, 'Writing the Body: Toward an Understanding of L'Ecriture feminine', in *The New Feminist Criticism*, ed. Showalter [1985], pp. 361–77 and Margaret Whitford 'Rereading Irigaray', in *Between Feminism and Psychoanalysis*, ed. Teresa Brennan [London, 1989], pp. 106–26 for two different treatments of the problem of essentialism.)

9. Jonathan Goldberg's important study, *Voice Terminal Echo* (New York, 1986), for example, never explicitly addresses the question of gender, even though his frequent allusions to Ovidian myth refer to women (Echo, Philomela, and Medusa). Notable exceptions are Elaine Showalter's *Speaking of Gender* (New York, 1989) and Nancy K. Miller's treatment of authorship in *Subject to Change* (New York, 1988).

10. I am indebted to Thomas M. Lennon for calling this reference to my attention.

11. Reginald Scot, *The Discoverie of Witchcraft* (Frontwell, Arundel, 1964), p. 120.

12. Plato, *Theaetetus, The Collected Dialogues of Plato*, ed. Edith Hamilton and Huntingdon Cairns (Princeton, NJ, 1961), pp. 853–4. [Further references are cited within the text. Ed.]

13. Kristeva offers a number of different definitions of the chora; in addition to the one I am working with here that figures the oneness of mother and child and refers to a moment in the subject's psychic development, she offers a second explanation, one that posits the internalisation of the mother, so that the chora becomes a 'mobile receptacle', organising and regulating the subject's drives (see Julia Kristeva, *Revolution in Poetic Language*, trans. Margaret Waller [New York, 1984], pp. 25–30). In 'Place Names' (in *Desire in Language*, ed. Leon S. Roudiez, trans. Thomas Gora, Alice Jardine and Leon S. Roudiez [New York, 1980]), Kristeva appears to offer a third interpretation of the chora, in which it becomes the site to which the subject relegates the mother; in this definition, the chora is associated most clearly with the semiotic, the repressed in language that resurfaces in poetic or psychotic language.

14. Julia Kristeva, in *Desire in Language*, ed. Roudiez, p. 240.

15. Elaine Scarry, 'Donne: "But yet the Body is his booke"', in *Literature and the Body: Essays on Populations and Persons*, ed. Elaine Scarry (Baltimore, MD, 1988), pp. 79–81.

16. Julia Kristeva, 'Stabat Mater', in *Tales of Love*, trans. Leon S. Roudiez (New York, 1987), p. 249. [Further references are cited within the text. Ed.]

17. Ian Maclean, *The Renaissance Notion of Woman* (Cambridge, MA, 1980), pp. 41–2.

18. Thomas Docherty's analysis is an exception. His interpretation is similar to mine in the sense that he, too, concentrates on the confusion or overlapping of Donne's name or voice and that of Elizabeth Drury. However, where I focus on maternity, pregnancy, and virginity, he discusses the relationship in terms of a marriage, the intersection between notions of the medium, the hymen, and the angel (pp. 227–31).

19. There has, of course, been a great deal of debate about the genre of the *Anniversaries*. Frank Manley (ed.) discusses the problem in *John Donne: The Anniversaries* (Baltimore, MD, 1963).

20. Much subsequent criticism has focused on identifying the idea represented by the woman, whether as historical figure (Queen Elizabeth), as archetype or symbol (Astraea, the Virgin, Christ, the indwelling logos), as allegory (Lady Wisdom, Lady Virtue, Lady Justice), as saint (Lucy,

pattern of Christian regeneration and illumination), or in terms of traditions like Neoplatonism and Petrarchism (Barbara Lewalski, *Donne's
Anniversaries and the Poetry of Praise* (Princeton, NJ, 1973), p. 108.

21. Ben Jonson, *Complete Poems*, p. 462.

22. Ibid., p. 208.

23. Mary Jacobus, *Reading Woman: Essays in Feminist Criticism* (New
York, 1986), p. 167.

24. Ibid., p. 169.

25. R. C. Bald, *John Donne: A Life* (Oxford, 1970), pp. 240–2; and
R. C. Bald, *Donne and the Drurys* (1959; rpt. Westport, CT, 1986),
pp. 85–103. [Further references to both books are cited within the
text. Ed.]

26. See Bald, *John Donne*, pp. 249–52. The child was buried on 24 January,
but Donne was still ignorant of what had happened in April.
Nevertheless, Donne's letters do indicate his profound concern for the
health of his wife and child.

27. Bald cites a letter from Lady Burghley, Sir Robert's sister, which speaks
of Lady Drury's 'great belly' (Bald, *Donne and the Drurys*, p. 103). The
pregnancy was apparently a rumour, but it appears that at least others
– if not the Drurys – were preoccupied with the possibility that she
would have another child.

28. His step-father was, after all, John Syminges, who had been President of
the Royal College of Physicians several times (Bald, *John Donne*, p. 37),
the house he moved to when he was eleven adjoined St Bartholomew's
Hospital (John Carey, *John Donne: Life, Mind and Art* [London, 1981],
p. 136), and he may well have had the chance to observe dissection
at first hand. His witnessing of executions seems to be registered in the
viscerality of his simile of the beheaded man that opens the *Second
Anniversarie*. For an account of the cultural history of anatomies and
'spectacular' nature of the anatomy theatre and its audience, see Jonathan
Sawday, 'The Fate of Masya: Dissecting the Renaissance Body', in
Renaissance Bodies: The Human Figure in English Culture c. 1540–1660,
ed. Lucy Gent and Nigel Llewellyn (London, 1990), pp. 111–35. See also
Don Cameron Allen's essay 'John Donne's Knowledge of Renaissance
Medicine', in *Essential Articles for the Study of John Donne's Poetry*, ed.
John R. Roberts (Hamden, CT, 1975).

29. William Harvey, *Disputations Concerning the Generation of Animals*,
trans. Gweneth Whitteridge (Oxford, 1981), pp. 8–9.

30. Jonathan Culler, 'Changes in the Study of the Lyric', in *Lyric Poetry:
Beyond New Criticism*, ed. Chaviva Hosek and Patricia Parker (Ithaca,
NY, 1985), p. 40.

8

Masculine Persuasive Force: Donne and Verbal Power

STANLEY FISH

'MY FEIGNED PAGE'

For a very long time I was unable to teach Donne's poetry. I never had anything good to say about the poems, and would always find myself rereading with approval C. S. Lewis's now fifty-year-old judgement on Donne as the 'saddest' and 'most uncomfortable of our poets' whose verse 'exercises the same dreadful fascination that we feel in the grip of the worst kind of bore – the hot eyed, un-escapable kind'.[1] Indeed my own response to the poetry was even more negative than Lewis's: I found it sick, and thought that I must be missing the point so readily seen by others. I now believe that to *be* the point: Donne is sick and his poetry is sick; but he and it are sick in ways that are interestingly related to the contemporary critical scene. In short, the pleasures of diagnosis have replaced the pleasure I was unable to derive from the verse.

Let's get the diagnosis out of the way immediately: Donne is bulimic, someone who gorges himself to a point beyond satiety, and then sticks his finger down his throat and throws up. The object of his desire and of his abhorrence is not food, but words, and more specifically, the power words can exert. Whatever else Donne's poems are, they are pre-eminently occasions on which this power can be exercised; they report on its exercise and stage it again in the reporting, and when one asks about a moment in the poetry, 'Why is it thus?' the answer will always be 'in order further to secure the control and domination the poet and his surrogates continually

157

seek'. This is, I think, what Judith Herz is getting at in a recent fine essay when she remarks that 'Donne ... will say anything if the poem seems to need it',[2] an observation I would amend by insisting that the need to be satisfied is not the poem's but the poet's, and that it is the need first to create a world and then endlessly to manipulate those who are made to inhabit it.

In more than a few of the poems Donne not only performs in this way but provides a theoretical explanation of his performance. Such a poem is the elegy usually entitled 'The Anagram', a variation on the topos of the praise of ugliness. What Donne adds to the tradition is an account of what makes it possible, the capacity of words to make connection with one another rather than with some external referent that constrains them to accuracy. Four lines teach the lesson and exemplify it:

> She's fair as any, if all be like her,
> And if none be, then she is singular.
> All love is wonder; if we justly do
> Account her wonderful, why not lovely too?
> (ll. 23–6)[3]

That is, if your mistress is indistinguishable from the indifferent mass of women, then say 'she's fair as any', and if she is distinguished by the oddness of her features, then say, 'she is singular', i.e., a rarity. In either case you will be telling the truth, not as it exists in some realm independent of your verbal dexterity, but as it has been established in the context *created* by that dexterity. This is even truer (if I can use that word) of the second couplet in which we are first invited to assent to an unexceptionable assertion ('All love is wonder') and then told that by assenting we have assented also to the infinite conclusions that might be reached by playing with the two words and their cognates. It is as if the copula operated not to form a proposition, but simply to establish an equivalence between two sounds that can then be related in any way that serves the interpreter's purpose. If love equals wonder, the so-called argument goes, the condition of being full of wonder should equal the condition of being full of love, but since loveful is not a proper word, let's make it lovely.

The obvious objection to this self-propelling logic of schematic figures is that it knows no constraints and is wholly unstable; meaning can be pulled out of a suffix or out of thin air, and the linear constraints of syntax and consecutive sense are simply overwhelmed. But Donne forestalls the objection by putting it into the poem, not however, *as* an objection but as a rationale for the interpretive fecundity of his 'method': 'If we might put letters but one way, / In the lean dearth of words, what could we say?' (ll. 17–18). The answer is that we could say only one thing at a time, and that the one thing we could say would be formed in relation to some prior and independent referent. By refusing to be confined by the lean dearth of words Donne becomes able to say anything or many things as he combines and recombines words and letters into whatever figurative, and momentarily real, pattern he desires. As Thomas Docherty has recently observed, in this poem 'anything we choose to call a stable essence is always already on its way to becoming something else'.[4] The result is an experience in which the reader is always a step behind the gymnastic contortions of the poet's rhetorical logic, straining to understand a point that has already been abandoned, striving to maintain a focus on a scene whose configurations refuse to stand still.

The case is even worse (or better) with another of the elegies, 'The Comparison'; for if the lesson of 'The Anagram' is that the 'lean dearth of words' is to be avoided, the lesson of this poem is that the lean dearth of words – the sequential fixing of meaning – can't be achieved. Structurally, the 'plot' of the poem couldn't be simpler: the poet's mistress is compared feature by feature to the mistress of his rival and declared to be superior; but this simplest of plots soon becomes radically unstable because the reader is often in doubt as to which pole of the comparison he presently inhabits. ...

It is an amazing performance, a high-wire act complete with twists, flips, double reverses, and above all, triumphs, triumphs at the expense of the two women who become indistinguishably monstrous when the poet makes it impossible for us to tell the difference between them ('the language of vilification contaminates that of praise');[5] and triumphs, of course, at our expense, as we are pushed and pulled and finally mocked by the incapacity he makes us repeatedly feel. But it is a triumph that has its cost, as the last half line of the poem makes clear:

> ... comparisons are odious.
> (l. 54)

This is a moment of revulsion, not from the women for whose features he is, after all, responsible, but from the act by which he makes of them (and us) whatever he wills. Comparisons are odious because they are too easy. Given the requisite verbal skill, it is impossible for them *not* to succeed, and their success carries with it a lesson that turns back on itself, the lesson of a plasticity in nature so pervasive that it renders victory meaningless. What pleasure can be taken in the exercise of a skill if it meets no resistance? And what security attends an achievement that can be undone or redone in a moment, either by the verbal artificer himself, or by the very next person who comes along?

It is a lesson that has just been learned by the speaker of *Elegy* 7, a complaint-of-Pygmalion poem in which the first-person voice discovers to his distress that the woman he has fashioned has detached herself from him and is now free to go either her own way or the way of another. He begins by recalling her as she was before they met, and remembers her exclusively in terms of the languages she did not then understand: 'thou didst not understand / The mystic language of the eye nor hand / ... I had not taught thee then, the alphabet / Of flowers, how they devisefully being set / ... might with speechless secrecy, / Deliver errands mutely' (ll. 3–4, 9–12). The point is not only that these were languages unknown to her, but that independently of them she was herself not known because she was as yet unformed. What she now understands now understands – in the sense of supporting or providing a foundation for – her; she is the sum of the signifying systems whose coded meanings and gestures now fill her consciousness and that is why her previous state is characterised as the *absence* of signification: 'ill arrayed / In broken proverbs, and torn sentences' (ll. 18–19). 'Arrayed' means both 'clothed' and 'set into order': by being clothed in *his* words she attains an order where before there was only linguistic – and therefore substantive – chaos, *broken* proverbs, *torn* sentences. Quite literally, his words give her life: 'Thy graces and good words my creatures be: / I planted knowledge and life's tree in thee' (ll. 25–6).

The horror is that after having in-formed her, he finds that she is no less malleable than she was when she was nothing but verbal bits and pieces waiting for someone who might make her into something intelligible. The two stages of creation – from incoherent fragments into sequenced discourse – are finally not so different from one another if the configuration achieved in the second stage is only temporary, if once having been planted, knowledge and sense can be *sup*planted by another gardener who brings new knowledge and an alternative sense. The poet cries out in dismay: 'Must I alas / Frame and enamel plate, and drink in glass? / Chafe wax for others' seals?' (ll. 27–9). In short, must others now 'write' you, inscribe you, as I have done? Cannot the work of signification be frozen once it has been accomplished? What the speaker here discovers, three hundred and seventy-five years before Derrida writes 'Signature Event Context', is the 'essential drift' of language, the capacity of any signifier to 'break with every given context, engendering an infinity of new contexts in a manner which is absolutely illimitable'.[6] Once an intelligible sign has been produced, one can always 'recognise other possibilities in it by inscribing it or *grafting* it onto other chains'. 'No context can ... enclose it', a truth the speaker of *Elegy 7* now ruefully acknowledges as the poem ends: 'Must I ... / ... break a colt's force, / And leave him then, being made a ready horse?' This final line and a half could not be more precise: the shaping power he exerted before the poem began is given its precise name – force – but once given, the name declares its own problematic; he who lives by force is precariously at the mercy of force wielded by others, by strangers. The grafting of signifiers – and, remember, that is all she is, a chain of signifiers – onto other chains cannot be stopped; and it cannot be stopped because there is nothing to stop it, no extralinguistic resistance to its inscribing power, a power the speaker once again displays when he uncreates what he has made by de-gendering it. He leaves his rival not with a 'her' but a 'him', a ready-made horse in place of the previously ready-made woman. It is as if he were attempting to forestall the reinscription of his creation by performing it himself and thus removing from the world the graces his words have placed there. It is a particularly nasty instance of someone saying, 'if I can't have her, no one will', with a decided emphasis on the will.

It should be obvious by now that in these poems the act of writing is gendered in ways that have been made familiar to us by recent feminist criticism. The male author, like God, stands erect before the blank page of a female passivity and covers that page with whatever meanings he chooses to inscribe. This is how the speaker of the elegies *always* imagines himself, as a centre of stability and control in a world where everyone else is plastic and malleable. But this self-dramatisation of an independent authority can be sustained only if the speaker is himself untouched by the force he exerts on others. Were that force to turn back and claim him for its own by revealing itself to be the very source of *his* identity (which would then be no longer his) he would be indistinguishable from those he manipulates and scorns; he would be like a woman and become the object rather than the origin of his own performance, worked on, ploughed, appropriated, violated. (This is in fact the posture Donne will assume in many of the *Holy Sonnets*.) The suspicion that this may indeed be his situation is continually surfacing in these poems, as when in 'The Comparison' the despised mistress is said to be 'like the first Chaos', an image that seems to place the poet in the preferred position of shaping creator, the bringer of order; but he cannot occupy that position unless chaos – the feminine principle – precedes him and provides him with the occasion of *self*-assertion. Chaos is thus *first* in a sense infinitely less comfortable than the one he allows himself to recognise;[7] for it is necessary both to the emergence of his being – such as it is – and to the illusion of his mastery, a mastery that is never more fragile than at those moments when it is most loudly proclaimed. ...

That is precisely what happens at the end of [*Elegy 3*] when he makes a perfect revolution from the stance of the opening lines to conclude 'change is the nursery / Of music, joy, life and eternity' (ll. 35–6). Critics complain that this conclusion seems inauthentic, that the 'work seems to come apart intellectually and emotionally',[8] but the complaint assumes the survival of a first-person voice of whom unity and integrity might be predicated. But that voice has been the casualty of its own poem, undone by the gymnastic virtuosity that impels both it and the poem forward. All that remains is what Sanders calls 'the serene beatitude of these lines', a beatitude that might mark an achieved coherence in a poem like Spenser's *Mutabilitie Cantos*, whose conclusion it resembles, but here marks only the dislodgement of the centred self by the fragmentary, ecphrastic discourse it presumed to control.[9] As Docherty puts it, there remains 'no identifiable "Donne", no identifiable or self-identical source or authority. ... Donne is that which is always the Other [to] himself.'[10]

The continual reproduction of a self that can never be the same, that can never be 'its own' is at once reported and repeatedly performed in the last of the elegies I shall consider, *Elegy 16*, 'On His Mistress'. The poem is an address to a woman who has offered to accompany the speaker on a journey disguised as his page, and commentary has foundered on the biographical speculation that the woman in question may have been Donne's wife. But the fact of the dramatic occasion is not revealed until line 15, and before that line the poem is focused neither on the woman nor on her proposed stratagem but on itself and on the other verbal actions that have preceded it.

> By our first strange and fatal interview,
> By all desires which thereof did ensue,
> By our long starving hopes, by that remorse
> Which my words' masculine persuasive force
> Begot in thee, and by the memory
> Of hurts, which spies and rivals threaten'd ne,
> I calmly beg: but by thy fathers wrath,
> By all pains, which want and divorcement hath,
> I conjure thee. ...
>
> (ll. 1–9)

This long syntactic unit is an extended oath, but while oaths typically invoke some extraverbal power or abstraction, this oath invokes previous oaths. Even when the verse names emotions that would seem to be prior to words, they turn out to have been produced by words: desires that proceed from interviews (exchanges of talk), hurts that flow from threats, pains fathered by the expressions of wrath. The lines call up a familiar Ovidian world of plots, dangers, crises, but the principal actors in that world are not the speaker or his mistress or her father, but the various speech acts in relation to which they have roles to play and meanings to declare. A phrase like 'fathers wrath' names a conventional linguistic practice, not a person, and when the speaker swears by it, indeed *conjures* by it, he acknowledges the extent to which the energy he displays is borrowed from a storehouse of verbal formulas that belong to no one and precede everyone.

Yet even as that acknowledgement is made, the speaker resists it by claiming that the power that is working in this scene has its source in him, or, more precisely, in the 'masculine persuasive force' by means of which he produces (begets) his mistress's character. The three words that make up this phrase are mutually defining and redundant. The masculinity he asserts is inseparable from his ability to persuade – that is, to control – and 'force' is just a name for the exercise of that control, an exercise that validates his independence and thereby confirms his masculinity. But even as the power of masculine persuasive force is asserted the line itself assigns that power to the *words* – 'my words' masculine persuasive force' – which thereby reserve for themselves everything the speaker would mark as his own, including his own identity. In the guise of telling a story about a man, a woman, and a proposed journey, the poem stages a struggle between its own medium and the first-person voice that presumes to control it. That struggle is enacted again in the next line and a half when the speaker declares that his words are subordinate to the inner reality of which they are the mere expressions: 'all the oaths which I / And thou have sworn to seal joint constancy' (ll. 9–10). The assertion is that the constancy is a feature of his character and is prior to the oaths that serve only as its outward sign; but no sooner has that assertion been made than it is flatly contradicted by the (speech) action of the next line: 'Here I unswear, and overswear them thus.' 'Overswear' means 'swear over', both in the sense of 'again' and in the sense of *re*inscribing, of writing over what has been written previously. Not only does this overswearing undermine the constancy that has just been claimed, it also renders empty the personal pronoun that stood as the sign of the claimant. A consciousness that can rewrite its own grounds in the twinkling of an eye is not a consciousness at all, but a succession of refigurings no different finally from the refigurings it boasts to have produced in others. ...

'ALL SIGNS OF LOATHING'

That irony is the subject of the *Satires*, despite the still influential account of them as spoken in the voice of one who 'consistently defends the spiritual values of simplicity, peace, constancy, and truth'.[11] Certainly there is much talk of these virtues in the poems, but they are invoked at the very moments at which the speaker is displaying their opposites; rather than naming his achievements, they name the states from which he is always and already distant, the state of being one thing (simplicity), of being that thing without conflict (in peace), and of being that thing forever and truly. The satires record the desperate and always failing effort of the first-person voice to distinguish himself from the variability and corruption – alteration from an original – he sees around him. The basic and (literally) self-defeating gesture of these poems is enacted in the very first lines of *Satire I*:

> Away thou fondling motley humourist,
> Leave me ...

The phrase 'fondling motley humourist' is made up of words that point to the same quality, instability; a humourist is a person of irregular behaviour, 'a fantastical or whimsical person' (*OED*); a fondling is a fool, someone dazed, incapable of focusing (in an earlier manuscript Donne wrote 'changeling'); and motley is what a fool wears because a cloth 'composed of elements of diverse or varied character' (*OED*) perfectly suits one who is without a centre. It also suits the traditional figure of the satirist, the writer of a random discourse who moves from one topic to another in ways that display no abiding rationale; the linking definition of satire as '*satura* medley' – a full dish of mixed fruit indiscriminately heaped up – was a standard one in the period and linked the satirist both with the court fool (as he appears, for example, in *King Lear*), and with the 'mirror' or recorder figure who reflects the disorder of a world without coherence and has no coherence of his own. (Here one might cite Skelton's Parrot). In short, what the first-person voice pushes away or tries (in an impossible effort) to push away is himself; rather than saying, as he would like to, 'Get thee behind me Satan', he is saying (in perfect *self*-contradiction), 'Get thee behind me me.' From the beginning he is protecting and defending an identity – a separateness from flux and surface – that he never really has.

In what follows, each declaration of distance and isolation is undermined even as it is produced. In line 11 he vows *not* to leave the 'constant company' of his library; but in the previous line that company is said to include 'Giddy fantastic poets', an acknowledgement that at once belies the claim of constancy and points once again to the giddiness (absence of stability) of the speaker, who is after all practising poetry at this very moment. In line 12 he is betrayed even by his own syntax:

> Shall I leave all this constant company,
> And follow headlong, wild uncertain thee?

Who is 'headlong' – that is, madly impetuous – the motley humorist or the speaker who (at least rhetorically) disdains him? Since 'headlong' can either be an adverb modifying 'I' or an adjective modifying 'thee' it is impossible to tell, and this impossibility faithfully reflects the absence of the difference the speaker repeatedly invokes.

The claim of difference is further (and fatally) undermined when the speaker without any explanation decides that he will follow along after all. As if to reaffirm his self-respect (and his self) he asks for assurances that he will not be left alone in the street (First swear ... / Thou wilt not leave me' [ll. 13–15]), but this weak (and, as he himself knows, futile) gesture only underlines the extent of his capitulation: the distance between 'leave me' and 'don't leave' has been travelled in only fifteen lines; the stutter rhythm of push away/embrace is now instantiated in the poem's narrative as the now indistinguishable pair prepares to exit together. Before they do, the speaker rehearses the dangers he hopes to avoid, but his recital of them is so detailed and knowledgeable that he seems already to have fallen to them, and when he once again reasserts his difference from the world he is about to enter – 'With God, and with the Muses I confer' (l. 48) – one cannot take him seriously. Immediately after uttering this line he says 'But' and performs the action he vowed never to perform in line 1:

> I shut my chamber door, and come, let's go.
> (l. 52)

Yet even here he hesitates, pausing on the threshold (which he has long since crossed) to analyse an action that he himself finds inexplicable; after all he knows his man too well to believe that he will be faithful, and he knows too that any fickleness will be accomplished by a justification for 'why, when, or with whom thou wouldst go' (l. 65). The real question, however, is why the *speaker* would go in the face of such knowledge, and he poses the question himself in the very act of going:

> But how shall I be pardoned my offence
> That thus have sinned against my conscience.
> (ll. 66–7)

There is no answer, merely the report that, finally, 'we are in the street' (l. 67), but the answer is all too obvious: if by conscience he means an inner integrity – an identity that holds itself aloof against all external temptations and assaults – then conscience is what he has not had ever since his first words revealed a mind divided against itself. Ironically, that mind is now unified (if that is the right word) when it accepts (certainly not the right word) its implication in the giddy and the variable, and ventures out into the world to encounter other versions of himself, others who, like him, are 'many-colored' and forever on the move. The fiction that it is not he but his fickle companion who refuses to stand still (l. 86) is rhetorically maintained by the distinction of pronouns, but even that distinction is collapsed in the final lines:

> He quarreled, fought, bled; and turned out of door
>   Directly came to me hanging the head,
>   And constantly a while must keep his bed.
>
> (ll. 110–12)

That is, he comes *home*, where he lives, to the speaker, and he comes 'directly', as if by instinct, and as he comes he shares with the speaker the pronoun 'me' – is it 'comes to me while hanging his head' or 'comes to me who am hanging my head'? The attribution of 'constancy' is mocked not only by the immediate qualification of 'a while', but by everything that has transpired in a poem where inconstancy rules and most spectacularly rules the voice who would thrust it from him ('Away ...'). ...

Moreover, insofar as the speaker's relationship to the world he scorns is precarious, so is Donne's, for nothing in the poem authorises us to perform the saving and stabilising move of formalist criticism in which a sharp distinction between the poet and his persona allows the former to stand outside the predicament of the latter. In Donne's poems, as Herz observes, 'inside and outside are no longer clearly fixed points',[12] and therefore we cannot with any confidence locate a place in which the poet is securely established as a controlling presence. This is particularly true of *Satire 4*, a poem in which the speaker plays with the dangers of displaying Catholic sympathies in a way that cannot be separated from the danger Donne – the Catholic-in-the-course-of-becoming-an-Anglican – risks in presenting such a speaker. Is it the satiric voice who begins by declaring 'Well; I may now receive' and then labours to render the suggestion of a forbidden ceremony metaphorical and jesting, or is it Donne? ...

What we do know is that once again a Donne poem presents a speaker who refuses to recognise himself in the indictment he makes of others. In this case the indictment is of those who go to court, which is the very first thing the speaker does in an action he finds as inexplicable as we do:

> My mind, neither with pride's itch, nor yet hath been
> Poisoned with love to see, or be seen.
> I had no suit there, nor new suit to show,
> Yet went to Court.
>
> (ll. 5–8)

The claim is, as in the earlier poems, a claim of interiority – he need not show himself in order to acquire value; he is content with what he

is in himself – and in order to maintain the claim, he at once min-
imises his sin and renders it something external by calling it 'my sin of
going' (l. 12). Characterised that way, the sin seems accidental to an
inner being it does not touch, something that 'happens' to that being
before it is even aware. Of course he knows what the commission of
this little sin will suggest to some, that he is 'As prone to all ill, and of
good as forget-/ful, as proud, as lustful, and as much in debt, / As vain,
as witless and as false as they / Which dwell at Court, for once going
that way' (ll. 13–16); but by insisting on the 'once', on the anomalous
nature of the event, he pushes the accusation away and reaffirms his
status as something apart from the scene he unwillingly enters.

It is in the service of the same affirmation that he labels everything
and everyone he meets 'strange' and a 'stranger', indeed 'Stranger than
strangers' (l. 23). That is to say, nothing I saw is like *me*, an assertion
belied by the very first person he encounters; that person wears coarse
clothes which leave him bare (l. 30); he 'speaks all tongues' (l. 35) and
has none of his own; rather he is 'Made of th' accents' (l. 37), a confection of 'pedant's motley' (l. 40). He is, in short, a satirist, affectedly
coarse, deliberately ill-attired, a mirror of everything around him, an
indiscriminate mixture. The speaker has met himself, and he responds
in language that at once admits the kinship and disclaims it:

> He names me, and comes to me; I whisper, 'God!
> How have I sinned, that thy wrath's furious rod,
> This fellow, chooseth me?'
>
> (ll. 49–51)

'He names me' is literal in its identification of the two, but of course
in so exclaiming the speaker intends only wonder at so unlikely an
act of recognition; but then he performs (unknowingly) the same
recognition when he 'names' the stranger 'thy wrath's furious rod',
for this is still another standard description of the satirist and his
purpose. Unable to free himself from this unwelcome companion,
he has recourse to behaviour that will he hopes drive the wretch
away: 'I belch, spew, spit, / Look pale, and sickly' (ll. 109–10);
but this is precisely the aspect the 'stranger' already bears, and it is
no wonder that upon meeting it in the speaker 'he thrusts on more'
(l. 111). The 'more' he produces is a compendium of stock satiric
themes – 'He names a price for every office paid; / He saith, our laws
thrive ill, because delayed; / That offices are entailed' (ll. 121–3) –
and as he listens to this version of himself even the speaker is close to
seeing the truth:

... hearing him, I found
That as burnt venomed lechers do grow sound
By giving others their sores, I might grow
Guilty. ...

(ll. 133–6)

Guilty, that is, not simply of going, but of being, or rather of nonbeing.

The thought is too horrible and he thrusts it away with a gesture that is its own allegory:

... I did show
All signs of loathing.
(ll. 136–7)

'All signs of loathing' is a formulation that definitively begs the question both for the speaker and for Donne. 'Signs' of loathing are precisely external indications of something that may be otherwise; whether the speaker *really* loathes is something we don't know and something *he* doesn't know either. The same holds for Donne: the entire poem constitutes *his* sign of loathing, *his* declaration of distance from the world he delineates and from the voice he projects: 'this is not me but my creature; this is not my world, but the world in which my creature is implicated in ways that he does not know; I, like you, know; I am in control.' But the only evidence he might cite in support of this declaration and its claim (the claim to be in possession of himself in contrast to his creature who is not) are his signs of loathing, his production of words, his *show*; but whether or not anything lies behind the show, whether the *signs* of loathing stand in for an authentic loathing or whether they constitute a ruse by which the true nature of Donne's impure being is concealed from us and from himself in exactly the manner of his fictional (or is it true?) surrogate, is something we cannot determine. *And neither can he.* As in the elegies, the foregrounding of the power of signs and of their tendency to 'compass all the land' catches the foregrounder in its backwash, depriving him of any independence of the forces he (supposedly) commands. The more persuasive is his account and exercise of verbal power the less able is he to situate himself in a space it does not fill, and he is left as we are, wondering if there is or could be anything real – anything other than artifice – in his performance (a word that perfectly captures the dilemma).

'TRUE GRIEFE'

The relationship between the exercise of power and the claims to independence and sincerity continues to be thematised in the *Holy Sonnets* although in these poems Donne occupies (or tries to occupy) the position of the creature and yields the role of the shaper to God. That difference, however, is finally less significant than one might suppose since the God Donne imagines is remarkably like the protagonist he presents (and I would say *is*) in the elegies, a jealous and overbearing master who brooks no rivals and will go to any lengths (even to the extent of depriving Donne of his wife) in order to secure his rights. It is as if Donne could only imagine a God in his own image, and therefore a God who acts in relation to him as he acts in relation to others, as a self-aggrandising bully. To be sure, in the sonnets the speaker rather than exerting masculine persuasive force begs to be its object ('Batter my heart, three person'd God'), but this rearrangement of roles only emphasises the durability of the basic Donnean situation and gives it an odd and unpleasant twist: the woman is now asking for it ('enthrall me', 'ravish me'). One might almost think that the purpose of the sonnets, in Donne's mind, is retroactively to justify (by baptising) the impulses to cruelty and violence (not to say misogyny) he displays so lavishly in his earlier poetry. In an important sense 'Thou hast made me and shall thy work decay' is simply a rewriting of 'Nature's lay idiot', which might itself be titled 'I have made you, and shall *my* work decay?' The plot is the same, an original artificer now threatened by a rival artisan ('our old subtle foe so tempteth me'), and a complaint against change in the name of a control that would be absolute. Of course in the 'sacred' version the complaint is uttered not by the about to be supplanted creator, but by the creature eager to remain subject to his power ('not one houre I can myself sustaine'); nevertheless the relational structure of the scene is the same, a structure in which masochism (and now sado-masochism) is elevated to a principle and glorified, earlier in the name of a frankly secular power, here in the name of a power that is (supposedly) divine. The fact that Donne now assumes the posture of a woman and like the church of 'Show me deare Christ thy spouse' spreads his legs (or cheeks) is worthy of note, but to note it is not to indicate a significant (and praiseworthy) change in his attitude toward women and power; it is rather to indicate how strongly that attitude informs a poetry whose centre is supposedly elsewhere.

Moreover, even as Donne casts himself in the female role, he betrays an inability to maintain that role in the face of a fierce and familiar desire to be master of his self, even of a self whose creaturely nature he is in the process of acknowledging. In a poem like 'As due by many titles I resigne / My selfe to thee', the gesture of resignation is at the same time a reaffirmation of the resigner's independence: considering well the situation, it seems proper that I choose to be subservient to you. As Hester has observed, this is not so much a resigning, but a re-signing, the production of a signature and therefore of a claim of ownership, if not of the self that was, as he says, 'made' (1.2), then of the act by which that self is laid down (a distinction without a difference).[13] Ostensibly the poem is an extended plea to be possessed (in every sense) by God, but in fact it is a desperate attempt to leave something that will say, like Kilroy, 'Donne was here'.

That desperation is the explicit subject of 'If faithfull soules be alike glorifi'd', a first line that enacts in miniature everything that follows it.[14] As it is first read, the question seems to be whether or not all faithful souls are glorified in the same way (are they alike?), but then the first two words of the second line – 'As Angels' – reveal that the likeness being put into question is between all faithful souls (now assumed to be glorified alike, but without any content specified for that likeness) and angels who are themselves glorified alike but perhaps not in the same manner (alike) as are faithful souls. If the pressure of interrogation falls on the notion of likeness and therefore on the issue of identity (one must know what something or someone uniquely is before one can say for certain whether or not it or he or she is like or unlike something or someone else), then the interrogation is from the very first in deep trouble when the word 'alike', meaning 'not different', turns out to be different from itself in the passage from line 1 to line 2.

The trouble is compounded as line 2 further unfolds:

> As Angels, then my fathers soule doth see

Whether or not his father's soul sees is still in doubt since the entire construction remains ruled by 'If'; and the fact of his father's being a Catholic reinvigorates the question that had been left behind in the turn of the second line: are faithful souls glorified alike even if they are faithful to papism? As a result, the status of his father's vision is doubly obscure; we don't know whether it is like the vision of other, more safely, faithful souls, and we don't know, should it pass that test, whether it is as perspicuous as the vision of angels.

It is in the context of that unsure vision that we meet the sight it may or may not see: ' That valiantly I hels wide mouth o'erstride' (l. 4). The line presents itself as an assertion of the way things really are – despite appearances I stand firm against the temptations of the world, flesh, and devil – but in the context of what precedes it, the assertion remains only a claim until it is confirmed by one who sees *through* appearances to the inner reality they obscure. Since, however, the question of whether his father is one who sees in that penetrating way has been left conspicuously open, neither he nor we can be sure of that confirmation, and there remains the suspicion that behind the sign of purity, behind the verbal report of spiritual valour, there is nothing; the suspicion that the truth about him is no deeper or more stable than his surface representation of it. It is this dreadful possibility that Donne (one could say 'the speaker', but it will come down to Donne in the end) raises explicitly in the next four lines:

> But if our mindes to these soules be descry'd
> By circumstances, and by signes that be
> Apparent in us, not immediately,
> How shall my mindes white truth to them be try'd?
>
> (ll. 5–8)

That is, if my father and other glorified souls (if he is, in fact, glorified and if all faithful souls are glorified alike) descry just as we on earth do, through a variety of glasses darkly, by means of signs, of representations, of what shows (is 'Apparent'), then there is no way that anyone will ever know what's inside me or indeed if there *is* anything inside me. A 'white truth' is a truth without colour, without coverings, without commentary, but if coloured, covered, and textualised truth are all anyone can see, then the white truth of his mind will continue to be an untried claim, and one moreover that is suspect, given the innumerable examples of those who feign commitments they do not have:

> They see idolatrous lovers weepe and mourne,
> And vile blasphemous Conjurers to call
> On Jesus name, and Pharisaicall
> Dissemblers feigne devotion.
>
> (ll. 9–12)

Anyone can *say* they are faithful or sincere or 'white', but such sayings, proffered as evidence of a truth beyond (or behind) signs, are themselves signs and never more suspicious than when they present the trappings of holiness. It is at this point (if not before) that the precarious situation of the poem becomes obvious; as a structure of signs it has done all the things it itself identifies as strategies of dissembling: it has wept, mourned, dramatised devotion; and then, as if it were following its own script, the poem closes by performing the most reprehensible of these strategies; it calls on Jesus' name:

> ... Then turne
> O pensive soule, to God, for he knowes best
> Thy true griefe, for he put it in my breast.
> (ll. 12–14)

There are at least two levels on which this is an unsatisfactory conclusion. First, there is no reason to believe that the turn to God is anything but one more instance of feigned devotion, one more *performance* of a piety for which the evidence remains circumstantial (that is, theatrical) and apparent, a matter of signs and show. To be sure, the structure of the sonnet lends these lines the aura of a final summing up, of a pronouncement ('Then') detached from the gestures that precede it; but nothing prevents us from reading the pronouncement itself as one more gesture, and therefore as a claim no more supported than the claim (that he valiantly o'erstrides hell's mouth) it is brought in to support. And even if we were to credit the sincerity of these lines and regard them not as dramatic projections but as spontaneous ejaculations, they would not provide what the poem has been seeking, a perspective from which we could discern once and for all what, if anything, was inside him; for all the lines say is that whatever there is in his breast, God knows it, which means of course that we don't, and that we are left at the end with the same doubt that his 'true griefe' (here just one more 'untry'd' claim) may be false, a confection of signs and appearances. As in the elegies and the satires, the relentless assertion and demonstration of the power of signs to bring their own referents into being – to counterfeit love and grief and piety – undermines the implicit claim of *this* producer of signs to be real, to be anything more than an effect of the resources he purports to control. ...

This is spectacularly the case in 'What if this present were the worlds last night?' This first line might well open one of the sermons Donne was later to write; it is obviously theatrical and invites us to imagine (or to be) an audience before whom this proposition will be elaborated in the service of some homiletic point. But in the second line everything changes abruptly. The theatricalism is continued, but the stage has shrunk from one on which Donne speaks to many of a (literally) cosmic question to a wholly interior setting populated only by versions of Donne:

> Marke in my heart, O Soule, where thou dost dwell,
> The picture of Christ crucified, and tell
> Whether that countenance can thee affright?
>
> (ll. 2–4)

Donne addresses his own soul and asks it to look in his heart, where will be found a picture he has put there, either for purposes of meditation or in the manner of a lover who hangs portraits of his lady in a mental gallery. But the meditation is curious in the way we have already noted: Donne does not direct it at his beloved, whether secular or spiritual, but to another part of himself. Although Christ's picture is foregrounded, especially in the lines (ll. 5–7) that rehearse its beauties in a sacred parody of the traditional blazon, in the context of the poem's communicative scene, the picture – not to mention the person it portrays – is off to the side as everything transpires between the speaker and his soul. The gesture is a familiar one in Donne's poetry; it is the contraction into one space of everything in the world ('All here in one bed lay'), which is simultaneously the exclusion of everything in the world ('I could eclipse and cloud them with a wink');[15] but here it seems prideful and perhaps worse, for it recharacterises the Last Judgement as a moment staged and performed entirely by himself: produced by Donne, interior design by Donne, case pled by Donne, decision rendered by Donne. Again, as in the elegies, Donne occupies every role on his poem's stage, and since the stage is interior, it is insulated from any correcting reference other than the one it allows. Thus protected from any outside perspective and from the intrusion of any voice he has not ventriloquised, Donne can confidently ask the poem's urgent question:

> And can that tongue adjudge thee unto hell,
> Which pray'd forgivenesse for his foes fierce spight?
>
> (ll. 7–8)

The question's logic assumes a distinction between 'that tongue' and 'thee' (i.e., me), but since Donne is here all tongues, the distinction is merely verbal and cannot be the basis of any real suspense. The answer is inevitable and it immediately arrives: 'No, no' (l. 9). But as John Stachniewski acutely observes, 'the argument of Donne's poems is often so strained that it alerts us to its opposite, the emotion or mental state in defiance of which the argumentative process was set to work'.[16] Here the mental state the poem tries to avoid is uncertainty, but its pressure is felt in the exaggerated intensity with which the 'No, no' denies it. Uncertainty and instability return with a vengeance in the final lines:

> ... but as in my idolatrie
> I said to all my profane mistresses,
> Beauty, of pitty, foulnesse onely is
> A signe of rigour: so I say to thee,
> To wicked spirits are horrid shapes assign'd,
> This beauteous forme assures a pitious minde.
> (ll. 9–14)

In the rhetoric of this complex statement, Donne's idolatry is in the past, but his words also point to the idolatry he has been committing in the poem, the idolatry of passing judgement on himself in a court whose furniture he has carefully arranged. The assertion that he is *not* now in his idolatry is undermined by the fact that he here says the very same things he used to say when he was. As he himself acknowledges, what he says is part of a seductive strategy, more or less on the level recommended in 'The Anagram': if your beloved's countenance is forbidding and harsh, impute to her a benign interior; and if her aspect is 'pitious', impute to her a consistency of form and content. In this poem, the suspect logic is even more suspect because it is directed at himself: the referent of 'thee' is his own soul, the addressee since line 2. The soul is asked to read from the signifying surface of Christ's picture to his intention, but since that surface is one that Donne himself has as-signed, the confident assertion of the last line has no support other than itself.

Indeed the line says as much in either of its two textual versions, 'This beauteous forme *assures* a pitious minde' or 'This beauteous forme *assumes* a pitious minde'.[17] In either variant 'This beauteous forme' refers not only to the form Donne has assigned to Christ's picture, but to the form of the poem itself; it is the poem's verbal felicity and nothing else that is doing either the assuring (which thus is no more than whistling in the dark) or the assuming (which as a word at least has the grace to name the weakness of the action it performs). The poem ends in the bravado that marks some of the other sonnets (e.g., 'Death be not proud'), but the triumph of the rhetorical flourish (so reminiscent of the ending of every one of the *Songs and Sonnets*) only calls attention to its insubstantiality. Once again, the strong demonstration of verbal power – of the ability to make any proposition seem plausible so long as one doesn't examine it too closely – undermines its own effects. In the end the poet always pulls it off but that only means that he could have pulled it off in the opposite direction, and *that* only means that the conclusion he forces is good only for the theatrical moment of its production. This is true not only for his readers but for himself; as the poem concludes, he is no more assured of what he assumes than anyone else, neither of the 'pitious minde' of his saviour, nor of the spiritual stability he looks to infer from the saviour's picture. The effort of self-persuasion – which is also at bottom the effort to confirm to himself that he is a self, someone who exceeds the theatrical production of signs and shows – fails in exactly the measure that his rhetorical effort succeeds. The better he is at what he does with words, the less able he is to claim (or believe) that behind the words – o'erstriding the abyss – stands a self-possessed being.

The realisation of radical instability ('the horror, the horror') is given full expression in 'Oh, to vex me, contraryes meete in one', a poem that desires to face the spectre down, but in the end is overwhelmed by it. The problem is succinctly enacted in the first line: if contraries meet in one, then one is not one – an entity that survives the passing of time – but two or many. This would-be-one looks back on its history and sees only a succession of poses – contrition, devotion, fear – no one of which is sufficiently sustained to serve as the centre he would like to be able to claim:

> ... to day
> In prayers, and flattering speaches I court God:
> To morrow I quake with true feare of his rod.
> (ll. 9–11)

These lines at once report on and reproduce the dilemma: 'prayers' seems innocent enough until 'flattering speaches' retroactively questions the sincerity of the gesture; and the same phrase spreads forward to infect the assertion of line 11; when he quakes with 'true fear', is the adjective a tribute to his artistry, to his ability to simulate an emotion in a way that convinces spectators (including himself) of its truth; or is the fear true in a deeper sense, one that would allow us to posit a moment (however fleeting) of authenticity in the midst of so many performances? The question is of course unanswerable, although as the poem ends (both with a bang and a whimper) there is one last attempt to draw the kind of line that would make an answer possible:

> So my devout fitts come and go away
> Like a fantastique Ague: save that here
> Those are my best dayes, when I shake with feare.
> (ll. 12–14)

'Devout fitts' recapitulates the problem: can devotion be genuine – heartfelt – if it comes and goes like the ever-changing scene of a fever? In the continual alternation of contradictory spiritual states, no one moment seems any more securely 'true' than any other. Nevertheless the poem proceeds to declare an exception with 'save that. ...' On one level the exception is to the comparison between spiritual and physical health: while in the illness of the body the best days are the days when convulsions subside, in spiritual matters the best days are marked by fearful agitation.[18] But the exception Donne here tries to smuggle in is one that would attribute authenticity to the fits he displays on some days as opposed to others: my life may be characterised by changeful humours, but among those humours one speaks the genuine me. In order for that claim to be strongly received, however, the last line must be disengaged from everything that has preceded it and be marked in some way with the difference it attempts so boldly to declare. But no such mark is available, and as we read it the line is drawn into the pattern from which it would distinguish itself. Either it refers backward to the 'true fear' of line 11, already identified as a theatrical production, or, if we give the word 'here' full force, it refers to itself – I am at this very moment of writing shaking with true fear – and asks us to accept as unperformed and spontaneous the obviously artful conclusion to a sonnet. In either case, one cannot rule out a reading in which the best days are the days when he best simulates the appropriate emotion ('look at how good I am at shaking with fear'), and we are as far from an emotion that is not simulated – from an emotion produced other than theatrically by someone other than a wholly theatrical being – than we were when he uttered the first self-pitying line, 'Oh, to vex me. ...'

Reading this same poem, Anne Ferry makes observations similar to mine but reaches a different conclusion. She takes the poem's lesson to be 'that what is grounded inward in [the speaker's] heart is at a distance from language used to describe it, which cannot render it truly', and she generalises this lesson into a Donnean theory of sincerity:

> ... what is in the heart cannot be interpreted or judged by outward signs, among which language is included, even when they are sincere. Inward states cannot therefore be truly shown, even by the speaker's own utterance in prayers or poems, cannot be defined by them, even to himself.[19]

Ferry assumes what it seems to me these poems put continually into question, that the 'inward experience' or *'real self'* is in fact there and the deficiency lies with the medium that cannot faithfully transcribe it. I have argued that the problem with language in these poems is not that it is too weak to do something, but that it is so strong that it does everything, exercising its power to such an extent that nothing, including the agent of that exercise, is left outside its sphere. I am not offering *this* as the insight Donne wishes to convey as opposed to the insight Ferry urges, but, rather, saying that it is not an insight at all – in the sense of something Donne commands – but the problematic in which he remains caught even when he (or especially when he) is able to name it as he does in this passage from a sermon delivered during his final illness:

> The way of Rhetorique in working upon weake men, ... is to empty [the understanding] of former apprehensions and opinions, and to shape that beliefe, with which it had possessed it self before, and then when it is thus melted, to powre it into new molds, ... to stamp and imprint new formes, new images, new opinions in it.[20]

Once again Donne identifies, this time by its proper name, the activity he has practised all his life, an activity propelled by a force that knows no resistance and simply writes over (overswears) whatever meanings and forms some previous, equally unstoppable, force has inscribed. Once again, he attempts to assert his distance from that force even as he exercises it and reports on its exercise, attempts to possess it without being possessed by it. And once again the attempt takes the form of an act of displacement by means of which his fears are pushed onto others, not this time onto women or Frenchmen or

Italians, but onto 'weake men'. Weak men are men whose convictions are so malleable, so weakly founded, that they can be shaped and reshaped by the skilled rhetorician who becomes, in an implied opposition, the very type of the strong man. But as we have seen, in the story that Donne's poems repeatedly enact, the skilful rhetorician always ends up becoming the victim/casualty of his own skill, and no more so than at those moments when his powers are at their height. The stronger he is, the more force-full, the more taken up by the desire for mastery, the less he is anything like 'himself'. The lesson of masculine persuasive force is that it can only be deployed at the cost of everything it purports to incarnate – domination, independence, assertion, masculinity itself.

In much of Donne criticism that lesson has been lost or at least obscured by a concerted effort to put Donne in possession of his poetry and therefore of himself. The result has been a series of critical romances of which Donne is the hero (valiantly o'erstriding the abyss). Ferry gives us one romance: the poet, ahead of his times, labours to realise a modern conception of the inner life. An older criticism gave us the romance of immediacy and the unified sensibility: the felt particulars of lived experience are conveyed by a verse that is at once tactilely sensuous and intellectually bracing. Often this romance was folded into another, the romance of voice in which a singular and distinctive Donne breaks through convention to achieve a hitherto unknown authenticity of expression. At mid-century the invention of the persona produced the romance of craft: Donne surveys the range of psychological experience and creates for our edification and delight a succession of flawed speakers. And the most recent scholarship, vigorously rejecting immediacy, voice, authenticity, and craft as lures and alibis, tempts us instead with the romance of postmodernism, of a Donne who is 'rigorously sceptical, endlessly self-critical, posing more questions than he answers'.[21] (This last is particularly attractive insofar as it transforms obsessive behaviour into existential heroism of the kind academics like to celebrate because they think, mistakenly, that they exemplify it.) As different as they are, these romances all make the mistake of placing Donne outside the (verbal) forces he sets in motion and thus making him a figure of control. In the reading offered here, Donne is always folded back into the dilemmas he articulates, and indeed it is the very articulation of those dilemmas – the supposed bringing of them to self-consciousness – that gives them renewed and devouring life.[22]

From *Soliciting Interpretation: Literary Theory and Seventeenth-Century English Poetry*, ed. Elizabeth D. Harvey and Katharine Eisaman Maus (Chicago, 1990), pp. 223–52.

NOTES

[Stanley Fish's essay discusses a wide range of generically distinct poems (elegies, satires, and religious sonnets) and discovers a common strand between them in the Donne who fashions reality through language, but who is anxious, at the same time, about the emptiness of his own rhetoric. In the highly mediated, highly textualised world of a Donne performance, there is, according to Fish, a continual effacement of 'prior and independent referent[s]' (see p. 159 above), including Donne himself. The gender hierarchy whereby Donne would ideally position himself as creator rather than created, essence rather than construct, subject rather than object of linguistic transformation, collapses to reveal a mutable 'sign', as available for linguistic appropriation as those he inscribes and re-inscribes via the use of analogy.

During the course of his commentary upon one of Donne's religious sonnets, Fish makes the interesting point that 'one must know what something or someone uniquely is before one can say for certain whether or not it or he or she is like or unlike something or someone else' (see p. 171 above). This position, anti-poststructuralist in its affirmation of a form of essentialism which holds that things and people possess their own unique and inviolable identities, is worth comparing and contrasting with the more attenuated essentialism of Elizabeth Harvey's and Barbara Estrin's feminist approaches.

For an interesting elaboration of Fish's theoretical position, see his 'What it Means to do a Job of Work', *English Literary Renaissance*, 25 (1995), 354–71. For further discussion and contextualisation of his essay, see Introduction, p. 18. Ed.]

1. C. S. Lewis, 'Donne and Love Poetry in the Seventeenth Century', in *Seventeenth Century English Poetry: Modern Essays in Criticism*, ed. William Keast (New York, 1962), pp. 98, 96.

2. Judith Herz, '"An Excellent Exercise of Wit that Speaks So Well of Ill": Donne and the Poetics of Concealment', in *The Eagle and the Dove: Reassessing John Donne*, ed. Claude J. Summers and Ted-Larry Pebworth (Columbia, MO, 1986), p. 5.

3. *John Donne: The Complete English Poems*, ed. A. J. Smith (Baltimore, MD, 1971). All further citations of the elegies and the satires are taken from this text.

4. Thomas Docherty, *John Donne, Undone* (New York, 1986), p. 68.

5. Arthur F. Marotti, *John Donne, Coterie Poet* (Madison, WI, 1986), p. 48.

6. Jacques Derrida, 'Signature Event Context', trans. Samuel Weber and Jeffrey Mehlman, *Glyph*, I (1977), 182, 185.

7. For a brilliant discussion of chaos as it operates in Renaissance literature in general and in Milton's *Paradise Lost* in particular, see Regina Schwartz, 'Milton's Hostile Chaos: "... And the Sea Was No More"', *ELH*, 52 (1985), 337–74.

8. Marotti, *Coterie*, p. 308.

9. Wilbur Sanders, *Donne's Poetry* (Cambridge, 1971), p. 41.

10. Docherty, *John Donne*, p. 60.

11. N. J. C. Andreason, 'Theme and Structure in Donne's *Satyres*', in *Essential Articles for the Study of John Donne's Poetry*, ed. John R. Roberts (Hamden, CT, 1975), p. 412.

12. Herz, 'Poetics of Concealment', p. 6.

13. M. Thomas Hester, 'Re-Signing the Text of the Self: Donne's "As due by many titles"', in *'Bright Shootes of Everlastingnesse': The Seventeenth-Century Religious Lyric*, ed. Claude J. Summers and Ted-Larry Pebworth (Columbia, MO, 1987), p. 69. Also see Docherty, *John Donne*, p. 139.

14. All citations from the *Holy Sonnets* are taken from *John Donne: The Divine Poems*, ed. Helen Gardner (Oxford, 1964).

15. 'The Sun Rising', ll. 20, 13.

16. John Stachniewski, 'John Donne: The Despair of the "Holy Sonnets"', *ELH*, 48 (1981), 691.

17. All manuscripts read *assures*, but the 1633 edition reads *assumes*.

18. Anne Ferry, *The 'Inward' Language* (Chicago, 1983), pp. 242–3.

19. Ibid., pp. 243, 249.

20. *Sermons*, ed. George R. Potter and Evelyn M. Simpson, 10 vols (Berkeley, CA, 1953–62), 2:282–3.

21. Docherty, *John Donne*, p. 29.

[22. I am grateful to Stanley Fish for his helpful suggestions for editing his essay. Ed.]

9

The *Figura* of the Martyr in John Donne's Sermons

NANCY WRIGHT

Nietzsche's perception that 'we are not getting rid of God because we still believe in grammar', a set of categories that defines our world, echoes a theory of language voiced in the sixteenth and seventeenth centuries.[1] He locates the origin of metaphysical concepts in the subject-predicate relation of grammar, whereas others had found the presence of God in the signification of the Bible's words, which, like the signs in the sacraments, could realise what they signified. This belief in the efficacy of religious discourse emerges from controversies involving Christian, legal, and political doctrines, a nexus of ideas found in Erastian societies such as Tudor and Stuart England that cited the Bible as the *auctor* of the divine *Logos* as well as of civic and ecclesiastical authority. That England's kings regulated the publication of grammars in the same manner in which they authorised and prohibited editions of the Bible suggests the special powers suspected of language. ...

In his 'Discourse on Language', Michel Foucault aptly characterises the restricting mechanisms used 'in every society [by means of which] the production of discourse is at once controlled, selected, organised, and redistributed according to a certain number of procedures, whose role is to avert its powers and its dangers, to cope with chance events'. In a society structured upon Erastian principles the effect of doctrine, which Foucault describes as a restrictive mechanism confining 'individuals to certain types of utterance while consequently barring them from all other', is particularly diffuse.[2] For example, Millar MacLure argues it is because of Erastian principles informing English society that from 1604 to 1622 'the statutes in any collection of government documents closely parallel the pronouncements from the pulpits and the injunctions in the Homilies. The two arms, ecclesiastical and secular, were joined in purpose; the welfare of the commonwealth was, in ideal, an accomplishment to God's glory, and obedience to the sovereign in all matters economic as well as political, a religious duty.'[3] Throughout his reign, King James relied upon the doctrine of his divine right to supreme authority in the government of the state and the Church of England to control the discourse of clergymen and civic deputies. The *Homily on Obedience*, preached throughout Jacobean England, confirmed that the sovereignty of the king had been instituted by 'God [who] hath assigned kings princes with other governors under them, all in good and necessary order'.[4] King James repeatedly pronounced that his divine right was conferred by 'the word of God it selfe' in order to establish it as orthodox religious and political doctrine, defended from controversy or questioning by the mechanism of commentary that limits doctrinal utterances to the 'reappearance, word for word (though ... solemn and anticipated) of the text commented on'.[5] Because doctrinal commentary claims its credibility from doctrine, its speaker cannot augment or contradict orthodox doctrine without forming a heretical statement that subverts its only claim to veracity. Because the doctrine of the king's divine right limited religious and political discourse in this manner, the Stuart kings, in the words of Charles I, valued '"Religion as the only firm foundation of all power"'.[6]

In 1622, however, King James implemented laws to censor discourse arising from a different conception of the 'Word of God', subscribed to by many Puritans. Although moderate Puritans conformed to the practices of the Church of England in matters considered *adiaphora* as long as the marks of the 'true' Church, the administration of the sacraments and the preaching of the Bible, were performed, they did not believe that the interpretation of scripture could be circumscribed by the king or his ministers. Moderate Puritans such as William Whitaker believed that 'the scripture is *autopistos*, that is hath all its authority and credit from itself; is to be acknowledged, is to be received, not only because the church hath so determined and commanded, but because it comes from God: and that we certainly know that it comes from God, not by the church, but by the Holy Ghost'.[7] The belief in immediate interpretation of scripture freed their discourse from restrictions and enfranchised the citation of biblical texts to criticise the king's political and religious policies. The king's foreign policy provoked dissent from his claim to be head of the Church of England when he failed to provide aid to restore his son-in-law, the Elector Palatine, a Protestant monarch, to the throne of Bohemia and consented to negotiate the marriage of Prince Charles to a Catholic princess. Because of criticism by moderate Puritan clergy of his 'divine right' to be head of the Church, King James published legal restrictions, both in a series of proclamations against 'meddling with speech or pen' in secrets of state and in *His Letter and Directions to the Lord Archbishop of Canterbury; Concerning Preaching and Preachers.* The latter ordinance commanded that no preacher could limit the 'Power, Prerogative, and Jurisdiction, Authority, or Duty of Soveraign Princes, and the People, than as are instructed and precedented in the Homilies of Obedience, and the rest of the Homilies, and Articles of Religion ... set forth by public Authority.'[8] In this manner he prohibited all discussion of his power except commentary upon texts confirming his legal and ecclesiastical authority such as the *Homilies* and the *39 Articles*. By also excluding all preachers below the rank of bishop or dean from discussing the doctrines of predestination, election, reprobation, and grace, King James severed the discourse of dissenting clergy from scripture, their source of ecclesiastical jurisdiction. Because, however, these prohibitions and exclusions limiting speech were external to the Bible, the *auctor* of religious discourse according to Calvinist theology, they revealed that the king's relation to discourse and doctrine was a secular, legal power.

The sovereign authority in sacred matters that moderate Puritans attributed to scripture diminished within secular, legal institutions, which also claimed absolute authority based upon a different concept of the truth revealed by language. Within courts of civil law and secular spheres of government, religious discourse is vulnerable to misinterpretation because the special powers of theological speech are denied. Only within the circumscribed and unchanging context of the liturgical cycle of the Church can words secure the coincidence of religious doctrine and discourse. The *nunc stans* that fixes time and meaning within the liturgy ensures that the words and ritual of the eucharist, for example, 'represent'

Christ, effectively making him present again so as to merge past and present, word and deed.[9] As Richard K. Fenn argues, beyond this sacred context, the forces shaping and controlling discourse sever the coincidence of language and event; 'instead of being able to "present again" words and deeds that are of crucial significance ... the lay person in court is allowed simply to "represent" that a certain statement conforms adequately to reality in the sense that others given the same opportunity to observe or understand, would say the same thing.'[10] As a result, not only the efficacy but also the meaning, the special theological significance of words, diminishes in juridical contexts and usage.

Language used by both the liturgy and the trial to define and appropriate the truth illuminates an origin of the conflict of juridical and religious discourse. Kenneth Burke has explained that religious terms had their origin in

> 'words' ... [that] have wholly naturalistic, empirical reference. But they may be used analogically, to designate a further dimension, the 'supernatural'. ... And in this state of linguistic affairs there is a paradox. For whereas the words for the 'supernatural' realm are necessarily borrowed from the realm of our everyday experiences, out of which our familiarity with language arises, once a terminology has been developed for special theological purposes the order can be reversed. We can borrow back the terms from the borrower, again secularising to varying degrees the originally secular terms that had been given 'supernatural' connotations.[11]

Words having secular referents require explication to determine and fix their theological significance within secular discourse. Renaissance theologians and rhetoricians such as Thomas Blundeville differentiate the analogical predication of religious terms from univocal and equivocal predication; analogical predication is 'unusual predication ... as wee read in the holy scriptures, God is man, the word was made flesh ... most essential and necessarie speeches, though not usuall in any other scyence than divinitie'.[12] Analogical predication establishes a proportionate relation between subject and predicate, divine and secular entities, that remains susceptible to secularisation beyond the liturgical context.

In his poetry John Donne reveals how pressure can be exerted upon religious significations in order to study their meaning, as in 'A Litany X *The Martyrs*':

> And since thou so desirously
> Didst long to die, that long before thou couldst,
>   And long since thou no more couldst die,
> Thou in thy scattered mystic body wouldst
>   In Abel die, and ever since
>   In thine, let their blood come
> To beg for us, a discreet patience
> Of death, or of worse life: for oh, to some
> Not to be martyrs, is a martyrdom.[13]

Here the literal, tropological, and anagogical meanings of 'martyr' are considered only with reference to the 'body' of the Church, the boundary of religious discourse. In the lyric 'The Funeral' Donne studies the religious significance formed by analogical predication of the term 'martyr' within the context of secular discourse. By means of the process of predication, the persona manipulates the meaning of signs and events. He calls into question the special religious significance of 'martyr' by his representation of his own death in his commands:

> Whoever comes to shroud me, do not harm
>   Nor question much
> That subtle wreath of hair, which crowns my arm;
> The mystery, the sign you must not touch,
>   For 'tis my outward soul
>   ...   .
> Whate'er she meant by it, bury it with me,
>   For since I am
> Love's martyr, it might breed idolatry,
> If into others' hands these relics came.
>   (ll. 1–5, 17–20)

The persona's definition of himself as 'love's martyr' exemplifies equivocal predication; in Aristotle's terms, the lover and the martyr 'have the name only in common, the definition (or statement of essence) corresponding with the name being different'.[14] By predicating the analogical, religious significance of martyr with a secular referent, Donne exposes the indeterminacy of religious discourse. As a result of this indeterminacy, the persona can manipulate the special meanings and powers attributed to religious terms, such as 'mystery' meaning a sacrament. By predicating 'the mystery, the sign' of a religious sacrament with a love token, the persona undermines the privileged religious signification and its efficacious powers.

These poems studying the word *martyria* or witness focus upon an important example of the confusion caused by 'borrowing' terms to express theological significations. According to classical rhetoricians, *martyria* signified one of the five inartificial proofs appropriate to forensic oratory, the rhetoric used in courts of law. As a rhetorical term, it referred to specific, recognised examples of discourse that Aristotle identifies as ancient and recent witnesses: 'By ancient I mean the poets and men of repute whose judgements are known to all. ... By recent witnesses I mean all well-known persons who have given a decision on any point, for their decisions are useful to those who are arguing about similar cases.'[15] Genres of discourse, proverbs, poems, oracles, and well-known authorities, function as time-proven and incorruptible sources of the truth, rhetorical witnesses relevant to a specific event in the present. In theological usage, however, the term μαρτυρία attributes special efficacy not only to discourse but also to the speaker. The verb μαρτυρέω and the nouns μαρτύριον and μάρτυς take on new significance in the New Testament through their reference to Christ and the apostles.[16] Both the speech and person of biblical *figurae* and Christ are identified, Donne says, as examples of a '*Martyr* ... [or] *Testis*, the very name of Martyr signifieth a *Witnesse*' (4:5, p. 151, ll. 218–19).

The Gospel's conflation of discourse and its human witness, the spoken and the speaker, in references to 'his servant John: who bare record of the word of God, and of the testimony of Jesus Christ, and of all things that he saw' (Rev. 1:1–2) and to 'Jesus Christ, who is the faithful witness, and the first begotten of the dead, and the prince of the kings of the earth' (Rev. 1:5) informs the discourse of preachers with powers that transform their speech and role. In the person of John the Baptist, a *figura* whose words prophesied the coming of the Divine *Logos*, the preacher finds an exemplum of the function of language as testimony. Among the names defining the responsibilities of John, Baptist, Prophet, and Preacher, Donne specifies that the most important was fulfilled by his

> *Vox clamantis, The voyce of him that cryes in the wilderness*. What names and titles soever we receive in the School, or in the Church, or in the State; if we lose our voice, we lose our proper name, our Christian name. But then, *John Baptists* name is not A voyce, Any voyce, but The voyce. ... Christ is *verbum*, The word; not A word, but The word: the Minister is *Vox*, voyce: not A voyce, but The voyce, the voyce of that word, and no other.
>
> (2:7, p. 172, ll. 299–306)

It is the duty of the preacher to give voice to the words and
mission of Christ by 'bringing the Gospel of Peace and Reparation'
(2:7, p. 172, ll. 309–10). The efficacy of their words has been
assured by Christ who was 'not onely a *Verball*, but an *Actuall*
manifester of former *Prophecies*, for all former Prophecies were
accomplished in his *Person*, and in his *deeds*, and *words*, in his
actions and *Passion*' (3:17, p. 349, ll. 56–8). The peculiar nature
of Christ as the Word that witnessed and realised prophecies
defines both the content and effect of the discourse of the preacher. Because the prophecies of the Bible have been revealed and
realised to the Church, the preacher does not form new prophetic
utterances but witnesses revealed truths in order to effect their
meaning in the present, just as liturgical speech acts effect an event
with the spoken word.

In three sermons spoken on the text John 1:8, 'He was not that
Light, but was sent to bear witness to that Light', John Donne
defines the duty, authority, and subject of the preacher with the
figura of John the Baptist, a type and witness of the Divine *Logos*.
Donne explains that

> *John Baptist* then had this competency, by knowledge infused by
> God, declared in former Prophecies, he knew the matter, which he
> was to testifie. Which is so essentiall, so substantiall a circumstance in
> matter of testimony, in what way soever we will be witnesses to God,
> as that no man is a competent witnesse for God, not in his *preaching*,
> not in his *living*, not in his *dying*, (though he be a witnesse in the
> highest sense, that is, a *Martyr*) if he do not *know, upon what ground*,
> he sayes, or does, or suffers that.
>
> (4:5, p. 147, ll. 87–95)

John's speech testifying to Christ's role as 'the light', signifying faith
and grace, confirms the Baptist's role as martyr or witness. Donne
insists that it is only by testifying to the literal, tropological, and anagogical meanings of scripture, the word of God and the mission of
Christ, that one can reveal his or her own significance as a martyr.
Donne denies the name of martyr to the Catholics who were ex-
ecuted for their attempt to kill King James in the Gunpowder Plot in
1605, although

> these men ... proclaim themselves to be *Martyrs*, witnesses for Christ
> in the highest degree; I say still, the Devill may be a witnesse, but I
> ground not my Faith upon that Testimony: A competent witnesse
> must be an honest man. This competency *John Baptist* had, the good

opinion of good men; And then, he had the seale of all, *Missus est*, he had his Commission, *He was sent to beare witness of that Light*.

(4:5, p. 155, ll. 374–80)

Because the conspirators did not testify to the words of scripture or Christ, their actions on behalf of their conscience and faith cannot be sanctified with the name of martyrdom. Although Donne argues that 'Every Christian is a state, a common-wealth to *himselfe*, and in him, the *Scripture* is his *law*, and the *conscience* is his *Judge*' (4:8, p. 216, ll. 229–30), he specifies that the individual's acts and words must accord with the word of God.

The importance of Donne's understanding of John the Baptist as a biblical *figura* of the preacher appears in his repeated use of John 1:8 as the text of three sermons within less than a year from the day of his 'defense' of the *Directions for Preachers*, spoken at the command of King James on 15 September 1622. By using John 1:8 as the text of his sermons on 25 December 1621, 24 June 1622, and 13 October 1622, the only example of Donne's repeated use of a biblical text in his extant sermons, he speaks urgently of his concern with the duty and discourse of the preacher. He divides the text of John 1:8 among the three sermons in order to explicate the relation of three witnesses: Christ, the witness of God's grace (3.17), John the Baptist, the witness of Christ's mission (4.5), and the preacher, the witness and instrument of faith who provides testimony to the Church (4.8). The sermons trace the transmission of a divine commission to bear witness from Old Testament *figurae* to John the Baptist, Christ, and preachers in later history. Donne understands that he and his contemporaries are 'also joyned in Commission with *John*, and we *cry out* still to you' (4:8, p. 224, ll. 523–4). He explains that testimony of God's word is not only the duty but also the vehicle of the preacher. For this reason, he defines the role of John and the preacher as both '*Testem*, and *Testimonium*, the *person*, and the *Office*; first, *who* the witnesse is, and then *what* he witnesses' (4:5, p. 145, ll. 9–11). Donne equates the words of Scripture and the role of the preacher in a manner similar to the discussion of John's testimony in Renaissance books of rhetoric. Henry Peacham's *Garden of Eloquence* cites John the Baptist as an example of the orator's means of confirming 'something by his own experience ... [speaking] of things removed from the knowledge of his hearers, and [alleging] his own testimony, grounded upon his own knowledge. ...'[17] To John Donne the rhetorical use of *testatio* or *martyria* as inartificial proof complements its special theological function as the use of language to voice his knowledge of the Divine *Logos* and thereby encourage others to 'bear witness for Christ'. According to Donne's explication, it was John the Baptist's speech as well as his act of 'laying down his life for the Truth ... that made him a witnesse, in the highest sense, a *Martyr*' (4:5, p. 160, ll. 568–9).

In his sermons defining the particular significance of John's speech and conduct, Donne emphasises 'that *John Baptists* Martyrdome, was not for the *fundamentall rock*, the body of the *Christian religion*, but for a *morall truth*, for matter of *manners*. A man may be bound to suffer much, for a lesse matter than the utter overthrow, of the whole frame and body of religion' (4:5, p. 160, ll. 572–6). This facet of John's act, his death testifying to the meaning of a tenet rather than the entire doctrine of Christianity, weighed heavily upon Donne during his sermon spoken in defence of the king's legal dictates prohibiting preachers to fulfil their divine commission to explicate Christian doctrine. Indeed, the sermon on 13 October 1622, following his defence of the king's ordinance, insists that 'the testimony of the messenger of God, the *preacher*, crying according to Gods ordinance' (4:8, p. 211, ll. 45–6) must obey divine rather than secular directions. Donne expounds the duty of the preacher as an obligation 'not to preach *our selves, but Christ Jesus*; not to preach for admiration, but for edification; not to preach to advance *civill ends*, without *spirituall ends*; to promote all the way the peace of all *Christian Kingdomes*, but to refer all principally to the Kingdome of peace, and the King of peace, the God of heaven' (4:8, p. 231, ll. 781–5). He dissociates civic concerns from the divine commission of the preacher that can only be fulfilled by testifying to the message of the Gospel. He uses the *figura* of John the Baptist as an exemplum for the preacher who must not deny his divine commission but provide 'Testimony; we confesse, and deny not, and say plainly, That our *own parts*, our *owne passions*, the purpose of great persons, the purpose of any State, is not Christ; we *preach Christ Jesus, and him crucified*; and whosoever preaches any other Gospell, or any other thing for Gospell, let him be accursed' (4:8, p. 231, ll. 787–91). By identifying the language of the preacher with testimony of Christ's Gospel, Donne suggests that 'God's Word' must supersede and, if necessary, transgress legal ordinances such as the king's secular *Directions for Preachers*.

Knowing that the king would censor and suppress any open disavowal of his right to restrict the clergy's words, Donne, in the

presence of King James on 15 September 1622, relies upon the use
of inartificial proof and the omission of biblical *figurae* to express
his intended meaning. The rhetorical amplification and high style of
the sermon distracts the auditor from the argument relating the legal
ordinance and the biblical text. In order to circumvent the ordinance against commentary about the king's jurisdiction, Donne
chooses an ambiguous and unusual text, Judges 5:20: 'They fought
from Heaven; The stars in their courses fou؛ht against Sisera.' This
prooftext affirming loyalty to God as the primary requirement for a
nation's security may be interpreted as an allegorical statement
confirming obedience either to a divinely appointed king or to
God's word. Donne leaves his position in regard to obedience to the
king's *Directions for Preachers* ambiguous; however, his auditors
may have suspected the reasons for his circumlocution. A contemporary who published a pamphlet under the pseudonym Tom Tell-
Troath advised King James, 'though there be orders given to preach
nothing but "court-divinity", yet a man may easily perceive by the
very choice of their texts and the very tears in their eyes that if they
durst they would speak their consciences'.[18] Tom Tell-Troath knows
that only his anonymity, protecting him from the king's proclamations limiting speech, allows such 'a free discourse touching the
manners of the time', a liberty unavailable to a preacher speaking
publicly at the king's command.[19]

Donne's sermon preached in explication of King James's
Directions for Preachers depends upon the testimony of biblical and
patristic prooftexts, examples of inartificial proof, to fulfil his divine
commission to speak the Word of the Gospel while defending a
legal ordinance that not only excludes testimony concerning Christ's
message of election and grace but also prescribes juridical subjects
external to the Bible. Throughout the first division of the sermon,
the literal explication of the biblical text, Donne employs biblical
and patristic texts to define the purpose and method of preachers. In
a passage dense with scriptural and patristic evidence, Donne commences with the example and words of Christ concerning

> Preaching, He himselfe was anointed for that, *The Spirit of the Lord is
> upon me, because the Lord hath anointed mee to preach*: His unction
> was his function. Hee was anointed with that power, and hee hath
> anointed us with part of his owne unction: *All power is given unto
> me*, says he, *in Heaven and in Earth*; and therefore (as he adds there)
> *Go ye, and preach*: Because I have all power, for preaching, take yee
> part of my power, and preach too. For, Preaching is *the power of*

God unto Salvation, and the savour of life unto life. When therefore the *Apostle* saies, *Quench not the Spirit, Nec in te, nec in alio*, say *Aquinas*; Quench it not in your selfe, by forbearing to heare the Word preached, quench it not in others, by discouraging them that doe preach. For so Saint *Chrysostome*, (and not he alone) understood that place, *That they quench the spirit, who discountenance preaching, and dishearten Preachers*.

(4:7, p. 195, ll. 568–81)

The cumulative evidence of the prooftexts testifying to the Divine *Logos*, the words not only of the apostles Matthew and Mark but also of patristic exegetes such as Aquinas and Chrysostom, intimates that the power and commission of the preacher are divinely given and beyond restrictions imposed by legal decrees and limitations. By concluding this passage with the observation, 'Preaching then being *Gods Ordinance*, to beget Faith, to take away preaching, were to disarme *God*, and to quench the spirit; for by that *Ordinance, he fights from heaven*' (4:7, p. 195, ll. 590–2), Donne confirms his divine commission rather than his civic obligations to the king's ordinance.

Donne equivocates in his acknowledgement of the jurisdiction of civil ordinances used to determine the minister's orders and fix a 'constant course of conteyning Subjects in their Religious and Civill duties, by preaching' (4:7, p. 194, ll. 559–61). He argues that preachers must speak the words of the Gospel as 'onely *God* ordain'd. ... Christ when he sent his *Apostles*, did not give them a particular command, *Ite orate,* goe and pray in the publique Congregation ... he onely said, *Sic orabitis*, Not go, and pray, but, *when you pray, pray thus*, he instructed them in the forme' (4:7, p. 194, ll. 561–7). Throughout the first section of the sermon, the literal explication of the biblical text, Donne emphasises that 'Preaching is *Gods* ordinance' (4:7, p. 192, l. 480), a divine command that indicates Christian conduct in both civil and religious matters. By means of the use of biblical texts, Donne affirms that the preacher must pronounce the words of Scripture in his devotions according to the forms and order prescribed by the examples of Christ and the apostles rather than those ordained by secular laws.

Donne abandons the use not only of biblical *figurae* but also of scriptural and patristic texts as witnesses in the second section of the sermon concerning the king's legal ordinance. Ambivalence characterises his defence of the subjects and forms of worship prescribed and prohibited by King James. The only witness quoted as evidence of a king's ecclesiastical authority is Aquinas, whose statement, '*Ordo semper dicitur ratione principii: Order alwayes presumes a head'* (4:7, p. 198, ll. 707–8), alludes, in Donne's usage, to King James's position as 'Head of the Church'. The tenuous basis for the application of the biblical text of the sermon, Judges 5:20, to the subject of the *Directions for Preachers* is evident in the paucity of patristic, scriptural, and personal testimony used in the five pages of exegesis developing this subject. The unusually limited testimony offered for the juridical statement against 'disorderly preaching' undercuts Donne's statements seeming to approve these prohibitions controlling religious discourse. By only citing examples of emperors and kings who previously had prescribed and augmented religious doctrine, Donne confines King James's authority and decree within a context of civil and secular jurisdiction.

It is significant that Donne prefaces to the application of the biblical text to the secular ordinance an adamant statement of the relation of civil and divine authority in the Church: 'a true *Christian* will never make *Contrarieties in fundamentall things indifferent*, never make foundations, and superedifications, the Word of *God*, and the Traditions of men, all one' (4:7, pp. 193–4, ll. 527–30). This passage speaks of the importance of differentiating true and fundamental doctrines by intimating the need to dissociate divine decrees from human dictates, such as King James's *Directions for Preachers*. Although Donne performs the sermon in obedience to secular, legal directions, as a 'godly' preacher, he commences the application of his text with his testimony not for civil and secular laws but only for fundamental religious doctrine; he affirms, in 'these proceedings ... I was not willing only, but glad to have my part therein, that as, in the feare of God, I have alwayes preached to you the *Gospell of Christ Jesus*, who is the *God* of your Salvation; So in the testimony of a good conscience, I might now preach to you, *the Gospell of the Holy ghost*, who is the *God of peace*, of unitie, and concord' (4:7, pp. 201–2, ll. 823–8). To define the subject and purpose of his testimony, Donne specifies only his intention to clarify Christian doctrine and Christ's directions for preachers.

Donne used similar means to circumvent secular restrictions and communicate his intended meaning when his sermon was printed at the king's command. In a dedicatory epistle addressed 'To the Right Honourable, George, Marquesse of Buckingham', Donne explained to the reader: *'For the first part of the* Sermon, *the* Explication *of the* Text, *my profession, and my Conscience is warant enough, that I have spoken as the* Holy Ghost *intended. For the second part, the*

Application *of the Text, it wil be warrant enough, that I have spoken as his Majestie intended, that your* Lordship *admits it to issue in your Name*' (4:7, pp. 178–9). Although Donne acknowledges his responsibility for the literal exegesis of the scriptural text, he divorces himself from its application to the king's *Directions for Preachers* by publishing this section of the sermon under the well-known names of its witnesses, Buckingham and King James. By means of rhetorical proof, Donne removes himself from the duty of testifying on behalf of the king's ecclesiastical jurisdiction in the printed text of the sermon.

Earlier in his career, Donne had warned the Church not 'To sin Grammatically, to tie sins together in construction, in a Syntaxis, in a chaine, and dependance, and coherence upon one another' (1:4, p. 225, ll. 94–6) by using language to augment or question doctrine.[20] He does not, however, avoid heterodox words that allow him to 'finde the voice and tongue of God, though in the mouth of the Devill, and his instruments' (10:4, p. 111, ll. 284–5). Through the secular ordinance and commands of King James, Donne, who confesses that he has 'beene ever kept awake in the meditation of Martyrdome', confirms the Bible to be the source of authority governing religious discourse.[21] He circumvents secular restrictions appropriating the authority and use of language by using biblical *figurae* and texts not only as rhetorical proof but also as exempla of a particular form of religious discourse, *martyria* or testimony. The setting and iconography of Paul's Cross where Donne spoke his sermon concerning the *Directions for Preachers* emphasised the veiled meaning of Donne's words. The 'Pulpit Crosse of timber, mounted upon steppes of stone, and covered with leade', an icon sanctifying the urban setting at Paul's Cathedral for religious services, visually reinforced Donne's role as a martyr whose speech effects the Word of the Gospel.[22] Standing within a pulpit representing the cross upon which Christ was martyred, Donne's sermon revealed the means of 'delivering our selves to Martyrdome, for the testimony of [Christ's] name, and advancing his glorie'.[23]

From *ELH*, 56 (1989), 293–309.

NOTES

[Nancy Wright's essay politicises and historicises the poststructuralist emphasis upon the volatile nature of language by drawing on Michel Foucault's insistence upon the inseparability of discourse from power.

Focusing in particular upon religious discourse, Wright argues that despite the attempts made by figures of authority, such as James I, to regulate the language of religion, the Jacobean period was one of linguistic and religious instability. Donne's sermons themselves contributed towards this state of de-regulation, by privileging the preacher's individual testimony to the Word of God over monarchial mediations of it. In Donne's reorientation of authoritative religious discourse, official uses of analogy, which perceived a likeness between God and monarch, are redeployed to empower an alternative correspondence between God and preacher.

Wright's essay further extends the range of genres discussed in the collection, and shows how texts beyond the orbit of those usually considered to be literary, and therefore deserving of close scrutiny, can be interestingly and provokingly read. The issues which Wright sees religion as raising, of language, authority, subjective testimony, and the role of analogy, also intersect with the concerns of several of the other essays (but see, in particular, William Kerrigan's). In terms of theoretical perspective, Wright's politicised and historicised poststructuralism may be usefully contrasted with Rajan's rather different application of similar theoretical insights. For further discussion and contextualisation of Wright's essay, see Introduction, pp. 19–20. Ed.]

I would like to thank Professors Heather Ross Asals and Paolo Valesio for their interest and suggestions concerning this article.

1. Friedrich Nietzsche, 'Twilight of the Idols', in *Twilight of the Idols and the Anti-Christ*, trans. R. J. Hollingdale (1968; rpt. Harmondsworth, 1983), p. 38. See Hollingdale's discussion of Nietzsche's ideas about language in Appendix C, pp. 190–1.

2. Michel Foucault, 'The Discourse on Language', in *The Archaeology of Knowledge*, trans. A. M. Sheridan-Smith (New York, 1972), pp. 216, 226.

3. Millar MacLure, *The Paul's Cross Sermons, 1534–1642* (Toronto, 1958), p. 123.

4. Quoted in E. M. W. Tillyard, *The Elizabethan World Picture* (New York, 1973), p. 88.

5. *The Political Works of James I*, ed. Charles H. McIlwain (Cambridge, MA, 1918), p. 283; Foucault, 'The Discourse on Language', p. 220.

6. Quoted in Christopher Hill, *The World Turned Upside Down* (Harmondsworth, 1975), p. 98.

7. William Whitaker, *A Disputation on Holy Scripture*, ed. William Fitzgerald (Cambridge, 1849), pp. 279–80.

8. *King James I His Letter and Directions to the Lord Archbishop of Canterbury; Concerning Preaching and Preachers...* (Thomas Walkeley, 16[2]2), 2. See the editors' discussion of sermons referring to King James's

foreign policy in *The Sermons of John Donne*, ed. George R. Potter and Evelyn M. Simpson, 10 vols (Berkeley and Los Angeles, 1959), 4:22–34. Throughout this essay, references to this edition of Donne's sermons will be identified in the text by volume, sermon, page, and line number.

9. Donne explains this understanding of liturgical speech acts in his commentary upon 'This present word, *Now*, [it] denotes an Advent, a new coming, or a new operation, other then it was before. ... It is an extensive word, *Now*; for though we dispute whether this *Now*, that is, whether an instant be any part of time or no, yet in truth it is all time; for whatsoever is past, was, and whatsoever is future, shall be in an instant; and did and shall fall within this *Now*' (2:12, p. 250, ll. 6–13). On the origins of the concept of the *nunc stans* in the writings of Boethius and Augustine, see J. G. A. Pocock, *The Machiavellian Moment* (Princeton, NJ, 1975), p. 7.

10. Richard K. Fenn, *Liturgies and Trials: The Secularization of Religious Language* (New York, 1982), p. 35.

11. Kenneth Burke, *The Rhetoric of Religion: Studies in Logology* (Berkeley and Los Angeles, 1970), p. 1.

12. Thomas Blundeville, *The Arte of Logike*, facsimile edn (Menston, 1967), p. 3. On the relation of logic and rhetoric in English Renaissance poetry, see Rosemond Tuve, *Elizabethan and Metaphysical Imagery* (Chicago, 1947) and Heather Ross Asals, *Equivocal Predication: George Herbert's Way to God* (Toronto, 1981).

13. John Donne, 'A Litany X *The Martyrs*', *John Donne: The Complete English Poems*, ed. A. J. Smith (1971; rpt. Harmondsworth, 1980), p. 320. All quotations of Donne's poems are taken from this edition.

14. Aristotle, *The Categories*, trans. H. P. Cook, Loeb Classical Library (Cambridge, 1938), p. 13.

15. Aristotle, *The 'Art' of Rhetoric*, ed. J. H. Freese, Loeb Classical Library (London and New York, 1926), 1.15.13–15.

16. On the etymology of *martyria* see *A Greek-English Lexicon of the New Testament*, ed. W. F. Arndt and F. W. Gingrich (Chicago, 1957), pp. 493–6.

17. Henry Peacham, *The Garden of Eloquence* (London, 1577), p. 85.

18. 'Tom Tell-Troath Or a free discourse touching the manners of the time', *Complaint and Reform in England, 1436–1714*, ed. A. H. Dunham, Jr and S. Pargellis (New York, 1938), p. 483. Donne's sermon on 15 September 1622 is his only sermon on a text from Judges.

19. 'Tom Tell-Troath', p. 481.

20. See Heather Ross Asals, 'John Donne and the Grammar of Redemption', *English Studies in Canada*, 5 (1978), 125–39, and *John Donne and the Theology of Language*, ed. P. G. Stanwood and Heather Ross Asals (Columbia, MO, 1986), pp. 69–71.

21. John Donne, *Pseudo-Martyr*, facsimile edn (New York, 1974), sig. 1.

22. John Stow, *Survey of London*, quoted from *The Sermons of John Donne*, 4.1. On the significance of such an icon, see Richard C. Trexler's study of the Renaissance concept of urban space as a land-scape lacking sacred places found in the natural environment, 'Ritual Behavior in Renaissance Florence: The Setting', *Medievalia et Humanistica: Studies in Medieval and Renaissance Culture*, n.s. 4 (1973), 125–44.

23. Donne, *Pseudo-Martyr*, ch. 1, p. 4.

10

The Fearful Accommodations of John Donne

WILLIAM KERRIGAN

Critics of John Donne have marked a peculiar violence in his sensibility not to be dissociated from the 'boldness' and 'daring' of his conceits. Among readers of the divine poems in particular this intemperate temperament has become an object of controversy. Qualities that made Donne a love poet of sublime egotism also, for some critics, damaged his religious verse irreparably; 'The "Holy Sonnets" and the "Hymns"', argues a suspicious Douglas Bush, 'are focused, like the love poems, on a particular moment and situation, on John Donne, and the rest of life and the world is blacked out, does not exist.'[1] Moreover, the agoraphobic playfulness and unrelieved ingenuity so appealing in the context of human love have seemed less suitable to the doctrines of the Christian faith. It is one thing to run circles of wit about the straight-line orthodoxy of Petrarchan love poets, quite another to bend the cherished corners of dogma. Poems such as 'Batter my heart' and 'Show me deare Christ' may appear desperately inventive, the work of a histrionic convert who 'has to stimulate his awareness of God by dwelling on the awfulness of God'.[2] Like other Renaissance poets whose devotional verse has been assailed, Donne has been defended by scholars assuming (however implicitly) that negative evaluations are directed, whether by ignorance or design, against the religion itself. Louis Martz and Helen Gardner, locating a tradition of formal meditation intended to achieve sensual immediacy, interior drama, and intense emotion, have disarmed objections by subtly disarming the poems, revealing those idiosyncratic, 'tasteless' moments in the religious verse as the respectable, if passionate, consequences of devout contemplation.[3] Still, many readers – all those, in fact, who find in the tastelessness of Donne either the sure measure of his limitation or the problematic force of his greatness – will sympathise with the hesitations of Frank Kermode, who writes of 'Show me deare Christ': 'Perhaps we dislike this metaphor (Christ as *mari complaisant*) because the image of the Church as the Bride is no longer absolutely commonplace; but having accepted the image we are still unwilling to accept its development, even though we see that the main point is the *glorious* difference of this from a merely human marriage. Something is asked of us we can no longer easily give. Many of the Holy Sonnets have this perilous balance; their wit is always likely to seem indelicate as well as passionate.'[4] The 'we' of this passage is more just than it might first appear, for the great ambivalent power of Donne's sonnet depends on how, as the marital conceit develops toward holy adultery, the 'me' of the first line becomes the 'our sights' and 'most men' of the sestet, thus implicating readers in the express desire to woo the spouse of Christ.[5] The poem has been designed to force 'us' to participate in the alarming extension of a traditional metaphor. Drawn into uneasy complicity with the speaker, readers may find the '*glorious* difference' less compelling than the inglorious similarity.

The Ignatian exercises evoked to explain these violations of taste are in reality one minor consequence of the major theological problem of anthropomorphism. As we cannot conceive of God except in terms conceivable to a human mind, our apprehension of a timeless, infinite, unsearchably wise deity must be anthropomorphic to one degree or another – as, arguably, must all our apprehensions. ...

Christian theologians debated similar issues, distinguishing anthropomorphism as the emotional need of individual believers from anthropomorphism as the necessary condition of theological knowledge. Recognising the two directions implied by this discrimination, we may draw a useful line between those rational beings who keep always before them the difference between God as he is known and God as he is, and those more passionate for whom, in the ecstasies of devotion, the difference between a heavenly father and an earthly father tends to disappear. It is precisely the trespass of this fine line that complicates our response to 'Show me deare Christ'. For what disturbs Kermode, and what has disturbed critics of 'Batter my heart', is Donne's eagerness to display the most anthropomorphic consequences of anthropomorphism – in short, to imagine with some detail the sexuality of God. Approving the theological tenor, we suspect the anthropomorphic vehicle. Perhaps the Ignatian exercises, with their extraordinary reliance on the power of corporeal images, promoted unsettling formulations of this kind. But these impressive poems appropriately raise the larger question of how and why Donne thought of man while thinking of God. ...

Donne the preacher exhibited obvious delight in the imaginative consequences of accommodation. Excoriating the sins of pride, he undertook a curious digression proving that God, who is 'often by the Holy Ghost invested, and represented in the qualities and affections of man' in order 'to constitute a familiarity and commerce between man and God', never once submitted to the Satanic vice of pride.[6] God did, however, accept some other deadly ones, appearing in various passages of the Bible as slothful, prodigal, angry, vindictive, and drunk. Whenever 'those inordinate and irregular passions and perturbations, excesses and defects of man, are imputed to God', it is solely 'for the better applying of God to the understanding of man' (2:288). But this 'better applying' made God terrible even as it rendered Him comprehensible. Preaching on the 'terrible things' of Psalm 65.5, Donne argued that to preserve the 'stupendious, reverend, mysterious' aspects of worship, the Holy Spirit called us 'to all Acts, and Exercises of Religion' with fearful obscurity; 'terrible things' include both the promises of judgement and the 'Visions' or 'Similitudes' of the Bible that convey these promises (7:314). The Christian knowledge of God, 'a nearer approximation' than that of any other religion, dazzles beyond mere love: 'And therefore, the love of God, which is so often proposed unto us, is as often seasoned with the feare of God; nay, all our Religious affections are reduced to that one, To a reverentiall feare; If he be a Master, he cals for *feare*, and, If he be a Father, he calls for *honour*, and honour implies a reverentiall feare' (7:316). In effect, Donne has annihilated any distinction between the deliberate obscurity of prophetic visions and the deliberate simplicity of anthropomorphic metaphors. Both sorts of biblical language require, in his summary phrase, 'an awfull discrimination of Divine things from Civill' (7:316). The transference of temporal words to an eternal deity compels all Christians to 'make a difference' (7:314) in the meanings of those words. Yet from the convergence of familiar and divine significance arises 'a reverentiall feare' that seasons all our 'Religious affections'.

The consequences of this association between scriptural metaphor and reverent fear may be traced throughout the *Sermons*. Unquestionably Donne enjoyed imitating the 'third heavens of hyperboles' he so admired in the Bible. Addressing God in his *Devotions*, he wrote: 'all profane authors seem of the seed of the serpent that creeps, thou art the Dove that flies.'[7] But there was a terror in this appreciation. Often he wrenched his exegesis in the direction of the awesome, the unimaginable, the forbidden. He contrived, in a tone somewhere between delight and dread, the 'awful discrimination' of the human from the divine. Thus Donne on Jeremiah 9.1: 'It was God that was their Father, and it is God, their God that slew them; but yet, that God, their Father weepes over the slaughter. So in the person of Esay, God weepes again, I will bewaile thee with weeping, and I will water thee with teares. ... As though God had contracted an Irregularity, by having to do in a cause of blood, He sighs, he weeps when he must draw blood from them' (7:243). The passage winds up grief to a mysteriousness. Choosing to recognise God as a 'Father' at this moment, Donne formulates an 'irregular' situation – a father who, having murdered his children, mourns and vows revenge. Yet Donne remains well aware that his propositions cannot mean what, seemingly, they must mean. 'As though God had contracted an Irregularity. ...' It was left to the congregation to 'make a difference' between perverse human grief and impeccable divine grief.

The accommodated metaphor which Donne presented with unique force was that of God as lover or loved one. 'God is *Love*, and the Holy Ghost is amorous in his *Metaphors*' (7:87). He was most amorous, of course, in the Song of Songs. Luther, though careful to distinguish the historical from the allegorical sense, complimented the ancient interpretation of this book as the spiritual courtship of Christ and the church. The notion was 'delightful', 'ingenious and full of comfort': 'Let those who want to devise allegories follow this lead. ...'[8] Taking this advice, Donne found a brother in the example of Solomon: '... Solomon, whose disposition was amorous, and excessive in the love of women, when he turn'd to God, He departed not utterly from his old phrase and language, but having put a new, and spiritual tincture, and form and habit into all his thoughts, he conveys all his loving approaches and applications to God, and all Gods gracious answers to his amorous soul, into songs, and Epithalamions, and meditates upon contracts, and marriages between God and his Church, and between God and his Soul ...' (1:237). Of the many passages of 'old phrase and language' in the sermons of this reformed lover, the most revealing is the sermon of 1621 on Psalm 2.12, 'Kisse the Son, lest he be angry'. Now, the sanctification of a kiss in scriptural metaphor might not seem so bold an accommodation. Earthly experience, as we know, offers numerous instances of the asexual kiss – the sisterly, the chaste, the hurried – and Donne began by admitting that a lustless kiss was, in biblical times, a sign of deference to authority. Yet in order that his text be as disquieting as possible, Donne soon dropped the Psalmist's kiss into the depths of lewdness:

> They mistake the matter much, that thinke all adultery is below the girdle: A man darts out adultery with his eye, in a wanton look; and he wraps up adultery with his fingers, in a wanton letter; and he breaths in an adultery with his lips, in a wanton kisse. But though this act of love, be so defamed both wayes, by treachery, by licentiousness, Yet God chooses this Metaphore, he bids us *Kisse the Sonne*. It is a true, and an usefull Rule, that ill men have been Types of Christ, and ill actions figures of good: Much more, may things not ill in themselves, though deflected and distorted to ill, be restored to good againe; and therefore doth God, in more than this one place, expect our love in a kisse; for, if we be truly in love with Him, it will be a holy and an acceptable Metaphore unto us, els it will have a carnall and a fastidious taste.
>
> (3:318)

The unmistakable intent is to maximise the distance between a human and divine 'kiss', compelling listeners first to imagine carnal lust and then to imagine that lust 'restored to good againe'. When the sign of fleshly adultery becomes the sign of heavenly fidelity, this pure embrace will deflect the terrible divine wrath (3:324). But the word 'kiss', stretched with such tension between two diverse significations, almost snaps into incoherence. What might a kiss be without the desire to touch another's flesh intimately? Of what use is this accommodated metaphor? All the imaginative energy goes into evoking the carnal kiss of this world, while the sanctified kiss is defined solely by negation. The effect is bewilderment. Dividing the love we know from the love we should know, Donne has invested the imperative to kiss with a fear all its own – as if to think of kissing Christ with any carnal taint were to risk the consequences of 'lest he be angry'. In Holy Sonnet XIX Donne compared his 'prophane love' to his divine, judging his efforts to 'court God' less healthy for his spirit than to 'quake with true feare of his rod': 'Those are my best dayes, when I shake with feare.' Yet in the sermon on 'Kisse the Son', as in the poems I will consider next, love and fear are contraries that 'meete in one'.

Joan Webber has shown that Donne, in common with other Renaissance theologians, understood the verses of the Bible as 'enfolding' significance. In preaching manuals the word 'opening' referred to the division and interpretation of the text; the preacher merely exposed or dilated meanings assumed to be already present, though compressed, in the Bible itself. A sacred metaphor, like a seed bearing a tree, contained the full extension of its vehicle and the consequences of that extension for its tenor.[9] Perhaps this conception may help to describe that special way with conceits which we designate 'metaphysical wit', indicating how Jack Donne became Dr Donne without changing his habits of mind. For the way Donne presented the conventional metaphors of love poetry was exactly analogous to the way he 'unraveled' or 'opened' the sacred conceits of his sermons. In 'The Broken Heart', for example, Donne constructed an elaborate metaphor to describe his failure with a certain cold lady. His scorned heart shivers like glass. But where is it now? She has refused the heart, so its pieces must still reside in his breast: as a broken mirror shows many little faces instead of one large face, so his heart cannot love anymore, but only reflect lesser images in liking, wishing, and adoring. The poem unravels, unfolds, discloses, and displays what already exists, compressed in the hoary cliché 'You broke my heart'. Donne reinvigorated this dead trope by assuming its literal truth and proceeding to complicate the tenor (his relationship with the lady) to fit the extended vehicle (the broken mirror). In a sense, the witty developments of the poem pre-exist in the initial cliché, folded up in the weave of convention and waiting there for a curious expositor. Donne did not open the vehicle to include, or the tenor to respond to, the sweeping of shards, seven years bad luck, or the purchase of a new glass – but there was nothing in his method, no restraint in theory, to prevent him from doing so.[10]

Similarly, the disturbing rape in the last line of 'Batter my heart' should be understood as implicit in the ancient theological conceit of the righteous soul's marriage to God.[11] If the good man weds God, then the sinful man weds God's 'enemie', and if God would claim this recalcitrant soul, then he must grant divorce and possess her by force. Given Donne's conception of sacred metaphor, the accommodated marriage would enfold infidelity, divorce, and even imprisonment. It would compress all the things which attend earthly marriages, the only ones we know and the only ones our language can properly signify. More specifically, it may be appropriate to mention, but absurd to continue mentioning, that Donne was in fact imprisoned by the father of his bride and that this poem resembles, with interesting shifts of identity and reattributions of virtue, the drama of his own marriage:

> Batter my heart, three person'd God; for, you
> As yet but knocke, breathe, shine, and seeke to mend;
> That I may rise, and stand, o'erthrow mee, 'and bend
> Your force, to breake, blowe, burn and make me new.
> I, like an usurpt towne, t'another due,
> Labour to'admit you, but Oh, to no end,
> Reason your viceroy in mee, mee should defend,
> But is captiv'd, and proves weake or untrue,
> Yet dearely'I love you, and would be lov'd faine,
> But am bethroth'd unto your enemie,
> Divorce mee, 'untie, or breake that knot againe,
> Take mee to you, imprison mee, for I
> Except you'enthrall mee, never shall be free,
> Nor ever chast, except you ravish mee.

To be sure, the poem is not so daring as it might have been. The phrase 'three person'd God', for example, identifies the male lover addressed in Trinitarian terms, themselves derived by accommodation from the earthly family.[12] I suppose that John Donne, in a certain mood, might have considered naming the holy lover as the 'father' of this hapless bride and played out the grotesque results in allusions to incest – but Donne, thankfully, was not Crashaw. Nevertheless, 'Batter my heart' does suggest by implication the details of its final phrase.

Though often described as a poem with three conceits of equal importance developed in successive quatrains, really the poem evolves from and toward a single metaphor. For the bride addressing her lover, equated to the soul addressing God, is the implicit situation throughout – unless we are to believe that suddenly and ridiculously, with the phrase 'Yet dearely'I love you', our speaker changes sex. Revealed with increasing clarity from l.9 to l.14, the figurative terms of this address are assumed in the 'heart' of the opening line and continue to be assumed in the formal simile of the second quatrain. Thus the actual tenor of 'Batter my heart' and 'like an usurpt towne' is not, as in the usual reading, an experience of conversion. These subsidiary conceits have primary reference to the love relationship, itself an accommodated vehicle for the spiritual life of the soul, and during most of the poem the true sense of this crucial primary reference is left unsettled.

So clear as vehicle and so loose as tenor, the language of the first two tropes is purposefully dislocated. This speaker would have her heart reformed by the tinker's tools. But what exactly is she inviting from 'three person'd God' when the terms of tinkering are translated to the terms of love? It will not suffice to recall the emblem tradition, where muscular arms wielding various tools reached from the clouds to batter or burn the miraculously suspended heart of the Christian Everyman, for the heart of this poem belongs to a misguided bride: the 'emblem', if such it is, must be reshaped within the figures of another and controlling 'emblem'.[13] The simile of the 'usurpt towne' would appear to be clearer, at least in its reference to the interior betrayal of 'weake or untrue' reason, since these words provide a semantic link between political intrigue and amorous infidelity. But 'Labour to'admit you' implies that 'three person'd God' is there at the gates, besieging the 'usurpt towne' in the person of a monarch reclaiming his territory. We must contend once again with the activity desired of the lover who is, in this second subsidiary trope, a warfaring king. What do the propositions of the second quatrain mean when transferred, as they must be transferred, to the love relationship? The language hovers, referentially uncertain, until fixed upon the desired event of the final line. There drama and definition coincide. 'That I may rise, and stand, o'erthrow mee', 'breake, blowe, burn and make me new', and 'Labour to'admit you' – the drifting metaphors of the poem strike anchor in that ravishment which would make the speaker newly 'chaste'.

The root problem in interpreting this sonnet is not whether its tripartite development conceals some allusion to the Trinity. Probably it does. What readers must confront, as fearlessly or fearfully as the poem itself, is the way Donne has unbalanced his central equation by choosing to detail the physical violation. Though metaphors be equations, we do not understand them as such: one term of this conceit must have linguistic, philosophical, and psychological priority and be, as we say, the theme, subject, or motive of the poem. Because of the personified 'Reason', because 'three person'd God' is named as the lover, we recognise that sexual rape is here a metaphor for the forcible entrance of the deity into an otherwise impenetrable soul. But the design of the poem grants extraordinary emphasis to the penetration of a tight body. Insofar as the tropes reach out of local context to describe the climactic invitation, that sexual event acquires the force of a tenor. The intercourse of the speaker and God becomes virtually a 'real' presence in the poem, a final repository of reference – the shore on which the gathering wave of implication finally breaks. Donne has turned his anthropomorphic conceit toward actual event, generating what might be termed a 'cumulative metaphor'. As the tinkering and the besieging express a desire for renewal and reclamation, looking forward to the ravishment, so do the very instruments and objects of attack progress logically toward the sexual. A paradigm of this linguistic mobility, the opening phrase undergoes successive redefinitions. 'Batter my heart' is addressed first to God the tinker, then becomes doubly applicable to the warrior God of ll. 5 and 6. She would 'admit' the just ruler, but to 'no end': by inference she wishes the monarch to reclaim his city with some 'battering' engine of war, most likely a battering ram. Finally she 'would be lov'd faine', though her heart is hard and her gates are closed, and the initial phrase becomes synonymous with the plea for ravishment, *heart* being not uncommon as a slang word for *vagina* during this period. The commands of the poem proceed through a series of transformations in assaulter and thing assaulted. The vehicles of her wishes flow together. The battered heart becomes the attacked city which becomes the ravished vagina. The tinker's tools become the monarch's engine which becomes, indeed, the penis of God. Donne's accumulation of assaults and batteries rests precisely there. We have the effect, in psychoanalytical terms, of moving from sublimation to cathexis or, in theological terms, of moving from relatively 'safe' accommodations – God the tinker, God the king – to a 'dangerous' accommodation made all the more evocative by the scheme of the movement itself. Donne has contrived a most 'awful discrimination' of the human from the divine. Though all of sexuality, even prostatitis and moniliasis, may in theory lie folded within the ancient metaphor of spiritual marriage, Donne has opened a suggestiveness near to crude anthropomorphism. And crude anthropomorphism is another name for outright blasphemy.

Recognising how overtly this poem dares the forbidden, we can appreciate the uncommon power of its closing paradox. The equation of ravishment and chastity deflects the perilous situation reached through the unravelling of accommodated love; having painted himself into a corner, Donne extricated himself by switching colours. We should eschew all interpretations that diminish the mystery of chaste ravishing. The word 'chaste' here does not denote Spenserian chastity, the sanctification of sexuality in lawful marriage. More to the point, if we must have analogues, are the legends of the hagiographical tradition, which often represent the restoration of innocence to fallen female saints, or the discussion early in *The City of God* of the ravished martyrs who retained their physical purity.[14] For as 'make me new' would suggest, 'nor ever chaste' concerns the recovery of virginity. Donne created this paradox by applying the traditional logic of accommodation. In Milton's formulation, we may participate without error in accommodated speech so long as 'weakness when viewed in reference to ourselves' is understood as 'most complete and excellent when imputed to God'. What does it mean when, in the unfolding of anthropomorphic metaphors, the God we believe to be perfect would appear to be irregular? When God himself takes on those qualities he would suppress in us? With the conviction that God is the author of goodness alone, one can only say that human imperfection has obscured divine perfection. But how can we understand divine perfection? Since we know only human perfection, we can indicate our recognition of the failure of accommodation by conflating earthly weakness with earthly virtue: we can reaccommodate the failed accommodation. Therefore the rape of 'Batter my heart' must preserve, rather than destroy, chastity. The God who violently ravishes must be the God who honourably abstains, the possessed soul a virgin soul. To escape from an irregular anthropomorphism, Donne introduces a 'complete and excellent' anthropomorphism, equating the imputed human vice to the appropriate and opposite human virtue. Anthropomorphism twice applied eludes anthropomorphism altogether. God, unlike any man, can be at once lustful and honourable. The soul, unlike any body, can be at once ravished and chaste. Beautifully calculated, the final line of 'Batter my heart' presents the word 'chaste' before 'ravish me', relaxing anxieties an instant before the revelation that focuses them. As we read the last phrase, the human act we comprehend has already been diverted to a superhuman paradox. All at once we see the base and the miraculous.

The strategy of 'Batter my heart' – approaching the forbidden, reaching a moment of dangerous anthropomorphism, deflecting that danger, just before the moment appears, with an equation between carnality and virtue – also informs 'Show me deare Christ'. Here the passionate speaker desires to enjoy the true church promised in the Bible, ending the miserable schisms of history.[15] In the accommodated terms of the poem, this desire becomes the eager sexuality of the 'amorous soule':

> Show me deare Christ, thy spouse, so bright and cleare.
> What, is it she, which on the other shore
> Goes richly painted? or which rob'd and tore
> Laments and mournes in Germany and here?
> Sleepes she a thousand, then peepes up one yeare?
> Is she selfe truth and errs? now new, now outwore?
> Doth she, 'and did she, and shall she evermore
> On one, on seaven, or on no hill appeare?
> Dwells she with us, or like adventuring knights
> First travaile we to seeke and then make love?
> Betray kind husband thy spouse to our sights,
> And let myne amorous soule court thy mild Dove,
> Who is most trew, and pleasing to thee, then
> When she'is embrac'd and open to most men.

Until the final three lines the revelation sought is only distantly sexual. The speaker wishes to view the 'bright and cleare' spouse in her radiant nakedness, not to possess her. Donne might have discontinued the unfolding of his conceit at the provocative but inexplicit 'Betray ... to our sights', since the word 'betray' carries a sexual implication neatly subordinate to its primary meaning as a synonym for 'Show' in l. 1. Moreover, the activity of seeing was itself invested with sexual significance in the classical optics Donne inherited. The word 'propagation' referred to the multiplication of the visual image in the spatial continuum between the object and the eye – seeing was making love to the world. 'Making babies' in Elizabethan slang denoted the mutual gaze of lovers. And certainly the Italianate love poetry of the sixteenth century had established gazing, glancing, glimpsing, peering, peeking, and peeping as a kind of sexual activity, a foreplaying near in effect to a consummation, electric as lightning and magnetic as the lodestone, sufficient to cause both orgasmic ecstasy and postvisual depression: Cupid's poets appreciated the many arrows in the quiver of an eye. However, as 'make love' in l. 10 foreshadows, the poem shifts from subdued implication to overt proposition. Much resembling the sweep toward ravishment in 'Batter my heart', there is a sense of inexorable progression in these lines, an unveiling of desire to match the unveiling desired.

The conceit of 'Show me deare Christ' extends beyond the tradition of its origin. In the common formulation the church is the bride of Christ, and by joining the church a man becomes metaphorically a woman; he becomes a 'member' of the earthly body of the bride. Whereas Donne accepted a figurative womanhood in 'Batter my heart', here he has made the marriage of the church a triangular affair by insisting on his actual, rather than symbolic, sexuality. Given this fundamental revision, the argument unfolds with pseudological exactitude. Because the church triumphant has yet to appear, Christ must be guarding his bride from other men; and because such jealousy is contrary to the true nature of Christ, he can be wooed into compliance with human wishes. So Christ is asked to become at last a 'kind husband', generously betraying his wife to his friends. She will please him 'most' when she is 'embrac'd and open to most men'. Reminiscent of many of the *Songs and Sonnets*, the wit of the concluding passage depends upon our ability to deduce the fallacious argument which must have preceded the statement before us. The doors of a church remain open; the more men who enter, the more pleased Christ is. Moving freely from object to concept and tenor to vehicle, the speaker offers a proposition admirable as religious desire but startling as sexual desire.

The bride of 'Batter my heart' wished to be penetrated by an eager male. The eager male of 'Show me deare Christ' wishes to possess an 'open' bride and he assumes the collective voice of 'most men', convincing the husband to permit this betrayal in the interests of his own pleasure. With 'a reverentiall feare' we again confront 'an awful discrimination of Divine things from Civill'. And again there is the balm of paradox. The bride is 'most trew' when most unfaithful: she is at one time 'selfe truth' and yet 'errs'. The husband finds her 'most ... pleasing' when human cuckolds find their wives most abhorrent: in her openness she will please him as a 'most trew' spouse. Just at the moment of its definition, twisted adultery, in accord with the principles of accommodated speech, becomes equated with exemplary fidelity.

The reversal from vice to virtue differs ever so subtly from that of 'Batter my heart', yet the difference is telling. For virginity and ravishment are forever incompatible on this earth. The conclusion of the earlier sonnet, anthropomorphically nonanthropomorphic, translates readers from the familiar life of the body to the inexpressible life of the soul. We approximate transcendence with the aid of a marvellous proportion: as ravishment is to the body, so chastity is to the soul. Similarly, no wife imaginable can be at once 'most trew' and 'open to most men'. Yet this wife has been imagined, to our exquisite amazement, and she seems worthy to be the wife of Christ. However, the second reversal of 'Show me deare Christ' does not escape from human categories. It is indeed possible for a human husband to consider his spouse 'most ... pleasing' when most untrue, and not only in the Darien, Connecticut, of modern America. Augustine put this case to his interlocutor in the dialogue *On Free Choice of the Will*:

> **Evodius** I know that adultery is an evil because I myself would be unwilling to allow adultery in the case of my wife. And whoever does to another what he does not wish done to himself, does evil.
>
> **Augustine** What if someone's lust is so great that he offers his own wife to another and willingly allows her to be seduced by the man with whose wife he in turn wants to have equal license? Don't you think that he does evil?
>
> **Evodius** Yes, the worst evil!
>
> **Augustine** By the rule you mentioned such a man does not sin, for he does nothing that he would not endure. You must find some other reason by which to prove that adultery is evil.[16]

Donne must find some other reason by which to prove that cuckoldry is miraculous. The Christ of the closing passage does not elude a recognisable and unhealthy human attitude. Donne has generated a paradox in the sense of 'a proposition contrary to orthodoxy' – for husbands pleased by infidelity are rare – but not a paradox in the sense of 'a proposition true but impossible'. We are left with an awful similarity rather than an awesome discrimination; the fine balance of danger and relief at the conclusion of 'Batter my heart' does not recur. I feel that this difficulty accounts for the lingering dissatisfaction of Frank Kermode and accounts indirectly for the popularity of Helen Gardner's interpretation of the sonnet, which turns attention away from the problems of ll. 10–14 to concentrate instead upon the theological and topical significance of ll. 1–9.[17] The last passage, beautiful as it is, nearly crumbles. Donne almost loses control of his reader's imagination and therefore of his intentional meaning. The lame paradox of 'and pleasing to thee, then' threatens to undermine the triumphant 'most trew', for if we can imagine a human *mari complaisant*, we can also imagine his willing wife. This activity pushes 'most trew' away from 'most faithful' toward 'most true to your desires'. By now the poem is close, too close, to the tactless exercises in accommodated devotion we find in Crashaw, daring with no sense of danger, creating neither mystery nor wit, but leaving us aghast at the combination of great verbal power, unquestioned faith, neurosis, and stupidity. We finish 'Show me deare Christ' with a twinge of the wrong sort of 'reverentiall feare.'

Human terms were the only ones he had. Donne could not conceive of God without discovering, somewhere in the folds of his conception, human vice. It may be objected that the two poems I have discussed do not unravel metaphors inherent in Christian theology; one may dismiss the religious implications of these fearful accommodations by supposing that Donne, acting out some private compulsion, deliberately generated the inessential images of God the rapist and Christ the willing cuckold. But consequences of anthropomorphism as grotesque as these lie coiled in the most central Christian doctrines. The *De ecclesiastica rhetorica* of Valerio, a popular manual for preachers, alerted its readers to this contingency by forbidding the wanton, though logical, 'opening' of doctrines such as the redemption:

> There are, however, many warnings which the orator must heed in the use of metaphors. First that they be not taken from remote things. ... Finally that they do not originate from anything unseemly, as when someone would call God the killer of Christ; for he commanded that he should die for the sins of men so that he satisfy by that death divine justice and open the gates of Heaven to believing men. He ought not for that reason to be called killer; and, in short, easy metaphors, taken from beautiful things and applied with judgement, which wise men have called the essence of prudence, illuminate the sermon.[18]

As a 'father' God raises his 'son' to a position of full equality. But as a 'father' God also requires the sacrificial murder of his 'son' to atone for our disobedience. Of course, to the extent that God the Father appears sadistic, to that extent he is not to be apprehended as a human being. When the metaphor turns perverse, God vacates the metaphor. Yet again, without the metaphor – and it is one sanctioned by the Bible, the exegetical tradition, the liturgy, and the prayers of many generations – we cannot think of God at all. It may be 'the essence of prudence' to confine oneself to 'easy metaphors'.

But there is, as Valerio realised, a dreadful logic to be avoided as we expound the most comforting doctrine of the Christian faith.

Donne was the one great poet of the English Renaissance to exploit the fearful consequences of accommodation in his devotional verse. Spenser, Herbert, Milton, and Marvell were careful to avoid imputing vice to God. When they unfolded anthropomorphic metaphors, they did so with evident caution. The Christ of Herbert's 'The Sacrifice' exhibits an inhuman sense of humour, but in comprehending his ironies we admire without qualification the intelligence and self-possession they imply. In the devotional lyrics of Herbert accommodated vice never remains, at the end of the poem, to trouble our conception of the God addressed, since by then all blasphemies have redounded upon the speaker. More comparable to Donne in this regard was Ben Jonson, whose lyric 'To Heaven' addresses God as an accommodated 'judge' dispensing something less than justice.[19] But Jonson did not, in the manner of his contemporary, emphasise the distance between true and false human judgement. Donne alone explored the difference between God as we know him and God as we must believe him to be, compelling us to recognise the conjunction of vice and virtue as the necessary condition of our knowledge of the deity. Accommodation for Donne was both our gift and our curse. He wrote of the two faces of God in his brilliant Holy Sonnet XIII, superimposing the compassionate Son upon the vengeful Father:

> Marke in my heart, O Soule, where thou dost dwell,
> The picture of Christ crucified, and tell
> Whether that countenance can thee affright,
> Teares in his eye quench the amasing light,
> Blood fills his frownes, which from his pierc'd head fell,
> And can that tongue adjudge thee unto hell,
> Which pray'd forgivenesse for his foes fierce spight?

Tears extinguish the fearful light, blood hides the frowns, the tongue of judgement prays for mercy – it is a lovely definition of the Atonement, the cancellation of Old Testament wrath by New Testament love. Christ incarnate perfected the accommodated speech of the Bible, embodying God in human form and leaving an example of unambiguous virtue in this life. Yet for Donne that other face remained, hidden rather than vanquished, and while a 'beauteous forme' could not 'affright', the contorted visage of a wrathful God was there to be imagined behind the face of compassion. The paradoxes of 'Batter my heart' and 'Show me deare Christ' re-enact, within the particular terms of their anthropomorphism, this concealment: behind chastity is violation, behind fidelity is adultery. Mysteriously, our love for God is linguistically and psychologically inextricable from our lust.

Within the context of Christian time the fearful accommodation of God to man presupposes a mythic history. The primal likeness between God and man was genuinely harmonious. There was no grotesquerie to complicate our prelapsarian knowledge of the deity, because there was no human evil – no rape, adultery, or murder. Adam in his garden, the unfallen image of God, could understand his divine 'father' or 'friend' without fear of unravelling an 'awful discrimination' from these metaphors.[20] That first disobedience, defacing man, inevitably defaced his image of God:

> No more of talk where God or angel Guest
> With Man, as with his Friend, familiar us'd
> To sit indulgent, and with him partake
> Rural repast, permitting him the while
> Venial discourse unblam'd: I now must change
> These Notes to Tragic. ...[21]

So Milton began Book IX of his epic, announcing both the historical loss of 'Venial discourse unblam'd' and the loss within his own poem of unambivalent celebration. When the Fall turned all notes to tragic, harmonious likeness became fearful likeness. Because we know God in our own image and because that image, being corrupt, will at some time turn perverse when fitted to God, God must remain an object of dread for those unwilling to abjure the ancient privileges of analogy. It is true that God is fearful because he is incomprehensible. It is equally true that God is fearful because we can and do understand him. The creator, in this important sense, fell with the creature.

John Donne dramatised with special clarity the problems of all Christian devotion. Surely Aquinas was correct in his belief that a man with religious emotions ought to assume a divine 'personality' appropriate to receive them. The issue was where that assuming must halt. Sober men such as Calvin endeavoured to avoid the embarrassments of anthropomorphism by sealing up the Scriptures against unrestrained imaginations. Theologicallly this was doubtless the genteel position. But with insistent wit Donne, like other believers before and after him, made the old metaphors reveal their hidden grotesquerie. Such effects should be considered as neither the pathological impositions of a terror-struck convert nor the doctrinal expositions of a stolid conformist. Rather, the temperament and the religion unveiled each other. Donne arrived at these moments by permitting the traditional language of devotion to mean what it does mean and opening that language until, having proposed a fallen God, he raised his healing paradox. Behind the merciful face of God lay another face twisted in wrath and capable of the most fearsome acts. Finally, both faces belonged to man. For whenever his accommodated metaphors spoiled, his humanity had failed, not his God: in deference to this failure he conjured the image of man rectified. At such moments Donne worshipped human evil with the difficult faith that evil was, when predicated of God, perfection. 'The love of God begins in fear, and the fear of God ends in love; and that love can never end, for God is love' (6:113).

From *English Literary Renaissance*, 4 (1974), 337–63.

NOTES

[William Kerrigan's article, the second of two essays which focus exclusively upon Donne's religious writing, explores the issue of the anthropomorphic 'accommodation' or mediation of God within human language. Alive to the discursively *constructed* nature of all human perceptions in a way that anticipates some of the concerns of modern theory, Kerrigan asks the question: how can we know God except through human perceptions of him/her/it? Kerrigan shows how Christian theologians and writers from Augustine to Milton were themselves aware of the problem of anthropomorphism, and draws a distinction between those (constructivists) who translate God into one or another image of the human through the use of metaphor and analogy, and those (essentialists) 'who keep always before them the difference between God as he is known and God as he is' (see p. 199 above). Donne himself is located by Kerrigan in both categories, for the crude and outrageous anthropomorphism of some of his metaphors only demonstates their inappropriateness. Thus God remains elusive to the metaphors which might adequately translate him.

Kerrigan's discussion, within a religious context, of a constructivism (based on analogy), and an essentialism (based upon incommensurability), is worth setting alongside the differently oriented discussion of similar ideas in Wright's essay. Harvey and Fish also discuss the effects of Donne's use of analogy from a feminist perspective. For further discussion and contextualisation of Kerrigan's essay, see Introduction, p. 20. Ed.]

1. Douglas Bush, *English Literature in the Earlier Seventeenth Century*, revised edn (Oxford, 1962), pp. 140–1. See also T. S. Elliot's remarks about Donne as a preacher of 'impure motive', a 'sorcerer of emotional orgy' who 'lacked spiritual discipline', in *Selected Essays* (New York, 1960), p. 302.

2. J. B. Leishman, *The Monarch of Wit* (New York, 1965), p. 265.

3. I refer of course to Louis Martz, *The Poetry of Meditation* (New Haven, CT, 1954) and the similar argument in the introduction to John Donne, *The Divine Poems*, ed. Helen Gardner (Oxford, 1952).

4. Frank Kermode, *John Donne*, revised edn (London, 1961), p. 39. Kermode would also place 'Batter my heart' in this category.

5. Whenever quoting the Holy Sonnets, I use the text of Gardner and the numbering of H. J. C. Grierson (ed.), *The Poems of John Donne*, 2 vols (Oxford, 1912).

6. *The Sermons of John Donne*, ed. George Potter and Evelyn Simpson, 10 vols (Berkeley, CA, 1953–62), 2:288. Hereafter quotations from the *Sermons* are cited in my text by volume and page.

7. *Devotions Upon Emergent Occasions* (Ann Arbor, MI, 1959), p. 124.

8. Martin Luther, *Lectures on Genesis, Chapters 1–5*, in *Works*, ed. Joroslav Pelikan, trans. George V. Schick (St Louis, MO, 1958), pp. 233–4.

9. Joan Webber, *Contrary Music* (Madison, WI, 1963), *passim*, especially pp. 18, 146–7, 179.

10. Donald Guss considers Donne's 'literal' metaphors and their relationship to Italian poetry in *John Donne, Petrarchist* (Detroit, 1966). Michael McCanles studies Donne's pseudo-logical equations of object and concept in 'Paradox in Donne', *Studies in the Renaissance*, 13 (1966), 266–87.

11. Winfried Schleiner presents a concise account of this tradition in *The Imagery of John Donne's Sermons* (Providence, RI, 1970), pp. 157–9.

12. Indeed, the familial accommodation indicates one reason why theological arguments about the nature of the Trinity were so complex and often so tortuous: the abiding need was for a non-anthropomorphic formulation. I have a work in progress arguing that Milton arrived at his subordinationalist Christ by assuming the continuity of divine and human signification. The God of *De Doctrina* generated Christ because anterior fathers always generate posterior sons. Honouring the prior authority of God the Father, Milton imposed the sexual model of father creating son upon the deity, dismissing the orthodoxy of a co-essential and co-eternal Godhead – a rearrangement in keeping with his faith in the virtues of accommodated speech.

13. Mario Praz discusses the cult of the cordial emblem in *Studies in Seventeenth Century Imagery* (Rome, 1964), pp. 151–5; see also Gerhart Ladner, *The Idea of Reform: Its Impact on Christian Thought and Action in the Age of the Fathers* (Cambridge, MA, 1959), p. 91.

14. The legend of Mary Margaret of Egypt, who forfeited her virginity to cross the Jordan and regained her virginity to enter the temple, is recounted in *Aelfric's Lives of Saints*, ed. Walter W. Skeat, 2 vols (Oxford, 1890–1900), 2:2–53. Augustine considers the problem of ravished saints in *The City of God*, trans. Marcus Dodds (New York, 1950), 1:16–18.

15. *The Divine Poems*, pp. 121–7. It is just conceivable that the various false brides of the poem allude indirectly to Augustine's notion in *De bono conjugali*, xxi that Old Testament polygamy signified the future churches subject to one husband, Christ, while New Testament monogamy foreshadowed the coming unity of all churches and all men under Christ, a unity to be perfected only in the city of God.

16. Augustine, *On Free Choice of the Will*, trans. Anna S. Benjamin and L. H. Hochstaff (New York, 1964), p. 7.

17. See note 15.

18. Quoted in Schleiner, *The Imagery of John Donne's Sermons*, pp. 45–6.

19. See William Kerrigan, 'Ben Jonson Full of Shame and Scorn', *Studies in the Literary Imagination*, 6 (1973), 199–217.

20. Augustine states that our first parents lived with 'their love to God ... unclouded', entirely 'free from all perturbation' (*City of God*, 14:10). Being 'exempt from the vicissitudes of fear and desire', Adam and Eve found that 'true gladness ceaselessly flowed from the presence of God' (14:26). Augustine is echoed by Luther in *Lectures on Genesis*, pp. 61ff., 144, 165.

21. *Paradise Lost*, 9, ll. 1–6, from *The Complete Poems and Major Prose*, ed. Merritt Y. Hughes (New York, 1959), p. 378.

Further Reading

EDITIONS

Modern annotated editions of Donne's poetry:

The Elegies and Songs and Sonnets, ed. Helen Gardner (Oxford: Clarendon, 1965).

The Complete Poetry of John Donne, ed. John T. Shawcross (New York: Anchor, 1967).

The Satires, Epigrams and Verse Letters, ed. W. Milgate (Oxford: Clarendon, 1967).

The Songs and Sonets of John Donne, ed. Theodore Redpath, second edn (London: Methuen, 1983).

The Complete English Poems, ed. A. J. Smith (Harmondsworth: Penguin, 1984; first published, 1971).

The Variorum Edition of the Poetry of John Donne, Vol. 6: The Anniversaries and the Epicedes Obsequies, ed. Gary A. Stringer (Bloomington: Indiana University Press, 1995). This is the first volume (designated volume 6) of a projected eight volumes.

Editions of Donne's prose:

Essays in Divinity, ed. Evelyn M. Simpson (Oxford: Clarendon, 1952).

The Sermons of John Donne, ed. George R. Potter and Evelyn Simpson, 10 vols (Berkeley: University of California Press, 1953–62).

Ignatius His Conclave, ed. T. S. Healy (Oxford: Clarendon, 1969).

Devotions upon Emergent Occasions, ed. Anthony Raspa (Montreal: McGill/Queen's University Press, 1975).

Paradoxes and Problems, ed. Helen Peters (Oxford: Clarendon, 1980).

Biathanatos, ed. Ernest W. Sullivan (Newark: University of Delaware Press, 1984).

Pseudo-Martyr, ed. Anthony Raspa (Montreal: McGill/Queen's University Press, 1993).

BIBLIOGRAPHIES AND CROSS-PERIOD COLLECTIONS OF CRITICISM ON DONNE

Julian Lovelock (ed.), *Donne: Songs and Sonets* (London: Macmillan, 1973).

John Roberts, *John Donne: An Annotated Bibliography of Modern Criticism, 1912–1967* (Columbia: University of Missouri Press, 1982).

John Roberts, *John Donne: An Annotated Bibliography of Modern Criticism, 1968–1978* (Columbia: University of Missouri Press, 1982).

A. J. Smith (ed.), *John Donne: The Critical Heritage* (London: Routledge & Kegan Paul, 1975).

ASSESSMENTS OF TWENTIETH-CENTURY CRITICISM ON DONNE

Deborah Aldrich Larson, *John Donne and Twentieth-Century Criticism* (Rutherford: Fairleigh Dickinson University Press, 1989).

John Roberts, 'John Donne's Poetry: An Assessment of Modern Criticism', *John Donne Journal*, 1 (1982), 55–67.

ESSENTIALIST CRITICISM

This heading follows the account given in the Introduction of the differences between old and new critical approaches. By essentialist criticism, I mean those earlier forms of criticism which take literature to have a separate identity, and which represent literary criticism as distinct from other kinds of intellectual work. Defined thus, essentialist approaches include the New Criticism of Cleanth Brooks, the Modernist aesthetics of T. S. Eliot, and the combined utopianism and New Criticism of William Empson. It should be noted that these approaches are not as a-historical as they are sometimes alleged to be. However, the kind of history undertaken is one which tends to maintain, rather than subvert, the notion of literature as redemptive or transcendent.

Cleanth Brooks, 'The Language of Paradox', in *The Well Wrought Urn: Studies in the Structure of Poetry* (London: Dennis Dobson, 1969; first published, 1949), pp. 1–16.

T. S. Eliot, 'The Metaphysical Poets', in *Selected Essays*, 3rd edn (London: Faber and Faber, 1966; first published 1932), pp. 281–91.

William Empson, *Essays on Renaissance Literature*, vol. 1, ed. John Haffenden (Cambridge: Cambridge University Press, 1995; first published 1993).

F. R. Leavis, 'The Line of Wit', in *Revaluation* (Harmondsworth: Penguin, 1967; first published, 1936), pp. 17–41.

The following examples of more explicitly historical criticism are also included under the heading of essentialist criticism, since their contextualisation of Donne's writing (which often means his poetry), in terms of its perceived intellectual or literary affiliations, does not by and large call into question the assumption that literature, literary history and literary criticism have their own special characteristics. At the same time, the historicism of these approaches points forward (or sideways) to those recent forms of historicist criticism which more stridently question literature's separateness.

Helen Gardner (ed.), 'General Introduction', in *The Elegies and Songs and Sonnets* (Oxford: Clarendon, 1965), pp. xvii–lxii.

Herbert Grierson (ed.), 'Introduction', in *The Poems of John Donne* (London: Oxford University Press, 1933), pp. xiii–xlvii.

Donald Guss, *John Donne, Petrarchist* (Detroit: Wayne State University Press, 1966).

J. B. Leishman, *The Monarch of Wit* (London: Hutchinson, 1962; first published 1951).

Rosemond Tuve, *Elizabethan and Metaphysical Imagery* (Chicago: University of Chicago Press, 1947).

Murray Roston, *The Soul of Wit* (Oxford: Clarendon, 1974).

Arnold Stein, *John Donne's Lyrics: The Eloquence of Action* (Minneapolis: University of Minnesota Press, 1962).

RENAISSANCE STUDIES AND MODERN CRITICAL THEORY

The following books, essays and articles discuss and/or practically demonstrate the ways in which modern theoretical approaches have affected studies of the Renaissance.

Lynda E. Boose, 'The Priest, the Slanderer, the Historian and the Feminist', *English Literary Renaissance*, 25 (1995), 320–40.

Jonathan Crewe, 'The State of Renaissance Studies, or, A Future for ELR', *English Literary Renaissance*, 25 (1995), 341–53.

Margaret W. Ferguson, Maureen Quilligan and Nancy J. Vickers (eds), *Rewriting the Renaissance: The Discourses of Sexual Difference in Early Modern Europe* (Chicago: University of Chicago Press, 1987).

Valeria Finucci and Regina Schwartz (eds), *Desire in the Renaissance: Psychoanalysis and Literature* (Princeton, NJ: Princeton University Press, 1994).

Stanley Fish, 'What it Means to do a Job of Work', *English Literary Renaissance*, 25 (1995), 354–71.

Jonathan Goldberg, *Voice Terminal Echo: Postmodernism and English Renaissance Texts* (New York: Methuen, 1986).

Jonathan Goldberg (ed.), *Queering the Renaissance* (Durham, NC: Duke University Press, 1994).

Stephen Greenblatt (ed.), *Representing the English Renaissance* (Berkeley: University of California Press, 1988).

A. C. Hamilton, 'The Renaissance of the Study of the English Literary Renaissance', *English Literary Renaissance*, 25 (1995), 372–88.

Elizabeth D. Harvey and Katharine Eisaman Maus (eds), *Soliciting Interpretation: Literary Theory and Seventeenth-Century Poetry* (Chicago: University of Chicago Press, 1990).

Elizabeth Harvey, *Ventriloquized Voices: Feminist Theory and English Renaissance Texts* (London: Routledge, 1992).

Thomas Healy, *New Latitudes: Theory and English Renaissance Literature* (New York: Routledge, 1992).

Jean E. Howard, 'The New Historicism in Renaissance Studies', *English Literary Renaissance*, 16 (1986), 13–43.

Lisa Jardine, 'Strains of Renaissance Reading', *English Literary Renaissance*, 25 (1995), 289–306.

Katharine E. Maus, 'Renaissance Studies Today', *English Literary Renaissance*, 25 (1995), 402–14.
Kathleen E. McLuskie, 'Old Mouse-Eaten Records: The Anxiety of History', *English Literary Renaissance*, 25 (1995), 415–31.
Patricia Parker and David Quint (eds), *Literary Theory/Renaissance Texts* (Baltimore: The Johns Hopkins University Press, 1986).
Anne Lake Prescott, 'Divided State', *English Literary Renaissance*, 25 (1995), 445–57.
Debora Kuller Shuger, *Habits of Thought in the English Renaissance* (Berkeley: University of California Press, 1990).
Richard Strier, Leah Marcus, Richard Helgerson, and James G. Turner, 'Historicism, New and Old: Excerpts from a Panel Discussion', in Claude J. Summers and Ted-Larry Pebworth (eds), *'The Muses Common-Weale': Poetry and Politics in the Seventeenth Century* (Columbia: University of Missouri Press, 1988), pp. 207–17.
Raymond Waddington, 'What's Past is Prologue', *English Literary Renaissance*, 25 (1995), 458–68.

RECENT CRITICAL APPROACHES TO DONNE

The following texts have been chosen on the basis of the visibility of their theoretical and methodological concerns. The chosen headings should not be seen as mutually exclusive, but rather as indicating their primary orientation.

Forms of Historicism

Joan Faust, 'John Donne's Verse Letters to the Countess of Bedford: Mediators in a Poet–Patroness Relationship', *John Donne Journal*, 12 (1993), 79–99.
Anthony Low, 'Love and Science: Cultural Change in Donne's *Songs and Sonnets*', *Studies in the Literary Imagination*, 22 (1989), 5–16.
Anthony Low, 'John Donne: "Defects of lonelinesse"', in *The Reinvention of Love* (Cambridge: Cambridge University Press, 1993), pp. 31–64.
Arthur F. Marotti, 'John Donne and the Rewards of Patronage', in Guy Fitch Lytle and Stephen Orgel (eds), *Patronage in the Renaissance* (Princeton: Princeton University Press, 1981), pp. 207–34.
Arthur F. Marotti, *John Donne, Coterie Poet* (Madison: University of Wisconsin Press, 1986).
Arthur F. Marotti, 'John Donne, author', *Journal of Medieval and Renaissance Studies*, 19 (1989), 69–82.
David Norbrook, 'The Monarchy of Wit and the Republic of Letters: Donne's Politics', in Elizabeth D. Harvey and Katharine Eisaman Maus (eds), *Soliciting Interpretation: Literary Theory and Seventeenth-Century English Poetry* (Chicago: University of Chicago Press, 1990), pp. 3–36.
Ted-Larry Pebworth, 'John Donne, Coterie Poetry, and the Text as Performance', *Studies in English Literature*, 29 (1989), 61–75.
Annabel Patterson, 'All Donne', in Elizabeth D. Harvey and Katharine Eisaman Maus (eds), *Soliciting Interpretation: Literary Theory and Seventeenth-Century English Poetry* (Chicago: University of Chicago Press, 1990), pp. 37–67.

Annabel Patterson, '*Quod oportet* versus *quod convenit*: John Donne, Kingsman?', in *Reading Between the Lines* (London: Routledge, 1993), pp. 160–209.

David Hill Radcliffe, *Forms of Reflection: Genre and Culture in Meditational Writing* (Baltimore: The Johns Hopkins University Press, 1993), Introduction and chapter 1.

Mary Ann Radzinowicz, 'The Politics of John Donne's Silences', *John Donne Journal*, 7 (1988), 1–19.

Michael C. Schoenfeldt, 'The Poetry of Supplication: Toward a Cultural Poetics of the Religious Lyric', in John Roberts (ed.), *New Perspectives on the Seventeenth-Century English Religious Lyric* (Columbia: University of Missouri Press, 1994), pp. 75–104.

R. V. Young, '"O my America, my new-found-land": Pornography and Imperial Politics in Donne's *Elegies*', *South Central Review*, 4 (1987), 35–48.

Feminist Approaches

Ilona Bell, 'The Role of the Lady in Donne's *Songs and Sonets*', *Studies in English Literature*, 23 (1983), 113–29.

Diana Trevino Benet, 'Sexual Transgression in Donne's Elegies', *Modern Philology*, 92 (1994), 14–35.

David Blair, 'Inferring Gender in Donne's *Songs and Sonets*', *Essays in Criticism*, 45 (1995), 230–49.

Paula Blank, 'Comparing Sappho to Philaenis: John Donne's "Homo-poetics"', *PMLA*, 110 (1995), 358–68.

Helen Carr, 'Donne's Masculine Persuasive Force', in Clive Bloom (ed.), *Jacobean Poetry and Prose* (Basingstoke: Macmillan, 1988), pp. 96–118.

Barbara Correll, 'Symbolic Economies and Zero-Sum Erotics: Donne's "Sapho to Philaenis"', *English Literary History*, 62 (1995), 487–507.

Barbara Estrin, 'Donne's Injured "I": Defections from Petrarchan and Spenserian Poetics', *Philological Quarterly*, 66 (1987), 175–83.

Janet E. Halley, 'Textual Intercourse: Ann Donne, John Donne, and the Sexual Poetics of Textual Exchange', in Sheila Fisher and Janet E. Halley (eds), *Seeking the Woman in Late Medieval and Renaissance Writings* (Knoxville: University of Tennessee Press (1989), pp. 187–206.

Elizabeth Harvey, 'Ventriloquizing Sappho, or the Lesbian Muse', in *Ventriloquized Voices: Feminist Theory and English Renaissance Texts* (London: Routledge, 1992), pp. 116–34.

Deborah H. Lockwood, 'Donne's Idea of Woman in the *Songs and Sonets*', *Essays in Literature*, 14 (1987), 37–50.

Janel Mueller, 'Women among the Metaphysicals: A Case, Mostly, of Being Donne For', *Modern Philology*, 87 (1989), 142–58.

Janel Mueller, 'Troping Utopia: Donne's brief for lesbianism', in James Grantham Turner (ed.), *Sexuality and Gender in Early Modern Europe* (Cambridge: Cambridge University Press, 1993), pp. 182–207.

Maureen Sabine, *Feminine Engendered Faith: the poetry of John Donne and Richard Crashaw* (London: Macmillan, 1992).

Poststructuralist Perspectives

James Baumlin, *John Donne and the Rhetorics of Renaissance Discourse* (Columbia: University of Missouri Press, 1991).

Martin Coyle, 'The Subject and the Sonnet', *English*, 43 (1994), 139–50.

Thomas Docherty, *John Donne, Undone* (London: Methuen, 1986).

Judith Scherer Herz, '"An Excellent Exercise of Wit that speaks so well of Ill": Donne and the Poetics of Concealment', in Claude J. Summers and Ted-Larry Pebworth (eds), *The Eagle and the Dove: Reassessing John Donne* (Columbia: University of Missouri Press, 1986), pp. 3–14.

M. Thomas Hester, 'Re-Signing the Text of the Self: Donne's "As Due By Many Titles"', in Claude J. Summers and Ted-Larry Pebworth (eds), *'Bright Shootes of Everlastingnesse': The Seventeenth-Century Religious Lyric* (Columbia: University of Missouri Press, 1987), pp. 59–71.

Catherine Gimelli Martin, 'Pygmalion's Progress in the Garden of Love, or the Wit's Work is Never Donne', in Claude J. Summers and Ted-Larry Pebworth (eds), *The Wit of Seventeenth-Century Poetry* (Columbia: University of Missouri Press, 1995), pp. 78–100.

R. V. Young, 'Donne, Herbert, and the Postmodern Muse', in John Roberts (ed.), *New Perspectives on the Seventeenth-Century English Religious Lyric* (Columbia: University of Missouri Press, 1994), pp. 168–87.

Psychoanalysis

Ronald Corthell, 'The Obscure Object of Desire: Donne's *Anniversaries* and the Cultural Production of Elizabeth Drury', in Arthur Marotti (ed.), *Critical Essays on John Donne* (New York: G. K. Hall and Co., 1994), pp. 122–40.

Anthony Easthope, 'Foucault, Ovid, Donne: Versions of Sexuality, Ancient and Modern', in *Poetry and Phantasy* (Cambridge: Cambridge University Press, 1989), pp. 47–60.

William Shullenberger, 'Love as a Spectator Sport in John Donne's Poetry', in Claude J. Summers and Ted-Larry Pebworth (eds), *Renaissance Discourses of Desire* (Columbia: University of Missouri Press, 1993), pp. 46–62.

Elaine Perez Zickler, '"nor in nothing, nor in things": The Case of Love and Desire in John Donne's *Songs and Sonets*', *John Donne Journal*, 12 (1993), 17–40.

Alternative Perspectives

The following articles take issue, in an explicit way, with some of the recent approaches to Donne.

Gregory Dime, '"The New News at the New Court": Recent Historicist Interpretations of Metaphysical Poetry', *Essays in Literature*, 19 (1992), 3–19.

William Kerrigan, 'What Was Donne Doing?', *South Central Review*, 4 (1987), 2–15.

Richard Wollman, 'The "Press and the Fire": Print and Manuscript Culture in Donne's Circle', *Studies in English Literature*, 33 (1993), 85–97.

SOME RECENT BOOKS AND COLLECTIONS OF ESSAYS ON DONNE

For ease of reference, this section lists some recent books and collections of essays exclusively devoted to Donne. Where appropriate, I have also included them in the above sections to indicate the nature of their critical approach.

James Baumlin, *John Donne and the Rhetorics of Renaissance Discourse* (Columbia: University of Missouri Press, 1991).

Meg Lota Brown, *Donne and the Politics of Conscience in Early Modern England* (Leiden: E.J. Brill, 1995).

John Carey, *John Donne: Life, Mind and Art* (London: Faber and Faber, 1981).

Thomas Docherty, *John Donne, Undone* (London: Methuen, 1986).

M. Thomas Hester, *Kinde Pitty and Brave Scorn: John Donne's Satyres* (Durham, NC: Duke University Press, 1982).

Arthur F. Marotti, *John Donne, Coterie Poet* (Madison: University of Wisconsin Press, 1986).

Arthur Marotti (ed.), *Critical Essays on John Donne* (New York: G.K. Hall, 1994).

George Parfitt, *John Donne: A Literary Life* (London: Macmillan, 1989).

Terry Sherwood, *Fulfilling the Circle: A Study of John Donne's Thought* (Toronto: University of Toronto Press, 1984).

Claude J. Summers and Ted-Larry Pebworth (eds), *The Eagle and the Dove: Reassessing John Donne* (Columbia: University of Missouri Press, 1986).

Edward Tayler, *Donne's Idea of a Woman: Structure and Meaning in The Anniversaries* (New York: Columbia University Press, 1991).

SOME INTRODUCTIONS TO MODERN THEORY

Mary Eagleton (ed.), *Feminist Literary Criticism* (Harlow: Longman, 1991).

Maud Ellman (ed.), *Psychoanalytic Literary Criticism* (London: Longman, 1994).

Paul Hamilton, *Historicism* (London: Routledge, 1996).

Frank Lentricchia and Thomas McLaughlin (eds), *Critical Terms for Literary Study* (Chicago: University of Chicago Press, 1990).

Toril Moi, *Sexual/Textual Politics: Feminist Literary Theory* (London: Methuen, 1985).

Christopher Norris, *Deconstruction: Theory and Practice* (London: Methuen, 1982).

Ramon Selden, Peter Widdowson and Peter Brooker, *A Reader's Guide to Contemporary Literary Theory*, 4th edn (London: Prentice-Hall/Harvester Wheatsheaf, 1997).

Harold Veeser (ed.), *The New Historicism* (New York: Routledge, 1994).

Elizabeth Wright, *Psychoanalytic Criticism: Theory in Practice* (London: Methuen, 1984).

Notes on Contributors

David Aers is Professor of English at Duke University. His recent publications include *Community, Gender and Individual Identity in English Writing* (1988), and *The Powers of the Holy: Religion, Politics and Gender in Late Medieval English Culture*, with Lynn Staley (1996). He is also the editor of *Culture and History, 1350–1600* (1992).

Catherine Belsey chairs the Centre for Critical and Cultural Theory at the University of Wales, Cardiff. Her publications include *Critical Practice* (1980), *The Subject of Tragedy: Identity and Difference in Renaissance Drama* (1985), *John Milton* (1988) and *Desire: Love Stories in Western Culture* (1994).

Barbara L. Estrin is Professor of English at Stonehill College. Her publications include *Laura: Uncovering Gender and Genre in Wyatt, Donne and Marvell* (1994) and *The Raven and the Lark: Lost Children in Literature of the English Renaissance* (1985), as well as numerous articles on Renaissance and Modern topics.

Stanley Fish is Professor of English and Law at Duke University. His publications include *Surprised by Sin: The Reader in Paradise Lost* (1967, 1997), *Self Consuming Artifacts: The Experience of Seventeenth Century Literature* (1972), *Is There a Text in This Class? Interpretive Communities and the Sources of Authority* (1980), and *Doing What Comes Naturally: Change, Rhetoric, and the Practice of Theory in Literary and Legal Studies* (1989).

Achsah Guibbory is Professor of English at the University of Illinois, Urbana-Champaign. Her publications include *The Map of Time: Seventeenth-Century English Literature and Ideas of Pattern in History* (1986) and *Ceremony and Community from Herbert to Milton: Literature, Religion, and Cultural Conflict in Seventeenth-Century England* (1998).

Richard Halpern is Professor of English at the University of Colorado at Boulder. He is the author of *Shakespeare and the Moderns* (1997) and *The Poetics of Primitive Accumulation* (1991).

Elizabeth D. Harvey is Associate Professor of English at the University of Western Ontario. She is the author of *Ventriloquized Voices: Feminist*

Theory and English Renaissance Texts (1992) and co-editor of *Women and Reason* (1992) and *Soliciting Interpretation: Literary Theory and Seventeenth-Century English Poetry* (1990).

William Kerrigan is Professor of English at the University of Massachusetts at Amherst. His publications include *The Prophetic Milton* (1974), *The Sacred Complex: on the Psychogenesis of Paradise Lost* (1983), *Hamlet's Perfection* (1994), and with Gordon Braden, *The Idea of the Renaissance* (1989).

Gunther Kress is Professor of English/Education at the Institute of Education, University of London. His interests lie in the interrelations of forms of representation, culture, and subjectivity. Among his more recent publications are *Social Semiotics* (with Bob Hodge, 1988); *Reading Images: the Grammar of Visual Design* (with Theo van Leeuwen, 1996) and *Before Writing: Rethinking the Paths into Literacy* (1977).

Tilottama Rajan is Professor of English and Director of the Centre for the Study of Theory at the University of Western Ontario. She is the author of several articles, and of *Dark Interpreter: The Discourse of Romanticism* (1980), and *The Supplement of Reading: Figures of Understanding in Romantic Theory and Practice* (1990). She is also the co-editor of *Intersections: Nineteenth-Century Philosophy and Contemporary Theory* (1995), and *Romanticism, History and the Possibilities of Genre: Re-forming Literature 1789–1837* (1997).

Index

232INDEX

Sabine, Maureen, 221
Salisbury, Countess of, 132, 134n.
Sanders, Wilbur, 162, 181n.
Saussure, Ferdinand de, 12–13
Sawday, Jonathan, 156n.
Scarry, Elaine, 143, 155n.
Shawcross, John, 60n., 217
Schleiner, Winfried, 215n., 216n.
Schwartz, Regina, 181n., 219
Scot, Reginald, 138, 155n.
Sedgwick, Eve, 99, 103n.
Selden, Ramon, 22n., 23n., 223
Sellin, Paul, 44n.
Shakespeare, William, 29, 45, 71,
  79n., 90, 93, 97, 98, 99, 108,
  165
Sherwood, Terry, 223
Showalter, Elaine, 154n.
Shuger, Deborah, 18–19, 23n.,
  24n., 220
Shullenberger, William, 222
Sidney, Philip, 41n., 45, 58–9,
  103n., 141
Simpson, Evelyn, 21n., 61n., 181n.,
  196n., 215n., 217
Skelton, John, 165
Smith, A. J., 21n., 42n., 79n.,
  120n., 154n., 180n., 196n.,
  217, 218
Spenser, Edmund, 84–91, 94, 97,
  98, 102n., 136, 162, 207,
  212
Stachniewski, John, 21n., 175,
  181n.
Stallybrass, Peter, 43n.
Stanwood, P. G., 197n.
Stein, Arnold, 8, 22n., 47, 61n.,
  219
Stow, John, 197n.
Strier, Richard, 23n., 220
Stringer, Gary, 217
subjectivity: as appropriative,
  84–101, 103n., 140–53,
  158–62; and confession,

115–16; essentialist and anti-
  essentialist conceptions of,
  21–2n., 69–71, 122–33,
  135–7, 153n., 161–80; and
  gender, 25–40, 83–101,
  135–53, 159–62, 170–2; and
  language, 14, 66, 68–70,
  135–6, 160–80; in
  psychoanalytic theory, 14,
  65–77, 146–7; in religious
  context, 187–95
Sullivan, Ernest, 217
Summers, Claude, 223
Syminges, John, 156n.

Tayler, Edward, 223
Teubner, Gunther, 121n.
Theobald, Lewis, 117
Tillyard, E. M. W., 195n.
Toliver, Harold, 46, 60n.
Trexler, Richard, 197n.
Turner, James, 23n., 220
Tuve, Rosalind, 21n., 196n., 219

utopianism, 15, 46–52, 70–1, 74–5,
  83, 100–1n., 106, 112–13,
  142–3

Valerio, 211
Veeser, Harold, 23n., 223
ventriloquism, 138–53, 174–5; see
  also anthropomorphism;
  androgyny; subjectivity as
  appropriative
Vickers, Brian, 47–8, 61n.
Vickers, Nancy, 219

Waller, Marguerite, 82, 101n.
Walton, Izaak, 46, 148, 149
Warner, Marina, 146, 147
Webber, Joan, 203, 215n.
Whitaker, William, 183, 195n.
White, Allon, 43n.
Whitford, Margaret, 154n.